COCOA® PROGRAMMING FOR MAC® OS X

COCOA® PROGRAMMING FOR MAC® OS X

Aaron Hillegass

Addison-Wesley

Boston • San Francisco • New York • Toronto • Montreal
London • Munich • Paris • Madrid
Capetown • Sydney • Tokyo • Singapore • Mexico City

The publisher offers discounts on this book when ordered in quantity for special sales. For more information, please contact:

Pearson Education Corporate Sales Division
201 W. 103rd Street
Indianapolis, IN 46290
(800) 428-5331
corpsales@pearsoned.com

Visit AW on the Web: www.aw.com/cseng/

Library of Congress Cataloging-in-Publication Data

Hillegass, Aaron.
    Cocoa programming for Mac OS X / Aaron Hillegass.
        p. cm.
    ISBN 0-201-72683-1
    1. Mac OS. 2. Operating systems (Computers) 3. Macintosh
    (Computer)—Programming. I. Title

    QA76.76.063 H57145 2002
    005.26'8—dc21

ISBN 0-201-72683-1
Text printed on recycled paper
1 2 3 4 5 6 7 8 9 10—MA—0504030201
First printing, November 2001

For my son, Walden Carter Hillegass

CONTENTS

PREFACE

With the arrival of Mac OS X, Apple recommends that all new applications be written using Cocoa. Cocoa is a powerful collection of tools and libraries that will make writing new programs a much faster process.

The increased speed does not, however, come for free. The new technologies have a steep learning curve, and Apple's documentation leaves much to be desired. This book will guide you through the ideas and techniques that separate the great Cocoa programmers from the wanna-be's.

This book is written for programmers who already know C++ or Java and are curious about Cocoa. The reader is not expected to have any experience with Mac programming. It is a hands-on book and assumes that the reader has access to Mac OS X and the developer tools.

ACKNOWLEDGMENTS

Creating this book required the efforts of many people. I want to thank them for their help. Their contributions have made this a better book than I could have written alone.

First, I want to thank the students who took the Cocoa programming course at the Big Nerd Ranch. They helped me work the kinks out of the exercises and explanations that appear here. Their curiosity inspired me to make the book more comprehensive, and their patience made it possible.

Many people have read the drafts of this book and given me corrections and suggestions. They include: Mike Ferris, Erik Barzeski at CocoaDevCentral, Kris Jensen at Stone Design, Bill Bumgarner and everyone else at CodeFab, Michael Simmons, and Brandon Kirby at GroovePort. Each reader added something to what is here.

I used to work for NeXT Computer, and my department has since become Apple iServices Training. Renata Poray, who leads the department, has been a dear friend to me for many years. She sent me work when I needed to pay the rent, and left me alone when the book needed attention.

I had the great honor of working for several years with Kai Christiansen. He taught me many things about Cocoa and about teaching. Together, we wrote several courses on OpenStep and WebObjects. For me, writing this book was a natural continuation of our work. Although my hands were on the keyboard, Kai's voice was frequently what came out on the page.

The great people at Addison-Wesley took my manuscript and made it into a book. They put the book on trucks and convinced bookstores to put it on the shelves. Without their help, it would still be just a stack of papers in my office.

The final thank you is to my family. Some of the attention that would normally be given to my wife, Michele, was diverted into the creation of this book. By the time you read this, she will have given birth to our first child. I am thankful for her patience and all the other blessings she has brought into my life.

Chapter 1
COCOA: WHAT IS IT?

A Little History

The story of Cocoa starts with a delightful bit of history. Once upon a time, two guys named Steve started a company called Apple Computer in their garage. The company grew rapidly, so they hired an experienced executive named John Sculley to be its CEO. After a few conflicts, John Sculley moved Steve Jobs to a position where he had no control over the company at all. Steve Jobs quit to form another computer company, called NeXT Computer.

NeXT hired a small team of brilliant engineers. This small team developed a computer, an operating system, a printer, a factory, and a set of development tools. Each piece was years ahead of competing technologies, and the masses were excited and amazed. Unfortunately, the excited masses did not buy the computer or the printer. In 1993, the factory was closed, and NeXT Computer, Inc., became NeXT Software, Inc.

The operating system and the development tools continued to sell under the name NeXTSTEP. While the average computer user had never heard of NeXTSTEP, it was very popular with several groups: scientists, investment banks, and intelligence agencies. These were people who developed new applications every week, and they found that NeXTSTEP enabled them to implement their ideas faster than any other technology.

What was this operating system? First, NeXT decided to use Unix as the core of NeXTSTEP. They used the source code for BSD Unix from UC Berkeley. Why Unix? Unix crashed much less frequently than Microsoft Windows or Mac OS, and it came with powerful, reliable networking capabilities.

NeXT put the BSD Unix on top of a microkernel called *Mach*. Mach had been developed at Carnegie-Mellon University. The microkernel approach is a good way to sell Unix to the masses: Because everything that is not absolutely necessary is kept out of the kernel, no one should ever have to recompile it. OSF/1 Unix and the GNU HURD are also based upon the Mach microkernel.

Apple has made the source code to the Mach/Unix part of Mac OS X available. It is known as Darwin. There is a community of developers who are working to improve Darwin. You can learn more about Darwin at http://www.darwinfo.com or http://www.opensource.apple.com.

NeXT then wrote a *window server* for the operating system. A window server takes events from the user and forwards them to the applications. The application then sends drawing commands back to the window server to update what the user sees. One of the nifty things about the NeXT window server is that the drawing code that goes to the window server is the exact drawing code that would be sent to the printer. So a programmer only has to write the drawing code once and it can be used for display or printing. In the NeXTSTEP days, programmers were writing code that generated PostScript. With Mac OS X, programmers are writing code that generates commands in PDF. The Portable Document Format is an open standard for vector graphics created by the Adobe Corporation.

If you have used Unix machines before, you are probably familiar with the X window server. The window server for Mac OS X is completely different, but fulfills the same function as the X window server: It gets events from the user and forwards them to the applications and puts data from the applications onto the screen. At the moment, the X protocol has little support for things like antialiased fonts and transparency. This is why the Mac OS X window server looks so much better than an X window server.

NeXTSTEP came with a set of libraries and tools to enable programmers to deal with the window manager in an elegant manner. The libraries were called *frameworks*. In 1993, the frameworks and tools were revised and renamed *OpenStep*. (OpenStep has since been renamed *Cocoa*.)

As shown in Figure 1.1, the window server and your application are Unix processes. Cocoa enables your application to receive events from the window server and draw to the screen.

Programming with the frameworks is done in a language called *Objective-C*. Like C++, Objective-C is an extension to the C programming language that made it

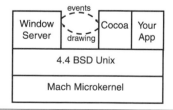

Figure 1.1   How Cocoa Fits In

object-oriented. Unlike C++, Objective-C is weakly typed and extremely powerful. With power comes responsibility: Objective-C also allows programmers to make ridiculous errors.

Programmers loved OpenStep. It enabled them to experiment more easily with new ideas. In fact, Tim Berners-Lee developed the first Web browser and the first Web server on NeXTSTEP. Securities analysts could code and test new financial models much, much more quickly. Colleges were developing the applications that made their research possible. I don't know what the intelligence community was using it for, but they bought thousands of copies of OpenStep. Because they were so useful, the OpenStep development tools were ported to Solaris and Windows NT, and the NeXTSTEP operating system was ported to most of the popular CPUs of the day: Intel, Motorola, HP's PA-RISC, and SPARC. (Ironically, OpenStep didn't run on a Macintosh until Mac OS X Server shipped in 1999.)

For many years, Apple Computer had been working to develop an operating system with many of the features of NeXTSTEP. This effort was known as Copeland. Project Copeland gradually spun out of control, and Apple finally decided to pull the plug and buy the next version of Mac OS from another company. After surveying the existing operating systems, they decided on NeXTSTEP. Since NeXT was small, Apple simply bought the whole company in December 1996.

Where do I fit into this story? I was writing code for NeXT computers on Wall Street until NeXT hired me to teach OpenStep programming to other developers. I was an employee at NeXT when it merged with Apple, and I taught many of the Apple engineers how to write applications for Mac OS X. No longer an Apple employee, I now teach Cocoa programming for Big Nerd Ranch, Inc.

NeXTSTEP became Mac OS X. It is Unix underneath, and you can get all the standard Unix programs (like the Apache Web server) on Mac OS X. It is more stable than Windows or Mac OS 9, and the user interface is spectacular. You, the developer, are going to love Mac OS X, because Cocoa will enable you to write full-featured applications faster than ever before.

Tools

You *will* love Cocoa, but perhaps not immediately. First, you will learn the basics. Let's start with the tools that you will use.

All the tools for Cocoa development come on the Mac OS X Developer CD-ROM. The developer tools will add about a dozen handy applications to your system, but you will use primarily the applications Project Builder and Interface Builder. Behind the scenes, the GNU C compiler (gcc) will be used to compile your code and the GNU debugger (gdb) will help you find your errors.

Project Builder tracks all the resources that will go into an application: code, images, sounds, and so on. You will edit your code in Project Builder, and Project Builder can compile and run your application. Project Builder can also be used to invoke and control the debugger.

Interface Builder is a GUI builder. It allows you to lay out windows and add widgets to those windows. It is, however, much more. Interface Builder allows the developer to create objects and edit their attributes. Most of those objects are UI elements like buttons and text fields, but some will be instances of classes that you create.

In this book, you will use Objective-C for nearly all of the examples. You can write Cocoa applications with Java, but the frameworks were written in Objective-C, and you will find them easier to understand if you know the Objective-C language. Objective-C takes two hours to learn if you already know C and an object-oriented language like Java or C++. In Chapter 25, we will discuss writing applications in Java.

The Objective-C code will be compiled by the GNU C compiler, gcc. The compiler allows you to freely mix C, C++, and Objective C code in a single file.

The GNU debugger, gdb, will be used to set breakpoints and browse variables at runtime. Objective-C gives you a lot of rope to hang yourself with; you will be glad to have a decent debugger.

Objects, Classes, Methods, and Messages

All Cocoa programming is done using object-oriented concepts. This section is a very brief review of terms used in object-oriented programming. If you have not done any object-oriented programming before, I recommend that you read *Object-Oriented Programming and the Objective-C Language*. The PDF file for the book is in the documentation that came with the developer tools. It is /Developer/Documentation/ Cocoa/ObjectiveC/ObjC.pdf.

What is an object? An *object* is like a C struct: It takes up memory and has variables inside it. The variables in an object are called *instance variables*. So when dealing with objects, the first questions we typically ask are "How do you allocate space for one?," "What instance variables does the object have?," and "How do you destroy the object when you are done with it?"

Some of the instance variables of an object will be pointers to other objects. These pointers enable one object to "know about" another.

Classes are structures that can create objects. Classes specify the variables the object has. Classes are responsible for allocating memory for the object. We say that the object is an *instance* of the class that created it (Figure 1.2).

An object is better than a struct, though; an object can have functions associated with it. We call the functions *methods*. To call a method, you send the object a *message* (Figure 1.3).

Frameworks

A framework is a collection of classes that are intended to be used together. They are compiled together into a reusable library of code. Any related resources are put into a directory with the library. The directory is renamed with the extension .framework. You can find the built-in frameworks for your machine in

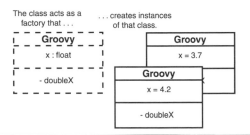

Figure 1.2 Classes Create Instances

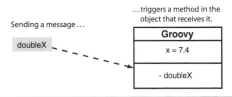

Figure 1.3 Messages Trigger Methods

`/System/Library/Frameworks`. All Cocoa applications use two of these frameworks: Foundation and AppKit.

> *Foundation*: Every object-oriented programming language needs the standard value, collection, and utility classes. Things like strings, dates, lists, threads, and timers are in the Foundation framework.

> *AppKit*: All things related to the user interface are in the AppKit framework. These include windows, buttons, text fields, events, and drawing classes. You will also see it called the *ApplicationKit*.

There are numerous other frameworks that handle things like encryption, QuickTime, and 3D rendering, but we will focus on Foundation and AppKit because they will be used by all Cocoa applications. Once you have mastered these two, the other frameworks will be easier to understand.

You can also create your own frameworks from the classes that you create. Typically, if a set of classes are used in several applications, you will want to make them into a framework.

How to Read This Book

When I sat down to write this book, I imagined that I was guiding a friend through activities that would help him understand Cocoa programming. This book acts as the guide through these activities. Often, I will ask you to do something and explain the details or theory afterwards. If you are confused, read a little more. Usually the help you seek is only a paragraph or two away.

If you are still stumped, you can get help on the Web site for this book. The URL is http://www.bignerdranch.com/Book. Errata, hints, and examples are listed there. Also, all the solutions for the exercises can be downloaded from there.

Each chapter will guide you through adding features to an application. This is not, however, a cookbook. This book teaches ideas, and the exercises are an example of these ideas in action. Don't be afraid to experiment.

There are about 120 classes in AppKit and about 80 in Foundation. These classes are documented in the online reference (see `/Developer/Documentation/Cocoa/Reference/`). Cocoa programmers spend a lot of time browsing through these pages. But until you understand a lot about Cocoa, it is hard to guess where to start to look for answers in the reference. Periodically as this book introduces you to a class, look that class up in the reference. You may not understand everything you find there, but browsing the reference will give you some appreciation for the richness of the frameworks. When you reach the end of this book, the reference will become your guide.

Typographical Conventions

To make the book easier to comprehend, I've used several typographical conventions.

In Objective-C, class names are always capitalized. In this book, I've also made them appear in a mono-bold font. In Objective-C, method names start with a lowercase letter. Method names will also appear in a mono-bold font. So, for example, you might see "The class **NSObject** has the method **dealloc**."

Other literals that you would see in code (including instance variable names) will appear in a regular mono font. Also, filenames will appear in this same font. Thus, you might see "In `MyClass.m`, set the variable `favoriteColor` to `nil`."

How to Learn

I have all sorts of people come to my class: the bright and the not so bright, the motivated and the lazy, the experienced and the novice. Regardless, the people who get the most from the class are always the ones who remain focused on the topic at hand.

The first trick to maintaining focus is to get enough sleep. I suggest ten hours of sleep each night while you are studying new ideas. Before dismissing this idea, try it. You will wake up refreshed and ready to learn. *Caffeine is not a substitute for sleep.*

The second trick is to stop thinking about yourself. While learning something new, many students will think, "Damn, this is hard for me. I wonder if I am stupid." Because stupidity is such an unthinkably terrible thing in our culture, the students will then spend hours constructing arguments that explain why they are intelligent yet are having difficulties. The moment you start down this path, you have lost your focus.

I used to have a boss named Rock. Rock had earned a degree in astrophysics from Cal Tech and had never had a job where he used his knowledge of the heavens. Once I asked him if he regretted getting the degree. "My absurd degree in astrophysics has proved to be very valuable," he said, "Some things in this world are just hard. When I am struggling with something, I sometimes think 'Damn, this is hard. I wonder if I am stupid,' and then I remember that I have a degree in astrophysics from Cal Tech; I must not be stupid."

Before going any further, assure yourself that you are not stupid and that some things are just hard. Armed with this silly affirmation and a well-rested mind, you are ready to conquer Cocoa.

Chapter 2
LET'S GET STARTED

M any books would start off by giving you a lot of philosophy. This would be a waste of precious paper at this point. Instead, I am going to guide you through writing your first Cocoa application. Upon finishing, you will be excited and confused... and ready for the philosophy.

Our first project will be a random number generator application. It will have two buttons labeled Seed random number generator with time and Generate random number. There will be a text field that will display the generated number. This is a simple example that involves taking user input and generating output. At times, the description of what you are doing and why will seem, well, terse. Don't worry, we will explore all of this in more detail throughout this book. For now, just play along.

Figure 2.1 shows what the complete application will look like.

In Project Builder

Assuming you have installed the developer tools, you will find Project Builder in `/Developer/Applications/`. Drag the application to the dock at the bottom of your screen; you will be using it a lot. Launch Project Builder.

As mentioned earlier, Project Builder will keep track of all the resources that go into your application. All these resources will be kept in a directory called the *project directory*. The first step in developing a new application is to create a new project directory with the default skeleton of an application.

Create a New Project

Under the File menu, choose New Project.... When the panel appears (see Figure 2.2), choose the type of project you would like to create: Cocoa Application. Notice that there are many other types of projects.

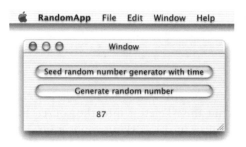

Figure 2.1 Completed Application

Figure 2.2 Choose Project Type

In this book, we will discuss the following major types of projects:

Application: A program that creates windows.

Tool: A program that does not have a graphical user interface. Typically, a tool is a command-line utility or a daemon that runs in the background.

Bundle or *Framework*: A directory of resources that can be used in an application or tool. A bundle is dynamically loaded at runtime. An application typically links against a framework at compile time.

For the project name, type in RandomApp, as in Figure 2.3. Application names are typically capitalized. You can also pick the directory into which your project directory will be created. By default, your project directory will be created inside your home directory. Click the Finish button.

A project directory will be created for you with the skeleton of an application inside. You will extend this skeleton into the source for a complete application and then compile the source into a working application.

Looking at the new project in Project Builder (Figure 2.4), you will see an outline view on the left side of the window. The folders in the view represent groups of resources. Most programmers group files based on their type. For example, most programmers keep the source code for their classes in the Classes group.

The skeleton of a project that was created for you will actually compile and run. It has a menu and a window. Click on the button with the hammer and screen to build and run the project as shown in Figure 2.5.

While the application is launching, you will see a bouncing icon in the dock. Then you will see the name of your application appear in the menu. This means that your application is now active. The window for your application may be hidden by

Figure 2.3   Name Project

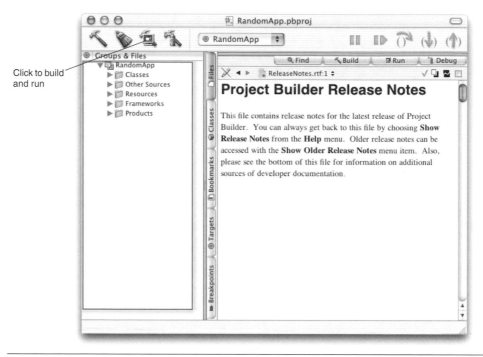

Figure 2.4   Skeleton of a Project

another window. If you do not see your window, choose Hide Others from the RandomApp menu. You should see an empty window as shown in Figure 2.6.

It doesn't do much, but notice that it is already a fully functional application. Quit the RandomApp and return to Project Builder.

The main Function

Under Other Sources, select main.m by single-clicking on it. The code will appear in the view on the right (Figure 2.7).

You will almost never modify main.m in an application project. The default **main()** simply calls **NSApplicationMain()**. **NSApplicationMain()** loads the user interface objects from a *nib file*. Nib files are created with Interface Builder. (Trivia: "NIB" stands for "NeXT Interface Builder." "NS" stands for "NeXTSTEP.") Once your application has loaded the nib file, it simply waits for the user to do something. When the user clicks or types, your code will get called automatically. If you have

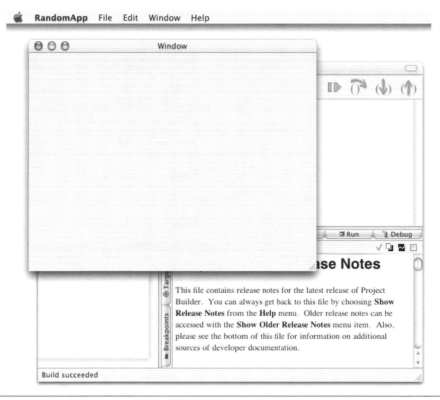

Figure 2.5   Project Built

never written an application with a graphic user interface before, this change will be startling: The user is in control. Your code simply reacts to what the user does.

In Interface Builder

In the outline view under Resources, you will find a nib file called MainMenu.nib. Double-click on it to open the nib in Interface Builder. Lots of windows will appear, so this is a good time to hide your other applications. In the Interface Builder menu, you will find Hide Others.

Interface Builder allows you to add and edit user interface objects (like windows and buttons) and save those objects into a file. You will also create instances of your custom classes and make connections between those instances and the standard user interface objects. When users interact with the user interface objects, the code in your classes will be executed.

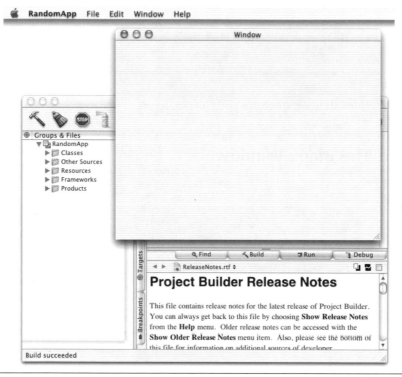

Figure 2.6 Running the Project

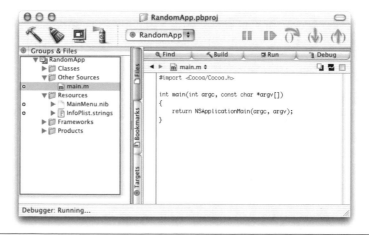

Figure 2.7 main() Function

The Standard Palettes

The palette window (Figure 2.8) is where you will find user interface widgets that can be dragged into your interface. For example, if you want a button, you can drag it from the palette window. Notice that there is a row of buttons at the top of the palette window. As you click the buttons, the various palettes will appear. In Chapter 26, you will learn to create your own palettes.

The Blank Window

The blank window (Figure 2.9) represents an instance of the **NSWindow** class that is inside your nib file.

Figure 2.8   Palette Window

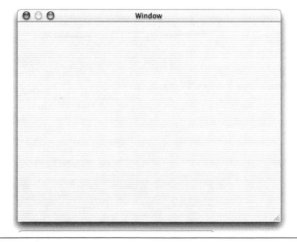

Figure 2.9   Blank Window

As you drop objects from the palettes onto the window, they will also be added to the nib file. After you have created instances of these objects and edited their attributes, saving the nib file is like "freeze-drying" the objects into the file. When the application is run, the nib file will be read and the objects will be revived. The cool kids say, "The objects are *archived* into the nib file and *unarchived* when the application is run."

Lay Out the Interface

Make the blank window smaller. Drag a button from the palette window and drop it onto the blank window. Double-click on the button to change its title to Seed random number generator with time. Drag another button out, and relabel it Generate random number. Drag out the text field that says Message Text and drop it on the window. Make the window smaller. Make it look like Figure 2.10.

The text field should be as wide as possible. Drag the left and right side of the text field toward the sides of the window. Notice that blue lines appear when you are close to the edge of the window. These are guides to help you conform to Apple's GUI guidelines (Figure 2.11).

To make the text field center its contents, you will need to use the Info Panel (also known as the "Inspector"). Select the text field, and choose Show Info from the Tools menu. Click on the center alignment button (Figure 2.12).

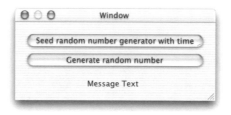

Figure 2.10   Completed Interface

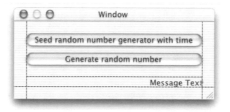

Figure 2.11   Resize Text Field

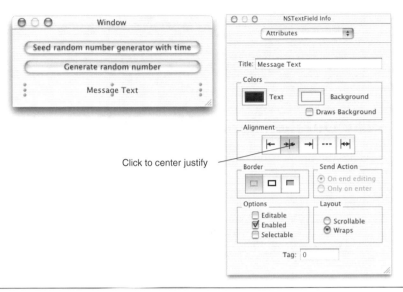

Figure 2.12   Center Justify Text Field

The Document Window

In your nib file, some objects (like buttons) are visible, and others (like your custom controller objects) are invisible. The icons that represent the invisible objects appear in the document window (Figure 2.13).

In the document window, you will see icons representing the main menu and the window. First Responder is a fictional object, but it is a very useful fiction. It will be

Figure 2.13   The Document Window

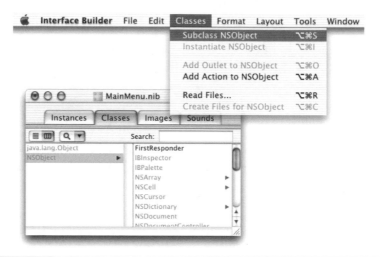

Figure 2.14 Foo is a Subclass of NSObject

fully explained in Chapter 16. File's Owner in this nib is the **NSApplication** object for your app. The **NSApplication** object is the one that takes events from the event queue and forwards them to the appropriate window. We will discuss File's Owner in depth in Chapter 7.

Create a Class

The document window also has a simple class browser that you will use to create a skeleton of your custom class. Click on the Classes tab and select **NSObject** (Figure 2.14). In the Classes menu, choose Subclass (pressing the return key will also work). Rename the new class **Foo**. Interface Builder now knows that you intend to create a subclass of **NSObject** called **Foo**. **NSObject** is the root class for the entire Objective-C class hierarchy. That is, all objects in the framework are descendants of **NSObject**.

Class names, by convention, are capitalized.

Next, you will add instance variables and methods to your class. Instance variables that are pointers to other objects are called *outlets*. Methods that can be triggered by user interface objects are called *actions*. If you select the **Foo** class and bring up the info panel, you will see a listing of the class's actions and outlets. Of course, your class doesn't have any outlets or actions, yet.

To add an outlet, click the + button next to the outlet table. Rename the new outlet textField. To add an action, click the + button next to the action table. Rename the new action **seed**. (When you press return, it will add a colon to the end of the action name. **seed:** is the actual name of the method that will be created.) Add a second action, and name it generate (see Figure 2.15).

By convention, the names of methods and instance variables start with lowercase letters. If the name would be multiple words in English, each new word is capitalized. For example, `favoriteColor`.

Now you will create the files for the class **Foo**. In Objective-C, every class is defined by two files: a header file and an implementation file. The header file, also known as the interface file, declares the instance variables and methods your class will have. The implementation file actually defines what those methods do.

Under the Classes menu, choose Create files... (Figure 2.16).

A save panel will appear. The default location (your project directory) is perfect. Save `Foo.h` (the header file) and `Foo.m` (the implementation file) there. Note that the files are being added to your RandomApp project (Figure 2.17).

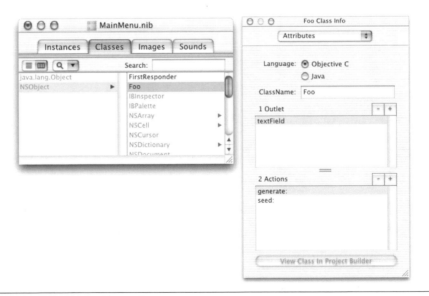

Figure 2.15   Create Outlets and Actions

Figure 2.16   Create Files

Figure 2.17   Choose a Location for the Files

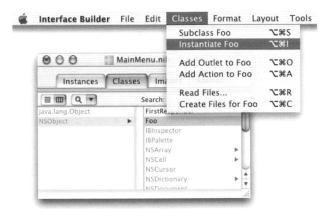

Figure 2.18   Create an Instance of Foo

Create an Instance

Next, you will create an instance of the class **Foo** in your nib file. Select **Foo** in the class browser and choose Instantiate from the Classes menu (Figure 2.18). Interface Builder will take you back to the Instances tab, and you will see a symbol representing your instance of **Foo** (Figure 2.19).

Make Connections

A lot of object-oriented programming has to do with which objects need to know about which other objects. Now you are going to introduce some objects to each other. Cocoa programmers would say, "We are now going to set the outlets of our

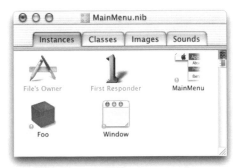

Figure 2.19   An Instance of Foo

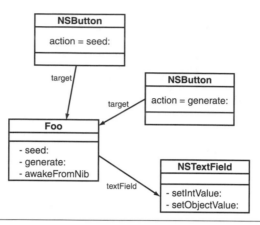

Figure 2.20 Object Diagram

objects." To introduce one object to another, you will control-drag from *the object that needs to know* to the object *it needs to know about*. Figure 2.20 is an object diagram that shows which objects need to be connected.

For example, you will set your **Foo**'s textField instance variable to point to the **NSTextField** object on the window that currently says Message Text. So control-drag from the symbol that represents your instance of **Foo** to the **NSTextField**. You will see the Info Panel appear. Choose textField in the view on the left, and click Connect. You should see a dimple appear next to textField (Figure 2.21).

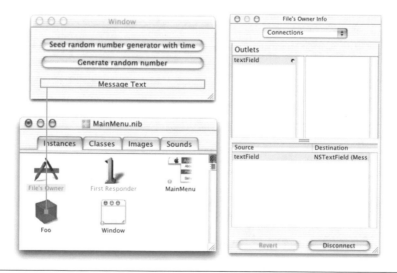

Figure 2.21   Set the textField Outlet

It is all about pointers: When you control-drag from A to B, you are setting a pointer in A to point to B. You have just set the pointer textField in your **Foo** object to point to the text field. This pointer will be set when the nib file is loaded.

Now you will set the Seed button's target instance variable to point to your instance of **Foo**. Furthermore, you want the button to trigger your **Foo**'s **seed:** method. Control-drag from the button to your **Foo**. Choose target in the view on the left and **seed:** in the view on the right. Click the Connect button to complete the connection. (Or you can double-click on the word **seed:**.) You should see a dimple appear next to **seed:** (Figure 2.22).

Similarly, you will set the Generate button's target instance variable to point to your instance of **Foo** and its action set to **generate:** method. Control-drag from the button to your **Foo**. Choose target in the view on the left. Choose **generate:** in the view on the right. Double-click on the action name (**generate:**) to complete the connection. Note the appearance of the dimple (Figure 2.23).

You are done with Interface Builder, so save the file and hide the application. Click on the Project Builder icon in the dock to bring Project Builder to the front.

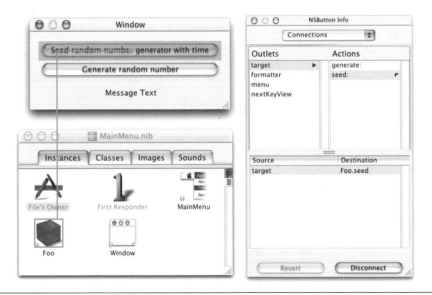

Figure 2.22 Set the Target and Action of the Seed Button

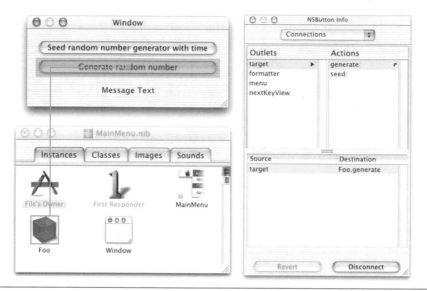

Figure 2.23   Set the Target and Action of the Generate Button

Back in Project Builder

In Project Builder, you will see that Foo.h and Foo.m have been added to the project. Most programmers would put these files under the Classes group (Figure 2.24). Drag the files into the Classes group if they aren't there already. Make sure that the circle to the left of the filename doesn't disappear. The file will be compiled into the application only if the circle is there. By clicking on the circle, you can make it appear and disappear.

In Java, a class would be declared like this:

```
import com.megacorp.Bar;
import com.megacorp.Baz;

public class Rex extends Bar implements Baz {
...methods and instance variables...
}
```

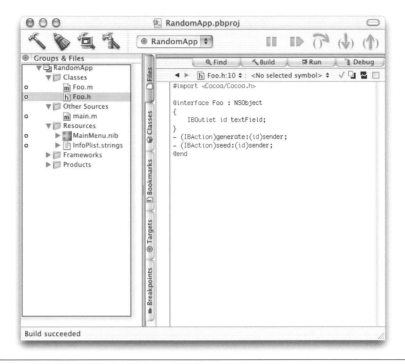

Figure 2.24   The New Class in Project Builder

This says, "The class **Rex** inherits from **Bar** and implements the methods declared in the **Baz** interface."

The analogous class in Objective-C would be declared like this:

```
#import <megacorp/Bar.h>
#import <megacorp/Baz.h>

@interface Rex: Bar <Baz> {
...instance variables...
}
...methods...
@end
```

If you know Java, Objective-C isn't so strange, is it? Like Java, Objective-C allows only single inheritance; that is, a class has only one superclass.

Types and Constants in Objective-C

Objective-C programmers use a few types that are not common in the rest of the C world. They are very simple.

- id is a pointer to any type of object.
- BOOL is the same as char, but is used as a boolean value.
  YES is 1.
  NO is 0.
- IBOutlet is a macro that evaluates to nothing. Ignore it. (IBOutlet is a hint to Interface Builder's parser.)
- IBAction is the same as void. It also acts has a hint to Interface Builder.
- nil is the same as NULL. We use nil instead of NULL for pointers to objects.

Edit the Header File

Click on Foo.h. Study it for a moment. You should see that it declares **Foo** to be a subclass of **NSObject**. Instance variables are declared inside the curly braces.

```
#import <Cocoa/Cocoa.h>

@interface Foo : NSObject
{
    IBOutlet id textField;
}
- (IBAction)generate:(id)sender;
- (IBAction)seed:(id)sender;
@end
```

Notice that there is an instance variable called textField of type id. As mentioned earlier, an id is a pointer to any type of object. Objective-C has very loose typing. In your code, you can try to send any message to any object. The compiler will happily compile it, and you will find the error while running the program. Thus you will need to be very careful when writing code. However, the dynamic nature of Objective-C makes it a very powerful tool. You can, for example, add new classes or add new methods to existing classes *while the application is running*. This is difficult or impossible in strongly typed languages like Java and C++.

If you would like to receive warnings about sending the wrong message to the wrong type of object, you can declare the variable more precisely. For example, you could change the type of textField from id to NSTextField *. The compiler will warn you when compiling code that sends messages to textField that an **NSTextField** object would not understand.

#import is like the C preprocessor's #include. #import, however, ensures that the file is only included once.

Notice that the declaration of the class starts with @interface. The symbol @ is not used in the C programming language. To minimize conflicts between C code and Objective-C code, many Objective-C-specific keywords are prefixed by @. Here are a few other Objective-C keywords that use it: @end, @implementation, @class, @selector, and @encode.

Edit the Implementation File

Now look at Foo.m. This is where the implementations of the methods are. Like C++ or Java, Objective-C is an object-oriented programming language. In C++ or Java, you might implement a method something like this:

```
public void increment(Object sender) {
    count++;
    textField.setIntValue(count);
}
```

In English, you would say "**increment** is a public instance method that takes one argument that is an object. The method doesn't return anything. The method increments the count instance variable and then sends the message **setIntValue()** to the textField object with count as an argument."

In Objective-C, the analogous method would look like this:

```
- (void)increment:(id)sender
{
    count++;
    [textField setIntValue:count];
}
```

Objective-C is a very simple language. It has no visibility specifiers: all methods are public, and all instance variables are private. (Actually, there are visibility specifiers for instance variables, but you will seldom see them used. The default is protected, and that works nicely.)

In the next chapter, we will explore Objective-C in all its beauty. For now, just copy the methods:

```
#import "Foo.h"

@implementation Foo

- (IBAction)generate:(id)sender
{
    // Generate a number between 1 and 100 inclusive
    int generated;
    generated = (random() % 100) + 1;

    // Ask the text field to change what it is displaying
    [textField setIntValue: generated];
}

- (IBAction)seed:(id)sender
{
    // Seed the random number generator with the time
    srandom(time(NULL));
    [textField setStringValue: @"Generator seeded"];
}

@end
```

(Remember that IBAction is the same as void. These methods don't return anything.)

Notice that because Objective-C is C with a few extensions, you can call functions from the standard C and Unix libraries.

Build and Run

Your application is done. To build the application, click on the hammer/screen icon at the upper left of the window (Figure 2.25). If it builds successfully, Build succeeded will appear in the lower left corner.

If your code has an error, you will see the compiler's message appear in the view in the upper right. If you click on the message, the erroneous line of code will be selected in the view on the lower right. In Figure 2.25, the programmer has forgotten a semicolon.

Launch your application. Click on the buttons and see the generated random numbers. Congratulations, you have a working application.

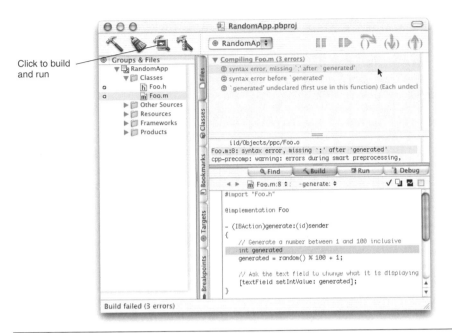

Click to build and run

Figure 2.25 Compiling

awakeFromNib

Notice that your application is flawed: when the application first starts, instead of anything interesting, the words Message Text appear in the text field.

Let's fix that problem: You are going to make the text field display the time and date that the application started. The nib file is a collection of objects that have been archived. When the program runs, the objects are brought back to life before the application handles any events from the user. After being brought to life and before any events are handled, all the objects are automatically sent the message **awakeFromNib**. You will add an **awakeFromNib** method that will initialize the textField's value.

Add the **awakeFromNib** method to Foo.m. For now, just type it in. You will understand it later on. Briefly, you are creating an instance of **NSCalendarDate** that represents the current time. Then you are telling the text field to set its value to the new calendar date object:

```
- (void)awakeFromNib
{
    NSCalendarDate *now;
    now = [NSCalendarDate calendarDate];
    [textField setObjectValue: now];
}
```

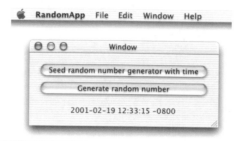

Figure 2.26 Finished Application

The order in which the methods appear in the file is not important. Just make sure that you add it after @implementation and before @end.

awakeFromNib gets called automatically. You will never have to call it. So build and run your application again. You should now see the date and time when the app runs (Figure 2.26).

Documentation

Before the wrap-up for this chapter, you should know where the documentation is. It may prove handy if you get stuck while doing an exercise later in the book. The online developer documentation is kept in the directory /Developer/Documentation/. The easiest way to get to it is by choosing Cocoa Help from Project Builder's Help menu (Figure 2.27).

What Have You Done?

You have now gone through the steps involved in creating a simple Cocoa application.

- Create a new project.
- Lay out an interface.
- Create custom classes.
- Connect the interface to your custom class or classes.
- Add code to the custom classes.
- Compile.
- Test.

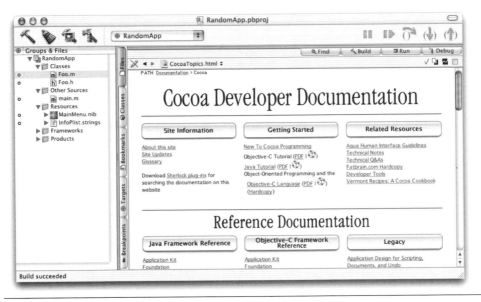

Figure 2.27   The Documentation

Let's briefly discuss the chronology of an application: When the process is started, it runs the **NSApplicationMain** function. The **NSApplicationMain** function creates an instance of **NSApplication**. There is a global variable called NSApp that points to that instance of **NSApplication**. NSApp reads the nib file and unarchives the objects inside. The objects are all sent the message **awakeFromNib**. Then NSApp checks for events. The timeline for these events appears in Figure 2.28.

When the window server receives an event from the keyboard and mouse, it puts the event data into the event queue for the appropriate application as shown in Figure 2.29. NSApp reads the event data from its queue and forwards it to a user interface object (like your button), and your code gets triggered. If this changes the data in a view, the view is redisplayed. Then NSApp checks its event queue for another event. This process of checking for events and reacting to them is known as the *main event loop*.

When the user chooses Quit from the menu, NSApp is sent the **terminate:** message. This ends the process, and all your objects are destroyed.

Puzzled? Excited? Move on to the next chapter so we can fill in some blanks.

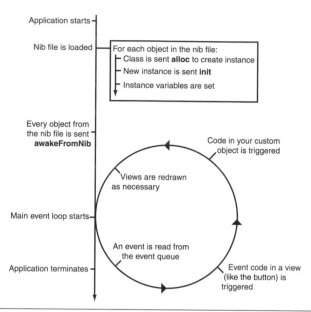

Figure 2.28   A Timeline

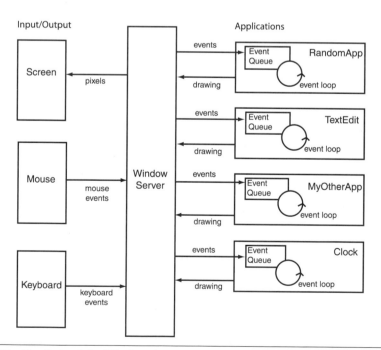

Figure 2.29   The Role of the Window Server

Chapter 3
OBJECTIVE-C

O nce upon a time a man named Brad Cox decided that it was time for the world to move toward a more modular programming style. C was a popular and powerful langauge. Smalltalk was an elegant untyped object-oriented language. Starting with C, Brad Cox added Smalltalk-like classes and message-sending mechanisms. He called the result *Objective-C*. Objective-C is a very simple addition to the C language. In fact, it was originally just a C preprocessor and a library.

Objective-C is not a proprietary language. It is an open standard that has been included in the Free Software Foundation's GNU C compiler (gcc) for many years. Cocoa was developed using Objective-C, and most Cocoa programming is done in Objective-C.

Teaching C and basic object-oriented concepts could consume an entire book. Instead of writing that book, this chapter assumes that you already know C and an object-oriented language like Java or C++ and introduces you to the basics of Objective-C. If you fit the profile, you will find learning Objective-C to be easy. If you do not, there are many great books on C and Apple's *Object-oriented Programming and the Objective-C Language* is an excellent, excellent book.

Creating and Using Instances

In Chapter 1, I mentioned that classes are used to create objects, that the objects have methods, and that you can send messages to the objects to trigger these methods. In this section, you will learn how to create an object, send messages to it, and destroy it when you no longer need it.

As an example, we will use the class **NSMutableArray**. You can create a new instance of **NSMutableArray** by sending the message **alloc** to the class like this:

```
[NSMutableArray alloc]
```

This method returns a pointer to the space that was allocated for the object. So you could hold onto that pointer in a variable like this:

```
NSMutableArray *foo;
foo = [NSMutableArray alloc];
```

While working with Objective-C, it is important to remember that foo is just a pointer. In this case, it points to an object.

Before using the object that foo points to, you would need to make sure that it is fully initialized. The **init** method will do this, so you might write code like this:

```
NSMutableArray *foo;
foo = [NSMutableArray alloc];
[foo init];
```

Take a long look at that last line; it sends the message **init** to the object that foo points to. We would say "foo is the receiver of the message **init**." Notice that a message send consists of a receiver (the object foo points to) and a message (**init**) wrapped in square brackets.

The method **init** actually returns the newly initialized object, so you will always nest the message sends like this:

```
NSMutableArray *foo;
foo = [[NSMutableArray alloc] init];
```

What about destroying the object when we no longer need it?

```
[foo release];
```

We will discuss **release** and what it really means later in this chapter.

Some methods take arguments. If a method takes an argument, the method name (called a *selector*) will end with a colon. For example, to add objects to the end of the array, you will use the **addObject:** method. (Assume bar is a pointer to another object.)

```
[foo addObject:bar];
```

If you have multiple arguments, the selector will have multiple parts. For example, to add an object at a particular index, you could use

```
[foo insertObject:bar atIndex:5];
```

Note that **insertObject:atIndex:** is one selector, not two. It will trigger one method with two arguments. This is strange to most C and Java programmers, but should be familiar to Smalltalk programmers.

Methods can also return values. For example, if you wanted to know how many objects were in foo, you would use the method **count**:

```
int x;
x = [foo count];
```

You are now at a point where you can read simple Objective-C code, so it is time to write a program that will create an instance of **NSMutableArray** and fill it with ten instances of **NSNumber**.

Using Existing Classes

If it isn't running, start Project Builder. Close any projects that you were working on. Under the Project menu, choose New Project.... When the panel pops up, choose to create a Foundation Tool (Figure 3.1).

Figure 3.1   Choose Project Type

Figure 3.2   Name Project

Name the project lottery (Figure 3.2). Unlike the names of applications, most tool names are lowercase.

A *foundation tool* has no graphical user interface and typically runs on the command line or in the background as a daemon. Unlike in an application project, you will always alter the main.m file of a foundation tool.

When the new project appears, select main.m under Source. It should look like Figure 3.3.

Edit main.m to look like this:

```
#import <Foundation/Foundation.h>

int main (int argc, const char * argv[])
{
    NSMutableArray *array;
    int i;
    NSNumber *number;

    NSAutoreleasePool * pool = [[NSAutoreleasePool alloc] init];

    array = [[NSMutableArray alloc] init];
    for ( i = 0; i < 10; i++) {
        number = [[NSNumber alloc] initWithInt:(i*3)];
```

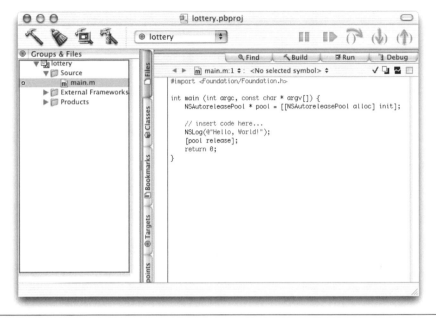

Figure 3.3   main.m

```
      [array addObject:number];
  }
  NSLog(@"array = %@", array);
  [array release];

  [pool release];
  return 0;
}
```

Here is the play-by-play for the code:

```
#import <Foundation/Foundation.h>
```

You are including the headers for all the classes in the Foundation framework. The headers are precompiled, so this is not as compute intensive as it sounds.

```
int main (int argc, const char *argv[])
```

The **main** function is declared just as it would be in any Unix C program:

```
  NSMutableArray *array;
  int i;
  NSNumber *number;
```

Here is the declaration of three variables: array is a pointer to an instance of **NSMutableArray**, i is an int, and number is a pointer to an instance of **NSNumber**. Note that neither the array object nor the number object exists yet. You have simply declared pointers that will refer to the objects once they are created.

```
NSAutoreleasePool *pool = [[NSAutoreleasePool alloc] init];
```

This declares a variable and attaches the variable to a new instance of **NSAutoreleasePool**. We will discuss the importance of autorelease pools later in the chapter.

```
for (i = 0; i < 10; i++) {
        number = [[NSNumber alloc] initWithInt:(i*3)];
        [array addObject:number];
}
```

Inside the for-loop, you have created an instance of **NSNumber** and made the variable number point to it. Then you have added that object to the array. Notice that this is a perfect example of the difference between the pointer and the object it points to. Here you have one variable of type NSNumber *, but you have ten instances of **NSNumber** (Figure 3.4).

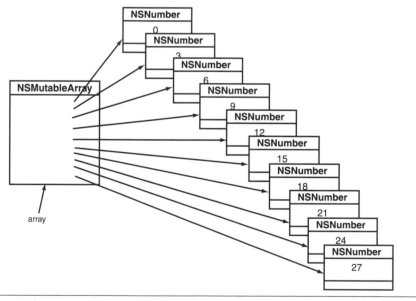

Figure 3.4 The Array of Number Objects

The array is not making copies of the **NSNumber** objects. Instead, it is simply keeping a list of pointers to the **NSNumber** objects. Objective-C programmers make very few copies of objects. It is seldom necessary.

```
NSLog(@"array = %@", array);
```

Here you are printing the contents of the array to the console. **NSLog** is a function much like **printf()**; it takes a format string and a comma-separated list of variables to be substituted into the format string. When displaying the string, **NSLog** prefixes the generated string with the name of the application and a time stamp.

In **printf**, for example, you would use a %x to display an integer in hexadecimal form. With **NSLog**, we have all the tokens from **printf** and the token %@ to display an object. The object gets sent the message **description**, and the string it returns replaces %@ in the string. We will discuss the **description** method in detail soon.

NSString Versus char*: If the @ before the quotes in @"array = %@" looks a little strange, remember that Objective-C is the C language with a couple of extensions. One of the extensions is that strings are instances of the class **NSString**. In C, strings are just pointers to a buffer of characters that ends in the null character. Both C strings and instances of **NSString** can be used in the same file. To differentiate between constant C strings and constant **NSStrings**, you must put @ before the opening quote of a constant **NSString**.

```
// C string
char *foo;
// NSString
NSString *bar;
foo = "this is a C string";
bar = @"this is an NSString";
```

You will use mostly **NSString**s in Cocoa programming. Wherever a string is needed, the classes in the frameworks expect an **NSString**. However, if you already have a bunch of C functions that expect C strings, you will find yourself using char * frequently.

One of the major benefits of **NSString** is that it can handle Unicode characters. The Unicode character set is much, much larger than ASCII and can represent text from many different languages. As long as you are dealing with only the standard ASCII character set, you can convert between C strings and **NSString**s:

```
// Create an NSString from a C string
bar = [NSString stringWithCString:foo];

// Create a C string from an NSString
foo = [bar cString];
```

All that said, you will nearly always use **NSString** in Cocoa programming.

Continuing with the code in **main()**, you have:

```
    [array release];
    [pool release];
    return(0);
}
```

When you no longer need the array or the autorelease pool, you send them the **release** message so that they will be deallocated.

Build and run the program (Figure 3.5).

Memory Management: Retain Count, Releasing, and Retaining

Let's discuss the **release** method. Every object has a retain count. The retain count is an integer. When an object is created by the **alloc** method, the retain count is set to 1. When the retain count becomes zero, the object is deallocated. You increment the retain count by sending the message **retain** to the object. You decrement the retain count by sending the message **release** to the object.

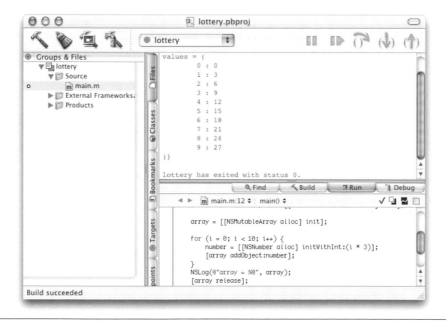

Figure 3.5 Completed Execution

Why is there a retain count at all? In C, after all, you would simply **malloc** memory and then **free** the memory when it is no longer needed. Imagine for a moment that you are an object that would be useful to several other objects. They are willing to share you, but how will you get deallocated when none of the other objects needs you any more? When an object gets a reference to you, it will send you a **retain** message. When an object no longer needs you, it will send you a **release** message. Thus, your retain count represents how many other objects have references to you. When the retain count becomes zero, this indicates that no one cares about you any more. You are deallocated so that the memory you were occupying can be freed.

The analogy that is commonly used is that of the dog and the leash. Each person who wants to ensure that the dog will stay around retains the dog by putting a leash around its neck. Many people can retain the dog, and as long as at least one person is retaining the dog, the dog will not go free. When zero people are retaining the dog, it will be freed. The retain count of an object, then, is the number of "leashes" on that object (Figure 3.6).

While Java has a garbage collector, Objective-C has this retain count mechanism. It gives the developer lots of control over how and when objects are freed, but it requires that you meticulously retain and release objects. You will spend some time every day walking through code and thinking about the retain count of the objects involved. If you release an object too much, it will be freed prematurely and your program will crash. If you retain an object too much, it will never get freed and you will waste memory.

When you ran your program a moment ago, it worked, didn't it? You would like to think that all the **NSNumber** objects neatly deallocated themselves when the array was released. You would be fooling yourself.

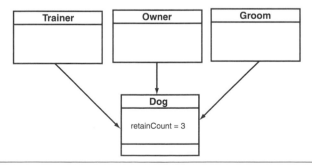

Figure 3.6   Objects Retain Each Other

An array does not make a copy of an object when it is added. Instead, the array stores a pointer to the object and sends it the message **retain**. When the array is deallocated, the objects in the array are sent **release**. (Also, if an object is removed from an array, it is sent **release**.)

We have a memory leak. Let's quickly go over the life of the **NSNumber** in your application:

- When the number object is created, it has a retain count of 1.
- When it is added to the array, its retain count is incremented to 2.
- When the array is deallocated, it releases the number. This decrements the retain count to 1.

The number object is not deallocated. In this example, the process ends an instant later, and the operating system reclaims all the memory. So it is not a big deal at all. However, in a program that ran a long time, a memory leak like this would be a bad thing. To practice being a tidy Objective-C programmer, fix the code.

After inserting the number into the array, release it. The for-loop should look like this:

```
for (i = 0; i < 10; i++) {
    number = [[NSNumber alloc] initWithInt:(i*3)];
    [array addObject:number];
    [number release];
}
```

Sending Messages to nil

In most object-oriented languages, your program will crash if you send a message to nil. In applications written in those languages, you will see many checks for nil before sending a message. In Java, for example, you frequently see the following:

```
if (foo != null) {
    foo.doThatThingYouDo();
}
```

In Objective-C, it is OK to send a message to nil. The message is simply discarded. This eliminates the need for these sorts of checks. So, for example, this will build and run without an error:

```
id foo;
foo = nil;
[foo count];
```

This is different from most languages, but you will get used to it.

Although you may send a message to nil, sending a message to a freed object will crash your program. For example, this code would not work:

```
id foo = [[NSMutableArray alloc] init];
[foo release];
[foo count];
```

Declaring Variables

Like C (but unlike C++ or Java), Objective-C requires that you declare variables at the beginning of a block. This, for example, will not compile:

```
int main(int argc, const char * argv[])
{
    int i = 6;
    i++;
    int j;
    return 0;
}
```

The line that increments i ends the declarations for the block. (A block is enclosed in curly braces.) The line that declares j is an error in C and Objective-C.

NSObject, NSArray, NSMutableArray, and NSString

Now, you have a fine program that uses a couple of the classes that came with Cocoa: **NSObject**, **NSMutableArray**, and **NSString**. (All classes that come with Cocoa have names with the "NS" prefix. Classes that you will create will *not* start with "NS.") These classes are all part of the Foundation framework. Figure 3.7 shows an inheritance diagram for these classes.

Let's go through a few of the commonly used methods on these classes. For a complete listing, you can access the online documentation in: /Developer/Documentation /Cocoa/Reference/Foundation/ObjC_classic/

NSObject

NSObject is the root of the entire Objective-C class hierarchy. Here are some commonly used methods on **NSObject**. (The method signature and its explanation must be on separate lines. This is consistent with Apple's documentation.)

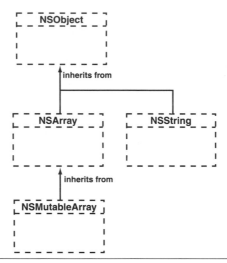

Figure 3.7 Inheritance Diagram

- (id)**init**

Initializes the receiver after memory for it has been allocated. An **init** message is generally coupled with an **alloc** message in the same line of code:

```
TheClass *newObject = [[TheClass alloc] init];
```

- (NSString *)**description**

Returns an **NSString** that describes the receiver. The debugger's print object (or "po") invokes this command. A good description method will often make debugging easier. Also, if you use %@ in a format string, the object that should be substituted in is sent the message **description**. What is returned from the **description** method is put into the log string. For example, this line in your main function

```
NSLog(@"array = %@", array);
```

is equivalent to

```
NSLog(@"array = %@", [array description]);
```

- (void)**release**

Decrements the receiver's reference count and sends it a **dealloc** message if its retain count becomes zero.

```
- (void)dealloc
```

Deallocates the object's memory. This is similar to a destructor in C++.

```
- (id)retain
```

Increments the receiver's reference count.

```
- (BOOL)isEqual:(id)anObject
```

`isEqual:` returns YES if the receiver and anObject are equal, NO otherwise. You might use it like this:

```
if ([myObject isEqual:anotherObject]) {
    NSLog("They are equal.");
}
```

But what does "equal" really mean? In **NSObject**, this method is defined to return YES if and only if the receiver and anObject are the same object, that is, if they are both pointers to the same memory location.

Clearly, this is not always the "equal" that you would hope for, so this method is overriden by many classes to implement a more appropriate idea of equality. For example, **NSString** overrides the method to compare the characters in the receiver and anObject. If the two strings have the same characters in the same order, they are considered equal.

Thus, if x and y are **NSStrings**, there is a big difference between these two expressions:

```
    x == y
```

and

```
    [x isEqual:y]
```

The first compares the two pointers. The second compares the characters in the strings. Note, however, that if x and y are instances of a class that has not overridden **NSObject**'s `isEqual:` method, the two expressions are equivalent.

NSArray

An **NSArray** is a list of pointers to other objects. It is indexed by integers. If there are n objects in the array, the objects are indexed by the integers 0 through $n-1$, and you cannot put a nil in an **NSArray**. (Note that this means that there are no "holes" in an **NSArray**. This confuses some programmers who are used to Java's Object[].) **NSArray** inherits from **NSObject**.

An **NSArray** is created with all the objects that will ever be in it. You can neither add nor remove objects from an instance of **NSArray**. We say that **NSArray** is *immutable*. (Its mutable subclass, **NSMutableArray**, will be discussed next.) Immutability is nice in some cases. Because it is immutable, a horde of objects can share one **NSArray** without worrying that one object in the horde might change it. **NSString** and **NSNumber** are also immutable. Instead of changing a string or number, you will simply create another one with the new value. (In the case of **NSString**, there is also the class **NSMutableString** to get around this problem.)

Here are some commonly used methods implemented by **NSArray**.

- (unsigned)**count**

Returns the number of objects currently in the array.

- (id)**objectAtIndex:**(unsigned)i

Returns the object located at index i. If i is beyond the end of the array, you will get an error at runtime.

- (id)**lastObject**

Returns the object in the array with the highest index value. If the array is empty, nil is returned. (Remember: nil is the same as NULL.)

- (BOOL)**containsObject:**(id)anObject

Returns YES if anObject is present in the array. This method determines whether an object is present in the array by sending an **isEqual:** message to each of the array's objects and passing anObject as the parameter.

- (unsigned)**indexOfObject:**(id)anObject

Searches the receiver for anObject and returns the lowest index whose corresponding array value is equal to anObject. Objects are considered equal if **isEqual:** returns YES. If none of the objects in the array are equal to anObject, **indexOfObject:** returns NSNotFound.

NSMutableArray

NSMutableArray inherits from **NSArray** and adds the ability to add and remove objects. Objects are retained when added and released when removed. To create a mutable array from an immutable one, use **NSArray**'s **mutableCopy** method.

Here are some commonly used methods implemented by **NSMutableArray**.

- (void)**addObject:**(id)anObject

Inserts anObject at the end of the receiver. You are not allowed to add nil to the array.

- (void)**addObjectsFromArray:**(NSArray *)otherArray

Adds the objects contained in otherArray to the end of the receiver's array of objects.

- (void)**insertObject:**(id)anObject **atIndex:**(unsigned)index

Inserts anObject into the receiver at index. If index is already occupied, the objects at index and beyond are shifted up one slot to make room. index cannot be greater than the number of elements in the array. You will get an error if anObject is nil or if index is greater than the number of elements in the array.

- (void)**removeAllObjects**

Empties the receiver of all its elements.

- (void)**removeObject:**(id)anObject

Removes all occurrences of anObject in the array. Matches are determined on the basis of anObject's response to the **isEqual:** message.

- (void)**removeObjectAtIndex:**(unsigned)index

Removes the object at index and moves all elements beyond index up one slot to fill the gap. You will get an error if index is beyond the end of the array.

NSString

An **NSString** is a buffer of Unicode characters. In Cocoa, all manipulations involving character strings are done with **NSString**. As a convenience, the Objective-C language also supports the @"…" construct to create a string object constant from 7-bit ASCII encoding:

```
NSString *temp = @"this is a constant string";
```

NSString inherits from **NSObject**. Here are some commonly used methods implemented by **NSString**.

- (id)**initWithFormat:**(NSString *)format, ...

Works like **sprintf**. format is a string containing tokens like %d. The additional arguments are substituted in for the tokens:

```
int x = 5;
char *y = "abc";
id z = @"123";
NSString *aString = [[NSString alloc] initWithFormat:
    @"Here's the int %d, the C String %s, and the NSString %@",
    x, y, z];
```

- (unsigned int)**length**

Returns the number of characters in the receiver.

- (NSString *)**stringByAppendingString:**(NSString *)aString

Returns a string object made by appending aString to the receiver. This code snippet, for example, would produce the string "Error: unable to read file."

```
NSString *errorTag = @"Error: ";
NSString *errorString = @"unable to read file.";
NSString *errorMessage = [errorTag stringByAppendingString:errorString];
```

"Inherits From" Versus "Uses" or "Knows About"

Beginning Cocoa programmers are often eager to create subclasses of **NSString** and **NSMutableArray**. Don't. Stylish Objective-C programmers almost never do. Instead, they use **NSString** and **NSMutableArray** as parts of larger objects. This is known as composition. For example, a **BankAccount** class could be a subclass of **NSMutableArray**. After all, isn't a bank account simply a collection of transactions? The beginner would do this. The old hand would create a class **BankAccount** that inherited from **NSObject** and has an instance variable called transactions that would refer to an **NSMutableArray**.

It is important to keep track of the difference between "uses" and "is a subclass of." The beginner would say, "**BankAccount** inherits from **NSMutableArray**." The old hand would say, "**BankAccount** uses **NSMutableArray**." In the common idioms of Objective-C, "uses" is much, much more common than "is a subclass of."

You will find it is much easier to use a class than it is to subclass one. Subclassing involves more code and a deeper understanding of the superclass. By using composition instead of inheritance, Cocoa allows developers to use very powerful classes without really understanding how they work.

In a strongly typed language like C++, inheritance is crucial. In an untyped language like Objective-C, inheritance is just a hack that saves the developer some typing. There are only two inheritance diagrams in this entire book. All the other diagrams are object diagrams that indicate which objects know about which other objects. This is much more important information to a Cocoa programmer.

Creating Your Own Classes

Where I live, the state government has decided that the uneducated have entirely too much money: You can play the lottery every week here. Let's imagine that a lottery entry has two numbers between 1 and 100, inclusive. You will write a program that will make up lottery entries for the next ten weeks. Each **LotteryEntry** object will have a date and two random integers (Figure 3.8). Besides learning how to create classes, you will build a tool that will certainly make you fabulously wealthy.

Creating the LotteryEntry Class

First you will create files for our **LotteryEntry** class. In the File menu, choose New file.... Select Objective-C class as the type (Figure 3.9).

Name the file LotteryEntry.m (Figure 3.10). Note that you are also causing a LotteryEntry.h to be created.

LotteryEntry.h

Edit the LotteryEntry.h to look like this:

```
#import <Foundation/Foundation.h>

@interface LotteryEntry : NSObject {
```

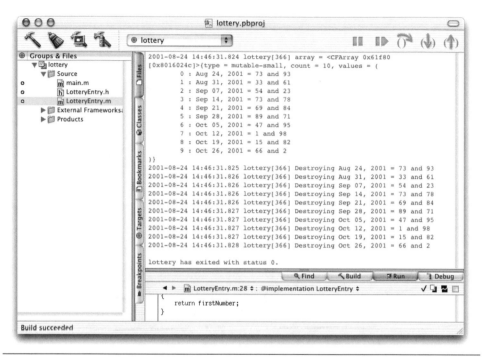

Figure 3.8 Completed Program

Figure 3.9 Choose Type of File

Figure 3.10   Name File

```
    NSCalendarDate *entryDate;
    int firstNumber;
    int secondNumber;
}
- (void)setNumbersRandomly;
- (void)setEntryDate:(NSCalendarDate *)date;
- (NSCalendarDate *)entryDate;
- (int)firstNumber;
- (int)secondNumber;
@end
```

You have created a header file for a new class called **LotteryEntry** that inherits from **NSObject**. It has three instance variables.

- entryDate is an **NSCalendarDate**.
- firstNumber and secondNumber are both ints.

You have declared five methods in the new class.

- **setNumbersRandomly** will set firstNumber and secondNumber to random values between 1 and 100. It takes no arguments and returns nothing.
- **entryDate** and **setEntryDate:** will allow other objects to read and set the variable entryDate. The method **entryDate** will return the value stored in the entryDate variable. **setEntryDate:** will allow the value of the entryDate

variable to be set. Methods that allow variables to be read and set are called *accessor methods*.

▪ You have also declared accessor methods for reading firstNumber and secondNumber.

LotteryEntry.m

Edit LotteryEntry.m to look like this:

```
#import "LotteryEntry.h"

@implementation LotteryEntry
- (void)setNumbersRandomly
{
    firstNumber = random() % 100 + 1;
    secondNumber = random() % 100 + 1;
}

- (void)setEntryDate:(NSCalendarDate *)date
{
    [date retain];
    [entryDate release];
    [date setCalendarFormat:@"%b %d, %Y"];
    entryDate = date;
}

- (NSCalendarDate *)entryDate
{
    return entryDate;
}
- (int)firstNumber
{
    return firstNumber;
}
- (int)secondNumber
{
    return secondNumber;
}
- (void)dealloc
{
    NSLog(@"Destroying %@", self);
    [entryDate release];
    [super dealloc];
}
@end
```

Here is the play-by-play for each method: **setNumbersRandomly** uses the standard **random** function to generate a pseudorandom number. You use the mod operator and add 1 to get the number in the range 1–100.

setEntryDate: releases the old date and retains the new one. Then you set the format on the date object so that it will display itself like this: "Feb 14, 1934." Then you set the `entryDate` variable to point to the new value.

The methods **entryDate**, **firstNumber**, and **secondNumber** simply return the values of variables.

dealloc

So far, the most interesting part of this class is the **dealloc** method. This method will get called automatically when the retain count becomes zero. The first thing in the method is the line

```
NSLog(@"Destroying %@", self);
```

By printing this message, you will know that the **dealloc** method got called.

Notice the use of `self`. Every method has an implicit local variable called `self`. `self` is a pointer to the object that is executing the method. You will commonly use `self` to have an object send a message to itself like this:

```
[self setNeedsDisplay:YES];
```

Continuing with the **dealloc** method, you come to the line

```
[entryDate release];
```

This line tells the **NSCalendarDate** object that you are no longer interested in it. This will decrement the retain count. If the retain count goes to zero, the **NSCalendarDate** object will also be deallocated.

Notice that you do not have to release the ints. They are inside the **LotteryEntry** object. When it is deallocated, the space will be freed. `entryDate`, on the other hand, is a pointer to an object that is outside the **LotteryEntry** object, so you must release it.

The last line is

```
[super dealloc];
```

This shows how we can call a superclass's implementation of a method. Here we are calling the superclass's **dealloc** method that will free the memory of the object.

Changing main.m

Now look at main.m. Many of the lines have stayed the same, but several have changed. The most important change is that now we are using **LotteryEntry** objects instead of **NSNumber** objects.

Here is the heavily commented code. (You don't have to type in the comments.)

```objc
#import <Foundation/Foundation.h>
#import "LotteryEntry.h"

int main (int argc, const char *argv[]) {
    NSMutableArray *array;
    int i;
    LotteryEntry *entry;

    NSCalendarDate *now;
    NSAutoreleasePool *pool = [[NSAutoreleasePool alloc] init];
    // Create the date object.
    now = [[NSCalendarDate alloc] init];
    // Initialize the random number generator.
    srandom(time(NULL));
    array = [[NSMutableArray alloc] init];

    for (i = 0; i < 10; i++){
        // Create a new instance of LotteryEntry
        entry = [[LotteryEntry alloc] init];
        [entry setNumbersRandomly];
        // Create a date/time object that is i weeks from now
        [entry setEntryDate: [now dateByAddingYears:0
            months:0 days:(i * 7) hours:0 minutes:0
            seconds:0]];
        // Add the LotteryEntry object to the array
        [array addObject: entry];
        // decrement the retain count of the lottery entry
        [entry release];
    }
    NSLog(@"array = %@", array);
    [array release];
    // Release the current time
    [now release];
    [pool release];
    return 0;
}
```

This program will create an array of LotteryEntry objects as shown in Figure 3.11.

Implementing a description Method

Build and run your application. You should see something like Figure 3.12.

Hmm. Not quite what we hoped for. After all, the purpose of the program is to see the dates and the numbers you should play on those dates, and you can't see either.

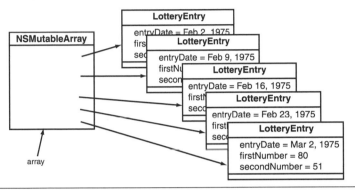

Figure 3.11   Object Diagram

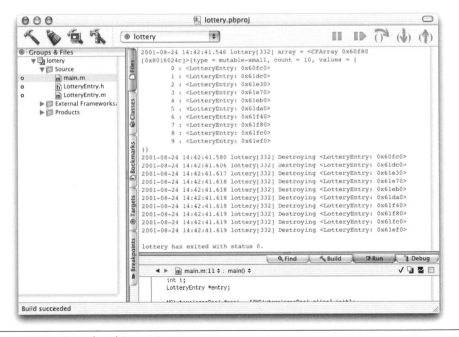

Figure 3.12   Completed Execution

Next you are going to make the **LotteryEntry** objects display themselves in a more meaningful manner.

Creating Autoreleased Objects

As we saw in the **NSObject** summary, every object has a **description** method that returns a string. The default method returns the name of the class and the hex address of the object. It would look like this: <LotteryEntry: 0x3da23>. So you are going to override the **description** method to return a more meaningful string.

A first attempt might look something like this:

```
- (NSString *)description
{
    NSString *result = [[NSString alloc] initWithFormat:@"%@ = %d and %d",
        entryDate, firstNumber, secondNumber];
    return result;
}
```

This would work perfectly well, but would result in an annoying memory leak. **alloc** always yields an object with a retain count of 1; thus the string being returned has a retain count of 1. Any object asking for the string would retain it. The string would then have a retain count of 2. When the object was no longer interested in the string, it would release it. The retain count would become 1. The string would never be deallocated.

Our next attempt might look something like this:

```
- (NSString *)description
{
    NSString *result = [[NSString alloc] initWithFormat:@"%@ = %d and %d",
        entryDate, firstNumber, secondNumber];
    [result release];
    return result;
}
```

This would not work at all. The string would be deallocated when sent the message **release**. The object asking for the string would get a pointer to a freed object.

The problem, then, is that you need to return a string, but you do not want to retain it. This is a common problem throughout the frameworks, which leads us to the **NSAutoreleasePool**.

Objects are added to the current autorelease pool when they are sent the message **autorelease**. When the autorelease pool is deallocated, it sends the message **release** to all the objects in the pool.

In other words, when an object is autoreleased, it is marked to be sent **release** sometime in the future. In particular, in a Cocoa application, an autorelease pool is created before every event is handled and deallocated after the event has been handled. Thus, unless the objects in the autorelease pools are being retained, they will be destroyed as soon as the event has been handled.

A correct solution then is

```
- (NSString *)description
{
    NSString *result = [[NSString alloc] initWithFormat:@"%@ = %d and %d",
        entryDate, firstNumber, secondNumber];
    [result autorelease];
    return result;
}
```

Rules Concerning Release

- Objects created by **alloc** or **copy** have a retain count of 1 and are not in the autorelease pool.
- If you get an object by *any* other method, assume that it has a retain count of 1 and is in the autorelease pool. If you do not wish it to be deallocated with the current autorelease pool, you must retain it.

Because you will frequently need objects that you are not retaining, many classes have class methods that return autoreleased objects. **NSString**, for example, has **stringWithFormat:**. The simplest correct solution then would be

```
- (NSString *)description
{
    return [NSString stringWithFormat:@"%@ = %d and %d",
        entryDate, firstNumber, secondNumber];
}
```

Note that this is exactly equivalent to the code from the previous version. Add this code to your LotteryEntry.m file. Build and run your application (Figure 3.13).

Temporary Objects

Notice that the autoreleased object won't be released until the event loop is over. This makes it perfect for an intermediate result. For example, if you had an array of

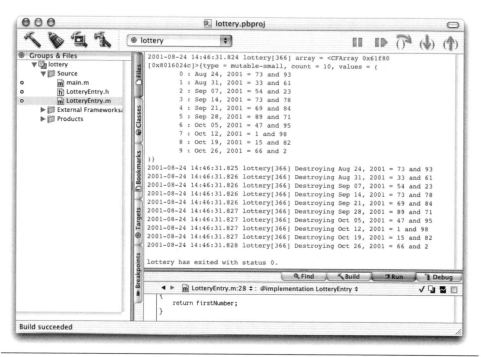

Figure 3.13   Completed Execution

NSString objects, you could create a string with all the elements in uppercase and concatenated together, like this:

```
- (NSString *)concatenatedAndAllCaps
{
    int i;
    NSString *sum = @"";
    NSString *upper;

    for (i=0; i < [myArray count]; i++) {
        upper = [[myArray objectAtIndex:i] uppercaseString]
        sum = [NSString stringWithFormat:@"%@%@",
                sum, upper];
    }
    return sum;
}
```

Notice that in this method, if you have 13 strings in the array, 26 autoreleased strings will be created (13 by **uppercaseString** and 13 by **stringWithFormat:**; the initial constant string is a special case and doesn't count). One of the resulting strings is returned and may be retained by the object that asked for it. The other 25 strings will be deallocated automatically at the end of the event loop.

Accessor Methods

An object has instance variables. Other objects cannot access these variables directly. To enable other objects to read and set an instance variable, an object will usually have a pair of accessor methods.

For example, if I have a class **Rex** that has an instance variable named `fido`, the class will probably also have two methods: **fido** and **setFido:**. The **fido** method enables other objects to read the `fido` variable. **setFido:** enables other objects to set the `fido` variable.

If you have a nonpointer type, the accessor methods are quite simple. For example, if your class has an instance variable called `foo` of type `int`, you would create the following accessor methods:

```
- (int)foo
{
    return foo;
}
- (void)setFoo:(int)x
{
    foo = x;
}
```

These methods will allow other objects to get and set the value of `foo`.

It gets more complicated if `foo` is a pointer to an object. In the setter method, you need to make sure that the new value is retained and the old value is released. If you assume that `foo` is a pointer to an **NSString**, there are three common idioms in setter methods. All three are fine, and you can probably find a couple of experienced Cocoa programmers who will argue the superiority of any one of them. I'll list the tradeoffs after each one.

The first is "Retain, Then Release":

```
- (void)setFoo:(NSString *)x
{
    [x retain];
    [foo release];
    foo = x;
}
```

Notice that it is important to retain before releasing. Imagine that you reverse the order. If x and foo are both pointers to the same object, the release would cause the object to be deallocated before it was retained. Tradeoff: If they are the same value, this method does an unnecessary retain and release.

The next is "Check Before Change":

```
- (void)setFoo:(NSString *)x
{
    if (foo != x) {
      [foo release];
      foo = [x retain];
    }
}
```

Here you are not setting the variable unless a different value is passed in. Tradeoff: An extra if statement.

The final idiom of the bunch is "Autorelease Old Value":

```
- (void)setFoo:(NSString *)x
{
    [foo autorelease];
    foo = [x retain];
}
```

Here, you autorelease the old value. Tradeoff: An error in retain counts will result in a crash one event loop after the error. This makes the bug harder to track down. In the previous versions, your crash will happen closer to your error. There is also a small performance overhead involved with **autorelease**.

You have read the tradeoffs, you can make your own decision on which to use. In this book, I will be using "Retain, Then Release."

The getter method for an object is the same as for a nonpointer type:

```
- (NSString *)foo
{
    return foo;
}
```

Most Java programmers would name this method **getFoo**. Don't. Objective-C programmers all call this method **foo**. In the common idioms of Objective-C, a method prefixed with "get" takes an address where data can be copied. For example, if you have an **NSColor** object and you want its red, green, blue, and alpha components, you would call **getRed:green:blue:alpha:** :

```
float r, g, b, a;

[myFavoriteColor getRed:&r green:&g blue:&b alpha:&a];
```

(For readers who might be a bit rusty with their C: "&" returns the address where the variable holds its data.)

If you used your accessor methods to read the variables, your **description** method would look like this:

```
- (NSString *)description
{
    return [NSString stringWithFormat:@"%@ = %d and %d",
        [self entryDate], [self firstNumber], [self secondNumber]];
}
```

This would be considered the "most correct" implementation of the **description** method.

NSCalendarDate

Before moving on to any new ideas, let's familiarize ourselves with **NSCalendarDate**. Instances of **NSCalendarDate** have a date and time, a time zone, and a format string. **NSCalendarDate** inherits from **NSDate**.

Instances of **NSCalendarDate** are basically immutable: You can't change the day or time of a calendar date once it is created. However, you can change its format string and its time zone. Because it is basically immutable, many objects often share a single calendar date object. There is seldom a need to create a copy of an **NSCalendarDate** object.

Here are some of the commonly used methods implemented by **NSCalendarDate**:

> \+ (id)**calendarDate**
>
> This method creates and returns a calendar date initialized to the current date and time in the default format for the locale. The time zone will be the time zone that the machine is set to. Remember that the returned object is autoreleased.

This is a *class method*. A class method is one that is triggered by sending a message to the class instead of an instance. This one, for example, could be used like this:

```
NSCalendarDate *now;
now = [NSCalendarDate calendarDate];
```

In the interface file, implementation file, and documentation, class methods are recognizable because they start with "+" instead of "-".

```
+ (id)dateWithYear:(int)year
        month:(unsigned)month
          day:(unsigned)day
         hour:(unsigned)hour
       minute:(unsigned)minute
       second:(unsigned)second
     timeZone:(NSTimeZone *)aTimeZone
```

This is another class method which returns an autoreleased object. This one creates and returns a calendar date initialized with the specified values. The year value must include the century (for example, 2001 instead of 1). The other values are the standard ones: 1 through 12 for months, 1 through 31 for days, 0 through 23 for hours, and 0 through 59 for both minutes and seconds. The following code fragment shows a calendar date created with a date on 3 August 2000, 4 PM, Pacific Standard Time (**timeZoneWithName:** returns the **NSTimeZone** object that represents the time zone with the specified name).

```
NSCalendarDate *hotTime = [NSCalendarDate dateWithYear:2000
    month:8 day:3 hour:16 minute:0 second:0
    timeZone:[NSTimeZone timeZoneWithName:@"PST"]];
```

```
- (NSCalendarDate *)dateByAddingYears:(int)year
                        months:(int)month
                          days:(int)day
                         hours:(int)hour
                       minutes:(int)minute
                       seconds:(int)second
```

This returns a calendar date with the year, month, day, hour, minute, and second offsets specified as arguments. A positive offset is the future, and a negative offset represents the past. You used this method in main.m. Here, we are creating a day six months after hotTime:

```
NSCalendarDate *coldTime = [hotTime dateByAddingYears:0
    months:6 days:0 hours:0 minutes:0 seconds:0];
```

- (int)**dayOfCommonEra**

Returns the number of days since the beginning of 1 A.D.

- (int)**dayOfMonth**

Returns a number that indicates the day of the month (1 through 31) of the receiver.

- (int)**dayOfWeek**

Returns a number that indicates the day of the week (0 through 6) of the receiver; 0 indicates Sunday.

- (int)**dayOfYear**

Returns a number that indicates the day of the year (1 through 366) of the receiver.

- (int)**hourOfDay**

Returns the hour value (0 through 23) of the receiver.

- (int)**minuteOfHour**

Returns the minutes value (0 through 59) of the receiver.

- (int)**monthOfYear**

Returns a number that indicates the month of the year (1 through 12) of the receiver.

- (void)**setCalendarFormat:**(NSString *)format

Sets the default calendar format for the receiver. A calendar format is a string formatted with date-conversion specifiers, as listed in Table 3.1.

- (NSDate *)**laterDate:**(NSDate *)anotherDate

This method is inherited from **NSDate**. Compares the receiver to anotherDate and returns the later of the two.

Table 3.1 Possible Tokens in the Calendar Format String

Symbol	Meaning
%y	Year without century (00–99)
%Y	Year with century ("1990")
%b	Abbreviated month name ("Jan")
%B	Full month name ("January")
%m	Month as a decimal number (01–12)
%a	Abbreviated weekday name ("Fri")
%A	Full weekday name ("Friday")
%w	Weekday as a decimal number (0–6), where Sunday is 0
%d	Day of the month as a decimal number (01–31)
%e	Same as %d but does not print the leading 0
%j	Day of the year as a decimal number (001–366)
%H	Hour based on a 24-hour clock as a decimal number (00–23)
%I	Hour based on a 12-hour clock as a decimal number (01–12)
%p	AM/PM designation for the locale
%M	Minute as a decimal number (00–59)
%S	Second as a decimal number (00–59)
%F	Milliseconds as a decimal number (000–999)
%x	Date using the date representation for the locale
%X	Time using the time representation for the locale
%c	Shorthand for %X %x, the locale format for date and time
%Z	Time zone name ("EST")
%z	Time zone offset in hours and minutes from GMT (HHMM)
%%	A '%' character

- (NSTimeInterval)**timeIntervalSinceDate:**(NSDate *)anotherDate

Returns the interval in seconds between the receiver and anotherDate. If the receiver is earlier than anotherDate, the return value is negative. NSTimeInterval is the same as double.

Writing Initializers

Notice the following lines in your **main** function:

```
entry = [[LotteryEntry alloc] init];
[entry setNumbersRandomly];
```

You are creating a new instance and then immediately calling **setNumbersRandomly** to initialize firstNumber and secondNumber. This is something that should really be handled by the initializer, so you are going to override the **init** method in your **LotteryEntry** class.

In the LotteryEntry.m file, change the method **setNumbersRandomly** into an **init** method like this:

```
- (id)init
{
    [super init];
    firstNumber = random() % 100 + 1;
    secondNumber = random() % 100 + 1;
    return self;
}
```

Notice that the **init** method calls the superclass's initializer at the beginning, initializes its own variables, and then returns self.

Now delete the line in main.m that says

```
[entry setNumbersRandomly];
```

In LotteryEntry.h delete the declaration

```
- (void)setNumbersRandomly;
```

Build and run your program to reassure yourself that it still works.

A few of the initializers in Cocoa will return nil if initialization was impossible. Also, a couple of the initializers in Cocoa return an object that is not the receiver. If a programmer is worried that the superclass's initializer may be one of these cases, he will create an initializer that is something like this:

```
- (id)init
{
    if (self = [super init]) {
        [self setFirstNumber: random() % 100 + 1];
        [self setSecondNumber: random() % 100 + 1];
    }
    return self;
}
```

This will always work and is considered the most correct form; however, none of the classes that you will subclass in this book require these checks. For simplicity, I will sometimes leave out the checks.

Initializers with Arguments

Look at the same place in main.m. It should look like this now:

```
entry = [[LotteryEntry alloc] init];
[entry setEntryDate: [now dateByAddingYears:0
                months:0 days:(i * 7) hours:0 minutes:0
                seconds: 0]];
```

It would be nicer if you could supply the date as an argument to the initializer. Change those lines to look like this:

```
entry = [[LotteryEntry alloc] initWithEntryDate: [now dateByAddingYears:0
                months:0 days:(i * 7) hours:0 minutes:0
                seconds: 0]];
```

First, declare the method in LotteryEntry.h:

```
- (id)initWithEntryDate:(NSCalendarDate *)theDate;
```

Now change the initializer:

```
- (id)initWithEntryDate:(NSCalendarDate *)theDate
{
    if (self = [super init]) {
      [self setEntryDate:theDate];
      firstNumber = random() % 100 + 1;
      secondNumber = random() % 100 + 1;
    }
    return self;
}
```

Build and run your program. It should work fine.

However, there is a problem with your class **LotteryEntry**. The problem is that you are going to e-mail the class to your friend Rex. Rex is going to use the class **LotteryEntry** in his program but might not realize that you have written **initWithEntryDate:**. If he made this mistake, he might write the following lines of code:

```
NSCalendarDate *today = [NSCalendarDate calendarDate];
LotteryEntry *bigWin = [[LotteryEntry alloc] init];
[bigWin setEntryDate:today];
```

This will not create an error. Instead, it will simply go up the inheritance tree until it finds an implementation of **NSObject**'s **init** method. The problem is that firstNumber and secondNumber will not get initialized properly. They will both be zero.

To protect Rex from his own ignorance, you will override **init** to call your initializer with a default date, like this:

```
- (id)init
{
    return [self initWithEntryDate:[NSCalendarDate calendarDate]];
}
```

Add this method to your LotteryEntry.m file.

Notice that **initWithEntryDate:** still does all the work. Since a class can have multiple initializers, we call the one that does the work the *designated initializer*. If a class has several initializers, the designated initializer typically takes the most arguments. You should clearly document which of your initializers is the designated initializer. Note that the designated initializer for **NSObject** is **init**.

> ### Conventions for Creating Initializers (Rules that Cocoa programmers try to follow regarding initializers)
>
> - You do not have to create an initializer in your class at all if the superclass's initializers are sufficient.
> - If you do decide to create an initializer, you must override the superclass's designated initializer.
> - If you create multiple initializers, only one does the work. It is the designated initializer. All other initializers call the designated initializer.
> - The designated initializer of your class will call its superclass's designated initializer.

The Debugger

The Free Software Foundation developed the compiler and the debugger that come with the developer tools. The compiler is gcc and the debugger is gdb. In this section we will talk about setting breakpoints, invoking the debugger, and browsing the values of variables.

While browsing code, you may have noticed a white margin to the left of your code. If you click in that margin, a breakpoint will be added at that line. Add a breakpoint in main.m at the line that reads (Figure 3.14):

```
[array addObject:entry];
```

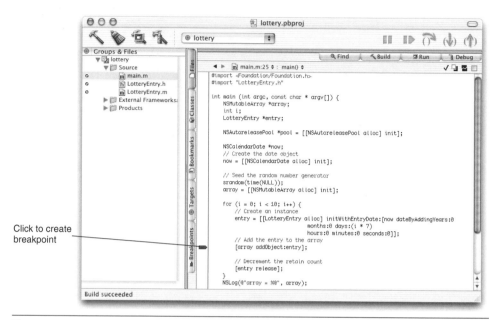

Click to create
breakpoint

Figure 3.14   Creating a Breakpoint

If your program is compiled, you can invoke the debugger by clicking on the button that looks like a can of bug spray in `Project Builder`. The debugger will take a few seconds to get started, and then it will run your program until it hits the breakpoint (Figure 3.15).

In the list on the left, you will see the frames on the stack. Because our breakpoint is in `main()`, the stack is not very deep. In the outline view on the right, you will see the variables and their values. Note that the variable i is currently 0.

The buttons above the stack information are for pausing, continuing, and stepping over, into, and out of functions. Click the continue button to execute another iteration of the loop. Click the step-over button to walk through the code line by line.

gdb, being a Unix thing, is usually run from a terminal. To see the terminal-like view of the gdb process, click on the tab labeled Console.

In the console, you have full access to all the capabilities of gdb. One very handy thing is "print-object," or just "po." If a variable is a pointer to an object, when you "po" it, the object is sent the message **description** and the result is printed in the console. Try printing the entry variable

```
po entry
```

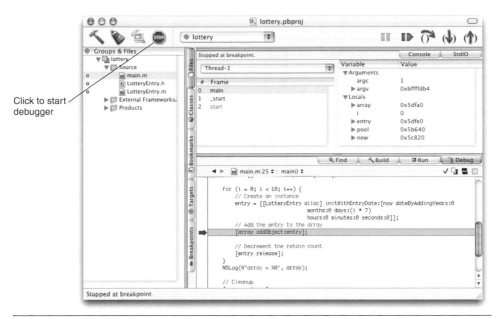

Figure 3.15 Stopped at a Breakpoint

You should see the result of your **description** method (Figure 3.16). (If you get a warning message from the debugger, ignore it.)

To remove the breakpoint, just drag it out of the margin. Remove your breakpoint and put another in **LotteryEntry**'s **dealloc** method next to the line that reads

```
NSLog(@"Destroying %@", self);
```

Click the continue button to run until the first **LotteryEntry** object executes its **dealloc** method. Notice that the stack is deeper this time. You can choose a frame in the stack in the list. The variables for that frame will appear in the outline view on the right.

That will get you started with the debugger. For more in-depth information, refer to the documentation from the Free Software Foundation (http://www.gnu.org/).

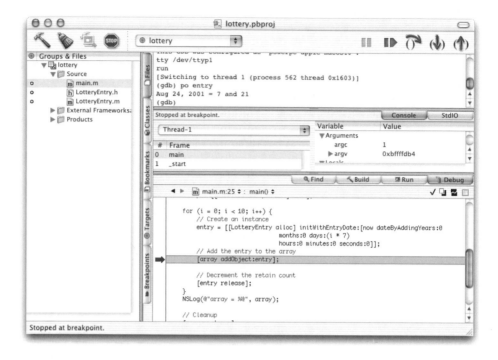

Figure 3.16   Using po

What Have You Done?

You have written a simple program in Objective-C. There was a **main** function that created several objects. Some of these objects were instances of **LotteryEntry**, which is a class that you created. The program logged some information to the console. You did not create an application: Your program has no event loop and didn't create any windows.

At this point, you have a pretty complete understanding of Objective-C. Objective-C is not a complex language. The rest of the book is concerned with the frameworks that make up Cocoa. From now on, you will be creating event-driven applications.

For the More Curious: How Does Messaging Work?

As mentioned earlier, an object is like a C struct. **NSObject** declares an instance variable called isa. Since **NSObject** is the root of the entire class inheritance tree, every object has isa. Thus isa is a pointer to the class structure that created the object (Figure 3.17). The class structure includes the names and types of the instance variables for the class. It also has the implementation of all the class's methods. The class structure has a pointer to the class structure for its superclass.

The methods are indexed by the selector. The selector is of type SEL. SEL is actually defined to be char *, but it is most useful to think of it as an int. Each method name is mapped to a unique int. For example, the method name **addObject:** might map to the number 12. When you look up methods, you will use the selector, not the string @"addObject:".

As part of the Objective-C data structures, there is a table that maps the names of methods to their selection as shown in Figure 3.18.

At compile time, the compiler looks up the selectors wherever it sees a message send.

```
[myObject addObject:yourObject];
```

becomes (assuming the selector for **addObject:** is 12).

```
objc_msgSend(myObject, 12, yourObject);
```

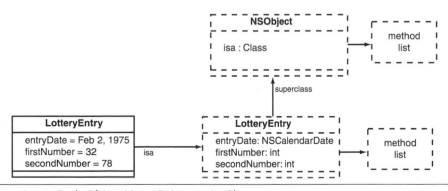

Figure 3.17   Each Object Has a Pointer to Its Class

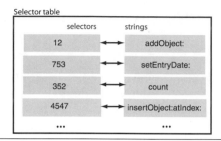

Figure 3.18   The Selector Table

objc_msgSend() looks at myObject's isa pointer to get to its class structure and looks for the method associated with 12. If it does not find the method, it follows the pointer to the superclass. If the superclass does not have a method for 12, it continues searching up the tree. If it reaches the top of the tree without finding a method, you receive an error.

Notice that this a very dynamic way of handling messages. These class structures can be changed at runtime. In particular, using the **NSBundle** class; it is relatively easy to add classes and methods to your program while it is running. This is a very powerful technique, and it has been used to create applications that can be extended by the user.

Challenge

Change the format string on the calendar date objects in your **LotteryEntry** class.

Create another loop in **main()** that removes all the **LotteryEntry** objects from the array. Notice that they are deallocated as they are removed.

Chapter 4
CONTROLS

Once upon a time, there was a company called Taligent. Taligent was created by IBM and Apple to develop a set of tools and libraries like Cocoa. About the time Taligent reached the peak of its mindshare, I met one of its engineers at a trade show. I asked him to create a simple application for me: A window would appear with a button, and when the button was clicked, the words "Hello, World!" would appear in a text field. The engineer created a project and started subclassing madly: subclassing the window and the button and the event handler. Then he started generating code: dozens of lines to get the button and the text field on to the window. After 45 minutes, I had to leave. The app still did not work. That day, I knew that the company was doomed. A couple of years later, Taligent quietly closed its doors forever.

Most C++ and Java tools work on the same principles as the Taligent tools. The developer subclasses many of the standard classes and generates many lines of code to get controls to appear on windows. Most of these tools actually work.

While writing an application that uses the AppKit framework, you will seldom subclass the classes that represent windows, buttons, or events. Instead, you will create objects that will work with the existing classes. Also, you will not create code to get controls on windows. Instead, the nib file will contain all this information. The resulting application will have significantly fewer lines of code. At first, this may be alarming. In the long run, most programmers find it delightfully elegant.

To understand the AppKit framework, a good place to start is with the class **NSControl**. **NSButton**, **NSSlider**, **NSTextView**, and **NSColorWell** are all subclasses of **NSControl**. A control has a *target* and an *action*. The `target` is simply a pointer to another object. The `action` is a message (a selector) to send to the `target`. Remember that you set the `target` and `action` for the two buttons in Chapter 2. You set your **Foo** object to be the `target` of both buttons, and you set the `action` on one to **seed:** (Figure 4.1) and the `action` on the other to **generate:**.

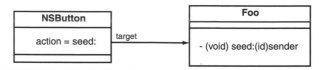

Figure 4.1 A Button Has a Target and an Action

When the user interacts with the control, it sends the `action` message to its `target`. So, for example, when the button gets pressed, the button sends the `target` its `action` message (Figure 4.2).

The action methods all take one argument: the sender. This enables the receiver to know which control sent the message. Often, you will call back to the sender to get more information. For example, a checkbox will send its action message when it is turned on and when it is turned off. After getting the action message, the receiver might call back to the button to find out if it is currently on or off:

```
- (IBAction)toggleFoo:(id)sender
{
    foo = [sender state];
}
```

To better understand **NSControl**, you should become acquainted with its ancestors: **NSControl** inherits from **NSView**, which inherits from **NSResponder**, which inherits from **NSObject**. Each member of the family tree adds some capabilities (Figure 4.3).

At the top of the class hierachy is **NSObject**. All classes inherit from **NSObject**, and this is where they get the basic methods like **retain**, **release**, **dealloc**, and **init**. **NSResponder** is a subclass of **NSObject**. Responders have the ability to handle events like **mouseDown:** and **keyDown:**. **NSView** is a subclass of **NSResponder**. An **NSView** has a place on a window, where it draws itself. You can create subclasses of **NSView** to do things like display graphs and allow the user to drag and drop data. **NSControl** inherits from **NSView** and adds the target and the action.

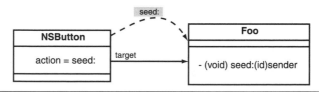

Figure 4.2 The Button Sends a Message

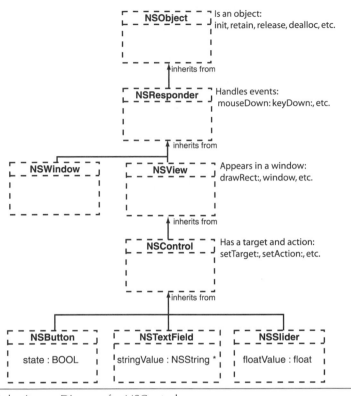

Figure 4.3   Inheritance Diagram for NSControl

Some Commonly Used Subclasses of NSControl

Before using some controls, let's take a brief look at the three most commonly used controls: **NSButton**, **NSSlider**, and **NSTextField**.

NSButton

Instances of **NSButton** can have several different appearances: oval, square, checkbox. They can also have different behavior when clicked: toggle (like a checkbox) or momentarily on (like most other buttons). Buttons can have icons and sounds associated with them. Figure 4.4 shows the Attributes info panel for an **NSButton** in Interface Builder.

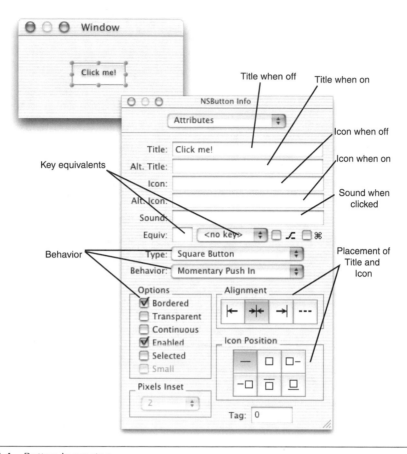

Figure 4.4 Button Inspector

Here are three methods that you will frequently send to buttons.

- (void)**setEnabled:**(BOOL)yn

The user can click on an enabled button. Disabled buttons are greyed out.

- (BOOL)**state**

Returns YES if the button is on, NO if the button is off. This is how you will see whether a checkbox is checked or unchecked.

- (void)**setState:**(BOOL)yn

Turns on or off the button. This is how you will check or uncheck a checkbox programmatically.

NSSlider

Instances of **NSSlider** can be vertical or horizontal. They can send the action to the target continuously while being changed, or they can wait to send the action until the user releases the mouse button. A slider can have markers, and it can prevent users from choosing values between the markers (Figure 4.5).

Here are two methods of **NSSlider** that you will use frequently.

- (void)**setFloatValue:**(float)x

Moves the slider to x.

- (float)**floatValue**

Returns the current value of the slider.

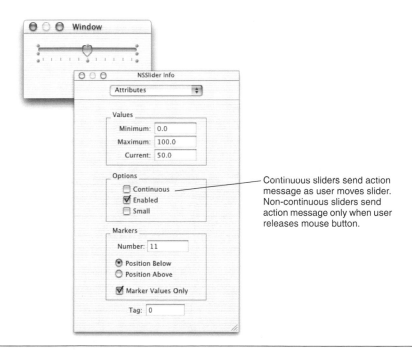

Figure 4.5   Slider Inspector

NSTextField

An instance of **NSTextField** can allow a user to type a single line of text. Text fields may or may not be editable. Uneditable text fields are commonly used as labels on a window. Compared to buttons and sliders, text fields are relatively complex. We will plumb the depths of the mysteries surrounding text fields in later chapters. Figure 4.6 shows the Attributes info panel for an **NSTextField** in Interface Builder.

Notice the Scrollable radio button. That means scrolling left to right, not up and down. If you want to have multiple rows of text, you will use an **NSTextView**, not an **NSTextField**.

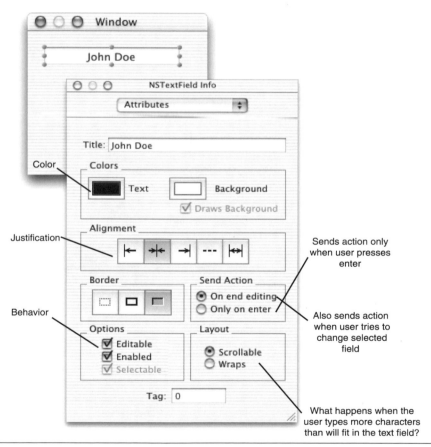

Figure 4.6   Text Field Inspector

NSSecureTextField is a subclass of **NSTextField**. **NSSecureTextField** is used for things like passwords. As the user types, bullets appear instead of the typed characters. You cannot copy or cut from an **NSSecureTextField**.

Here are a couple of the most commonly used **NSTextField** methods.

- (NSString *)**stringValue**

- (void)**setStringValue:**(NSString *)aString

These methods allow you to get and set the string data being displayed in the text field.

- (NSObject *)**objectValue**

- (void)**setObjectValue:**(NSObject *)

These methods allow you to get and set the data being displayed in the text field as an arbitrary object type. This is useful if you are using a formatter. **NSFormatter**s are responsible for converting a string into another type, and vice versa. If there is no formatter, these methods work with **NSString**s.

For example, you might use a text field to allow the user to type in a date. As the programmer, you don't want the string that the user typed in; what you want is an instance of **NSCalendarDate**. By attaching an **NSDateFormatter**, you ensure that the text field's **objectValue** method will return an **NSCalendarDate**. Also, when you call **setObjectValue:** with an **NSCalendarDate**, the **NSDateFormatter** will format it as a string for the user.

You will create a custom formatter class in Chapter 21.

Start the RaiseMan Example

As a simple example of using controls, you will be building an application to keep track of the people you manage and the raise that you intend to give them at review time. The app will look like Figure 4.7 when you are done with this chapter.

Figure 4.8 presents a diagram of the objects that you will create and their pointers to each other. Note that all the classes that start with "NS" are part of the Cocoa frameworks and thus already exist. Your code will be in the **Person** class and the **MyDocument** class.

In Project Builder, create a new project of type Cocoa Document-based Application (Figure 4.9). Name the project RaiseMan. A new project will appear.

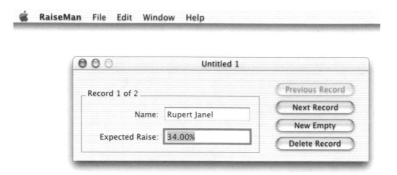

Figure 4.7   Completed Application

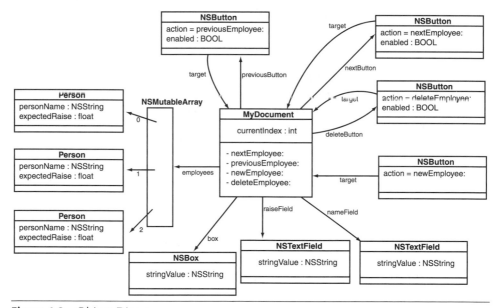

Figure 4.8   Object Diagram

Figure 4.9   Choose Project Type

The Interface File for MyDocument

The first thing to do is to add some declarations to the MyDocument.h file. Once you have typed in these declarations, Interface Builder can parse the file, and all the actions and outlets for your **MyDocument** class will be available to you when you make the connections. Edit MyDocument.h to look like this:

```
#import <Cocoa/Cocoa.h>

@interface MyDocument : NSDocument
{
    NSMutableArray *employees;
    int currentIndex;
    IBOutlet NSButton *deleteButton;
    IBOutlet NSButton *nextButton;
    IBOutlet NSButton *previousButton;
    IBOutlet NSTextField *nameField;
    IBOutlet NSTextField *raiseField;
    IBOutlet NSBox *box;
}
```

```
// Action methods
- (IBAction)nextEmployee:(id)sender;
- (IBAction)previousEmployee:(id)sender;
- (IBAction)deleteEmployee:(id)sender;
- (IBAction)newEmployee:(id)sender;

// Private methods
- (void)createNewEmployee;
- (void)updateEmployee;
- (void)updateUI;
@end
```

Notice the declarations of the variables:

- employees is the mutable array that will hold instances of your **Person** class.
- currentIndex is the index in the employees array of the person currently being displayed.
- The outlets deleteButton, nextButton, and previousButton are all pointers to **NSButton** objects. They will allow you to disable and enable the buttons. For example, if the user is viewing the first person in the array, the previousButton will be disabled. If they are viewing the last person in the array, the nextButton will be disabled. You will make sure that there is always one person in the list, so when there is only one person remaining, you will disable the deleteButton.

  Notice that the variable declarations specify that these are pointers to **NSButton** objects. You prefixed the declaration with IBOutlet. When Interface Builder parses this file, it will take that as a hint that you want to initialize these variables in Interface Builder. Because IBOutlet is a macro that evaluates to nothing, the compiler will ignore the hint. If you wanted to, you could have declared all these outlets like this:

  ```
  id deleteButton;
  id nextButton;
  id previousButton;
  id nameField;
  id raiseField;
  id box;
  ```

  By being more specific, other programmers will be able to comprend your code more quickly. Also, the compiler will give you more warnings.

- nameField is an outlet to the text field where the user will edit the person's name.
- raiseField is an outlet to the text field where the user will edit the person's expected raise.
- box is the box around the text fields. Its title will reflect which record is currently being displayed.

Then come the declarations of the action methods.

- `nextEmployee:` will read the edits the user has made, increment the `currentIndex`, and display the person at `currentIndex` in the array.
- `previousEmployee:` is like **nextEmployee:**, but it will decrement the `currentIndex`.
- `deleteEmployee:` will remove the person at `currentIndex`.
- `newEmployee:` will read any edits the user has made to the current person, add a new instance of **Person** to the array, and display the new instance.

Finally, you have the declarations of private methods. These will be called by the action methods.

- `createNewEmployee` creates an instance of **Person** and adds it to the array.
- `updateEmployee` reads the data in the text fields and saves it into the current person object.
- `updateUI` reads the data from the current person objects and sets the text fields accordingly.

Make sure you save the file. Now double-click on `MyDocument.nib` under Resources. It will open in Interface Builder.

Lay Out the Interface

The first thing to do in the new nib file is to tell it about the outlets and actions that you just typed in. To do this, under the Classes tab, select **MyDocument**. It is a subclass of **NSDocument**. Then in the Classes menu, choose Read files... (Figure 4.10).

The Parse panel will appear. It should default to your project directory, and you should see `MyDocument.h`. Select it and click the Parse button. When you have done that, you will see that your **MyDocument** class has all the outlets and actions that you typed into the file (Figure 4.11). Notice that `employees` and the `currentIndex` variables do not appear. Only variables tagged with `IBOutlet` or of type `id` are considered outlets. Similarly, note that only methods tagged with `IBAction` or those that were declared to take an `id` called `sender` as an argument and return `void` are considered action methods. Thus, you do not see **updateUI**.

If you do not see all the outlets and actions from `MyDocument.h`, there is probably a syntax error in the file. If you try compiling your application, the compiler will probably find your error.

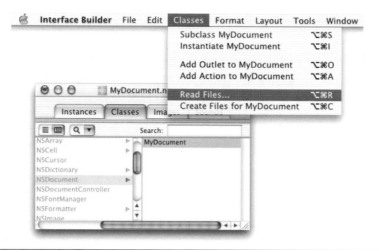

Figure 4.10   Parsing MyDocument.h

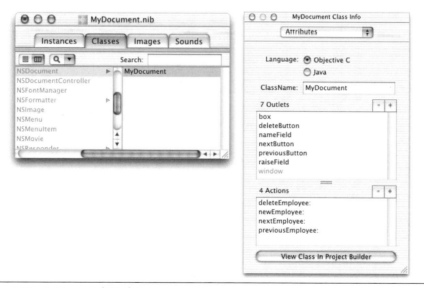

Figure 4.11   Actions and Outlets

(You could have also caused the file to be parsed by dragging it from Project Builder into Interface Builder.)

Notice that there are two ways to create outlets and actions. In Chapter 2, you created a class called **Foo** in Interface Builder. You added the actions and outlets in the class browser before generating the files Foo.m and Foo.h. In this exercise, you added the actions and outlets to Foo.h in Project Builder and then had Interface Builder parse it.

Creating the actions and outlets in Interface Builder would have involved less typing, but when you generated the files, the code that already existed in MyDocument.h and MyDocument.m would have been overwritten. (You would, however, get an alert panel before the destruction occurred.)

Now lay out the interface. In the next few pages, you will make your window look like Figure 4.12.

Drop four buttons on the window and label them. Drop two editable text fields on the window: one for the user to enter a name, and the other for the employee's expected raise. Drop two uneditable **NSTextFields** to act as labels for the editable text fields. (On the palette, the uneditable text field says "Message Text".) Select all four text fields and in the Layout menu choose Group In -> Box (Figure 4.13).

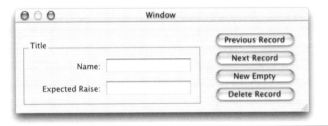

Figure 4.12   Completed Interface

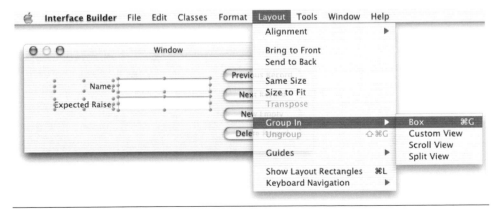

Figure 4.13   Group in Box

Using the Info Panel

Resizing the window would probably mess up your lovely layout, so you will want to eliminate the resize tab at the lower right of the window. To do this, you will need to use the info panel. Choose Show Info from the Tools menu. The info panel is context-sensitive. The attributes of whatever you select will appear in the info panel. You never have to close the info panel. Try it: Click on a text field and note that the info panel is now inspecting that text field. Now click on a button. The info panel is now inspecting that button. Notice that the title of the info panel changes as you change the selection (Figure 4.14).

The info panel has several pages which can be chosen with the popup. Take a look at the Connections page and the Size page. You should also see an Attributes page. Select the Attributes page.

To edit the attributes of the window, select the Window icon in the document window. To stop the window from resizing, turn off the checkbox labeled Resize. You will still see the resize tab in Interface Builder, but it will not appear at runtime.

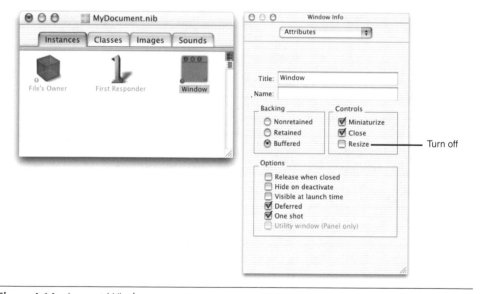

Figure 4.14 Inspect Window

Adding a Formatter

Next, drop an instance of **NSNumberFormatter** on the text field that will be displaying the expected raise. You will see the outline of the text field highlight when you are over it (Figure 4.15). Make sure that you drop the formatter while the text field is highlighted.

To look at the info for the formatter attached to the text field, select the Formatter page of the inspector. (If you do not see a Formatter page, you may not have successfully dropped the formatter on the text field. Go back and try again.) On this page, you can choose how you would like numbers to appear in the text field. Choose the format that is labeled 99.99% (Figure 4.16). That is, the expected raise will appear as a percentage with two digits after the decimal point.

Notice that there are two ways to alter the appearance and behavior of the UI objects. You can use the info panel to set its instance variables in Interface Builder. Or you can change the instance variables programmatically by sending messages to the objects in **awakeFromNib**. For example, instead of dropping the formatter on the text field in Interface Builder, you could have created an **awakeFromNib** method like this:

```
- (void)awakeFromNib
{
    NSNumberFormatter *formatter = [[NSNumberFormatter alloc] init];
    [formatter setFormat:@"0.00%"];
    [raiseField setFormatter:formatter];
    [formatter release];
}
```

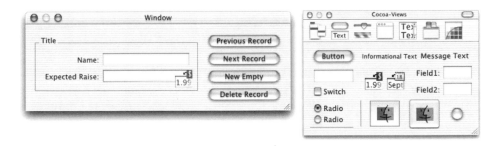

Figure 4.15   Drop NSNumber Formatter

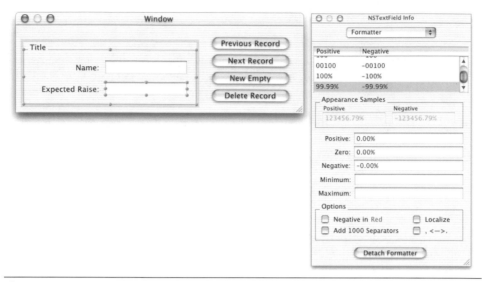

Figure 4.16   Inspect Formatter

Making Connections

When you chose Cocoa Document-based Application as your project type, Project Builder created the skeleton of an application where the user could have multiple documents open at a time. There are two nib files: MainMenu.nib and MyDocument.nib. MainMenu.nib has just enough information in it to get the menu up on the screen. The MyDocument.nib file will get read each time the user opens a new document. The default MyDocument.nib assumes that your **MyDocument** object is going to be created. You do not have to create an instance of **MyDocument**; the icon that says File's Owner represents an instance of **MyDocument**. You will learn more about the file's owner in Chapter 7.

For example, to set the target of the Previous Record button to be the instance of **MyDocument**, control-drag from the button to File's Owner. Choose target in the view on the left of the connection info panel, and **previousEmployee:**   in the view on the right (Figure 4.17). Click Connect.

Now you will create a connection in the reverse direction: To set the previousButton outlet on your **MyDocument** object, control-drag from the File's Owner to the Previous Record button. Choose previousButton in the connection info panel (Figure 4.18). Click Connect.

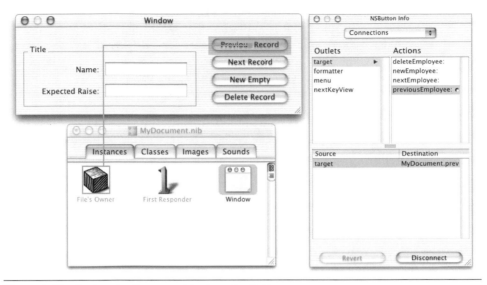

Figure 4.17 Setting the Target and Action of a Button

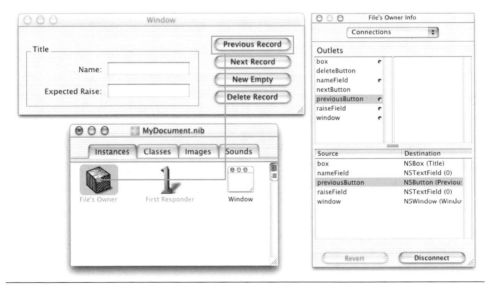

Figure 4.18 Setting an Outlet of the MyDocument Object

Notice that making a connection is like introducing people. You say, "Mrs. Robinson, this is Dr. Pepper." If it is important that Dr. Pepper also know Mrs. Robinson, you would continue with "Dr. Pepper, this is Mrs. Robinson." With objects in Interface Builder, you will control-drag from *the object that needs to know* to the object that *it needs to know about*. You might also control-drag the other way to create a connection back again, but not necessarily.

That last paragraph is so important that I am going to make you read it again: Making a connection is like introducing people. You say, "Mrs. Robinson, this is Dr. Pepper." If it is important that Dr. Pepper also know Mrs. Robinson, you would continue with "Dr. Pepper, this is Mrs. Robinson." With objects in Interface Builder, you will control-drag from *the object that needs to know* to the object that *it needs to know about*. You might also control-drag the other way to create a connection back again, but not necessarily.

For example, it was important for the Previous record button to know about the **MyDocument** object so that it can send it the **previousEmployee:** message when clicked. It is also important for the **MyDocument** object to know about the Previous Record button so that it can disable the button when the user is looking at the first person in the array. That is why you made connections in both directions. The New Empty button, on the other hand, needs to know about **MyDocument**, but **MyDocument** doesn't need to know about the New Empty button, because you will never disable the New Empty button. Figure 4.19 presents a diagram of the connections you need to create in the nib file.

Make connections from all the buttons to the **MyDocument** object. When a connection is completed, a dimple will appear next to the name of the variable that was set. Be sure as you make each connection that the dimple actually appears. Make connections from **MyDocument** to the three text fields, the Delete Record button, and the Next Record button.

In the nib window (where File's Owner appears), there are two buttons on the right edge. One gives you the view that you see now with icons to represent the different instances. The other button will give you an outline view of the instances. To the right of each object are triangles representing the outgoing and incoming connections. Click on the first triangle to see the outgoing connections. It should look like Figure 4.20. Note that the window outlet was set for you. The outlet window is declared in **NSDocument**. **MyDocument** inherits from **NSDocument**.

Now click on the second triangle to see the incoming connections. It should look like Figure 4.21. Notice that the delegate instance variable of the window was set to

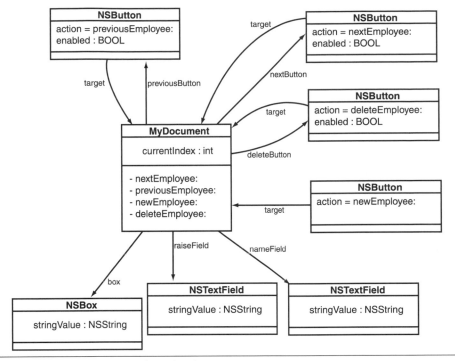

Figure 4.19   Connections in the Nib File

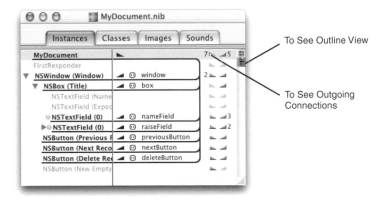

Figure 4.20   Check Outgoing Connections

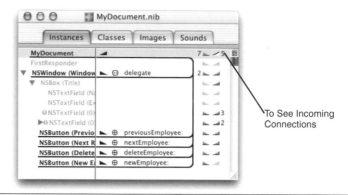

Figure 4.21   Check Incoming Connections

point to the **MyDocument** object before you opened the nib file. Go back to the icon view when you are done checking the connections.

NSWindow's initialFirstResponder Outlet

When your application runs and the new window appears, users should not have to click on a text field before they type. You can tell the window which view should be receiving keyboard events when the window appears. Control-drag from the window icon to the text field where the person's name will appear. Choose initialFirstResponder in the connection info panel (Figure 4.22).

NSView's nextKeyView Outlet

After users have typed in one text field, they may want to tab to the next. To indicate which text field to tab to, you will set the nextKeyView outlet on your text fields. First, control-drag from the Name field to the Expected raise field. Choose nextKeyView in the info panel (Figure 4.23).

Then create the connection back again: Control-drag from the Expected raise field to the Name field. Once again, choose nextKeyView.

Save your nib file. Now you can test the interface. You have not written any of the brains, so nothing interesting will happen, but you can see how the window will act when the application runs. Under the File menu, choose Test Interface. Try tabbing between the text fields. Type in a string in the Name field. Type in a number in the Expected raise field. Notice that the formatter neatly formats the number as a percentage. Notice that the window is not resizable.

Close the MyDocument.nib file.

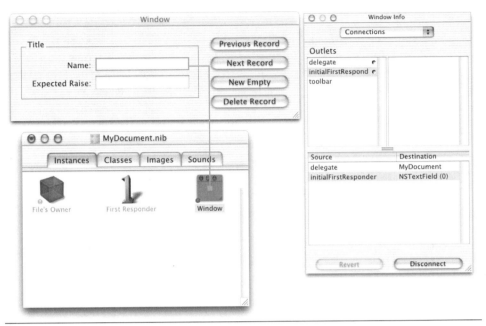

Figure 4.22   Set Window's Initial FirstResponder

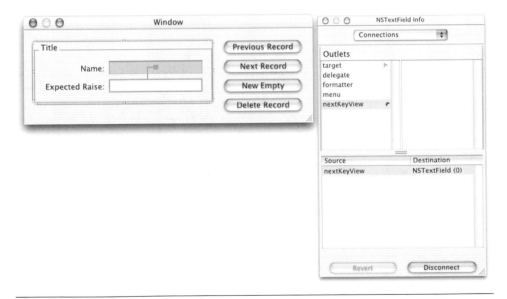

Figure 4.23   Set nextKeyView

Edit the Main Menu

Go back to Project Builder and open MainMenu.nib. This nib file has the menu for your application. Open up the menu and look at the different items. Notice that the leftmost menu has several items that should say RaiseMan but instead have the default NewApplication (Figure 4.24). Edit those items to say RaiseMan (Figure 4.25).

Save and close MainMenu.nib. Your interface is done; now you need to write some code.

Implementing the Person Class

You need to create a **Person** class. An instance of the **Person** class will have two instance variables: expectedRaise will be a float, and personName will be an **NSString**. You will need to create accessor methods that will allow other objects to

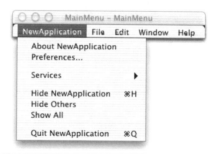

Figure 4.24   Original Menu

Figure 4.25   Corrected Menu

read and set the values of these two variables. In Project Builder, under the File menu, choose New File…. It will ask you what type of file you wish to create. Choose Objective-C Class. Name the new file **Person.m**.

The files should appear in your project. Edit Person.h to look like this:

```
#import <Foundation/Foundation.h>


@interface Person : NSObject {
    NSString *personName;
    float expectedRaise;
 }
- (NSString *)personName;
- (void)setPersonName:(NSString *)s;

- (float)expectedRaise;
- (void)setExpectedRaise:(float)f;

@end
```

Edit the Person.m file to look like this (You can leave out the comments. They are there to help you understand what you are reading.):

```
#import "Person.h"

@implementation Person

// init method makes sure that the instance variables are
// initialized to default values.
- (id)init
{
    if (self = [super init]) {
      // Call accessor methods with default values to
      //        initialize the instance variables
      [self setPersonName:@"New Employee"];
      [self setExpectedRaise: 0.0];
    }
    return self;
}

// Accessor methods for the variable personName
- (NSString *)personName
{
    return personName;
}
- (void)setPersonName:(NSString *)s
{
```

```
    // retain the new, then release the old
    [s retain];
    [personName release];
    personName = s;
}

// Accessor methods for the variable expectedRaise
- (float)expectedRaise
{
    return expectedRaise;
}
- (void)setExpectedRaise:(float)f
{
    expectedRaise = f;
}

// dealloc method ensures that all the memory being used by
// this object is freed.
- (void)dealloc
{
    // It is fun and educational to be informed of your object's destruction
    NSLog(@"Deallocing %@", personName);
    [personName release];
    [super dealloc];
}
@end
```

Overall, the **Person** class doesn't have a lot of smarts. It is just a place to hold data. You are going to put the smarts that make your application work into the **MyDocument** class.

Implementing the MyDocument Class

You have already declared the methods in the MyDocument.h file. So open up MyDocument.m and make it look like this (once again, you do not have to copy the comments):

```
#import "MyDocument.h"
#import "Person.h"

@implementation MyDocument

// initializer
- (id)init
{
    if (self = [super init]) {
```

```
        // Initialize the employees array
        employees = [[NSMutableArray alloc] init];
        // Put one blank record in the array to get the user started
        [self createNewEmployee];
    }
    return self;
}


// Action methods
- (IBAction)nextEmployee:(id)sender
{
    // Save the data from the text fields
    [self updateEmployee];
    // Increment the current index.
    // Don't worry about bounds check: button will be disabled
    // in updateUI if this operation would be illegal
    currentIndex++;
    // Display the data for the object at currentIndex
    [self updateUI];
}


- (IBAction)previousEmployee:(id)sender
{
    // Almost identical to nextEmployee:
    [self updateEmployee];
    // Decrement the currentIndex
    currentIndex;
    [self updateUI];
}


- (IBAction)deleteEmployee:(id)sender
{
    // Remove the record that the user is looking at
    [employees removeObjectAtIndex:currentIndex];
    // Unless the user is at the first record, move to the previous record
    if (currentIndex != 0){
        currentIndex;
    }
    // Display the data for the person at the currentIndex
    [self updateUI];
}


- (IBAction)newEmployee:(id)sender
{
    // Save the data from the text fields
    [self updateEmployee];
    // Create a new instance and add it to the array
    [self createNewEmployee];
    // Display the new instance
    [self updateUI];
}
```

```objc
// Private methods
- (void)createNewEmployee
{
    Person *newEmployee = [[Person alloc] init];
    [employees addObject:newEmployee];
    // Release the object. It is being retained by the array
    [newEmployee release];
    // Set the currentIndex to the index of the new object
    currentIndex = [employees count] - 1;
}

- (void)updateEmployee
{
    // Get hold of the person that is currently being displayed
    Person *currentEmployee = [employees objectAtIndex:currentIndex];
    // Read the text fields and set the variables of the currentEmployee
    [currentEmployee setPersonName:[nameField stringValue]];
    [currentEmployee setExpectedRaise:[raiseField floatValue]];
}

- (void)updateUI
{
    // Create a string to display what record the user is seeing
    NSString *recordText = [NSString stringWithFormat:
            @"Record %d of %d", currentIndex + 1, [employees count]];
    // Get hold of the person that is currently being displayed
    Person *currentEmployee = [employees objectAtIndex:currentIndex];
    // Read the data from the person object and set the text fields
    [nameField setStringValue:[currentEmployee personName]];
    [raiseField setFloatValue:[currentEmployee expectedRaise]];

    // Display the record number in the box's title
    [box setTitle:recordText];

    // The previousButton is enabled only if you are not at the
    //     first person in the array
    [previousButton setEnabled: (currentIndex > 0)];
    // The nextButton is enabled only if you are not at the
    //     last person in the array
    [nextButton setEnabled: (currentIndex < [employees count] - 1)];
    // The deleteButton is enabled only if there is more than
    //     one employee in the array
    [deleteButton setEnabled: ([employees count] > 1)];
}

- (NSString *)windowNibName {
    // This is the name of the nib file that will be displayed
    return @"MyDocument";
}
- (void)windowControllerDidLoadNib:(NSWindowController *) aController{
    [super windowControllerDidLoadNib:aController];
```

```
    // After the window appears, update the display
    [self updateUI];
}
- (NSData *)dataRepresentationOfType:(NSString *)aType {
    // Ignore this for now, but later we are going to use it to save
    // our array of people to a file
    return nil;
}
- (BOOL)loadDataRepresentation:(NSData *)data ofType:(NSString *)aType {
    // Ignore this for now, but later we are going to use it to load
    // arrays of people from a file
    return YES;
}
- (void)dealloc
{
    [employees release];
    [super dealloc];
}
@end
```

Your application is done. Build it and run it. Notice that you can create more than one window (Figure 4.26).

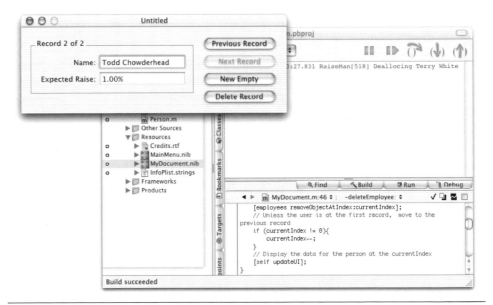

Figure 4.26 Run Completed Application

What Have You Done?

Notice that the classes of your application break into four basic groups.

- *Foundation*: The basic classes that act as collections (like **NSMutableArray**) and values (like **NSCalendarDate** and **NSString**).
- *View*: The classes that are visible on the screen (like **NSTextField**, **NSButton**, and **NSBox**).
- *Model*: The classes that represent ideas and hold onto data. Your **Person** class is part of your model.
- *Controller*: The classes that move data from the model into the views for the user to see and that take the user's edits from the views and move them into the model. The controller is also usually responsible for getting the model from a file or database. In this example, **MyDocument** was the controller.

You will see these same basic ideas emerge in many of the best object-oriented applications. The goal is to maximize reuse. In the language of object-oriented design patterns, this is the *Model-View-Controller pattern*.

The views can be reused in any application that has the standard GUI objects, like windows and buttons. That is because the controller creates the behavior that is specific to this application. Only occasionally will you have to subclass the standard view objects.

The model can be reused in any application that deals with the same types of data. For example, we might reuse our **Person** class in another application that deals with people and their expected raise. If you write a tool that runs on the command line that deals with people and their expected raises, you might reuse the **Person** class. By keeping specifics about the user interface out of the **Person** class, we have made this sort of reuse possible.

The controller for an application is the least likely candidate for reuse. Usually when you develop a new application, the hard part is creating the controller. Also, user requests most commonly result in changes to the controller. For example, when they ask "Could you bring up an alert sheet before deleting an employee?" you will have to change the controller. Do not expect to create many reusable controller objects.

If, however, you can partition out a particular behavior that is reusable into a separate class, the resulting controller could be reused in several applications. For example, you might create a controller that just handles the behavior of a find panel. This **FindPanelController** class could then be used in several applications.

When possible, the Model-View-Controller pattern should guide your designs. It will make code reuse more probable.

For the More Curious: Setting the Target Programmatically

Notice that the action of a control is a selector. There is a method in **NSControl**:

- (void)**setAction:**(SEL)aSelector

But how would you get a selector? @**selector** is an Objective-C compiler directive that will tell the compiler to look up the selector for you. For example, to set the action of a button to the method **drawMickey:**, you could do the following:

```
SEL mySelector;
mySelector = @selector(drawMickey:);
[myButton setAction:mySelector];
```

At compile time, @selector(drawMickey:) will be replaced by the selector for **drawMickey:**.

If you needed to find a selector for an **NSString** at runtime, you could use the function **NSSelectorFromString()**:

```
SEL mySelector;
mySelector = NSSelectorFromString(@"drawMickey:");
[myButton setAction:mySelector];
```

Challenge

This is an important challenge. You should actually do it before moving on. It is easy to follow my instructions, but eventually you will want to create your own applications. Here is where you start to develop some independence. Feel free to refer back to the exercises you have done, for guidance.

Create another application that will present the user with the window shown in Figure 4.27.

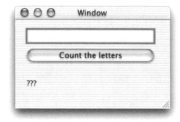

Figure 4.27   Before Input

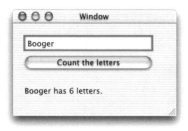

Figure 4.28   After

When the user types in a string and clicks the button, change the message text to display the input string and the number of characters it has (Figure 4.28).

You will use the following methods:

```
// NSTextField's
- (NSString *)stringValue;
- (void)setStringValue:(NSString *)aString;

// NSString's
- (int)length;
+ (NSString *)stringWithFormat:(NSString *),...;
```

You will create a controller object with two outlets and one action. (This is hard, and you are not stupid. Good luck!)

Chapter 5
HELPER OBJECTS

O nce upon a time (before *Baywatch*) there was a man with no name. KnightRider Industries decided that if this man were given guns and wheels and booster rockets, he would be the perfect crime-fighting tool. First they thought, "Let's subclass him and override everything we need to add the guns and wheels and booster rockets." The problem was that to subclass Michael Knight, you would need to know an awful lot about his guts so that you could wire them to guns and booster rockets. So instead, they created a helper object, the KnightRider Industries 2000 Super Car, or "Kitt."

Notice how this is different from the RoboCop approach. RoboCop was a man subclassed and extended. The whole RoboCop project involved dozens of surgeons to extend the man's brain into a fighting machine. This is the approach taken with many object-oriented frameworks.

While approaching the perimeter of an arms dealer's compound, Michael Knight would speak to Kitt over his watch-radio, "Kitt," he would say, "I need to get to the other side of that wall." Kitt would then blast a big hole in the wall with a small rocket. After destroying the wall, Kitt would return control to Michael, who would stroll through the rubble.

That is how many objects in the Cocoa framework are extended. There is an existing object (like a table view) that needs to be extended for your purpose (like displaying **Person** objects). Instead of subclassing the table view, you will simply supply it with a helper object. When the table view is about to display itself, it will turn to the helper object to ask things like "How many rows of data am I displaying?" and "What should be displayed in the first column, second row?"

NSTableView and Its Data Source

The user interface on the last example is awkward. It will be much more elegant if you use an **NSTableView**. In this example, you will make your application look like this (Figure 5.1).

An **NSTableView** has a helper object called a dataSource that must implement three methods.

```
- (int)numberOfRowsInTableView:(NSTableView *)aTableView;
```

The dataSource will reply with the number of rows that will displayed.

```
- (id)tableView:(NSTableView *)aTableView
     objectValueForTableColumn:(NSTableColumn *)aTableColumn
                          row:(int)rowIndex;
```

The dataSource will reply with the object that should be displayed in the row rowIndex of the aTableColumn.

```
- (void)tableView:(NSTableView *)aTableView
    setObjectValue:(id)anObject
    forTableColumn:(NSTableColumn *)aTableColumn
              row:(int)rowIndex;
```

The dataSource takes the input that the user put into row rowIndex of aTableColumn. You do not have to implement this method if your table view is not editable.

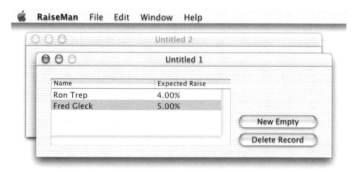

Figure 5.1   Completed Application

Notice that you are taking a very passive position in getting data to appear. Your data source will wait until the table view asks for the data. Most programmers when they start to work with **NSTableView** (or **NSBrowser**, which works in a very similar manner) want to boss the table view around and tell it "You will display 7 in the third row in the fifth column." It doesn't work that way. When the table view is ready to display the third row and the fifth column, it will ask its dataSource for the object to display.

How, then, will you get the table view to fetch updated information? You will tell the table view to **reloadData**. This will cause it to reload all the rows that the user can see.

MyDocument Interface File

Open the project you created in the last chapter. You are going to make your instance of **MyDocument** the dataSource of the table view (Figure 5.2). This is involves two parts: implementing the three methods listed above and setting the table view's dataSource outlet to the instance of **MyDocument**.

First, you are going to add the declaration of a few methods and instance variables to MyDocument.h. You will also delete a few methods and instance variables.

```
#import <Cocoa/Cocoa.h>

@interface MyDocument : NSDocument
{
    NSMutableArray *employees;
    IBOutlet NSTableView *tableView;
    IBOutlet NSButton *deleteButton;
}
// Action methods
- (IBAction)deleteEmployee:(id)sender;
- (IBAction)newEmployee:(id)sender;
```

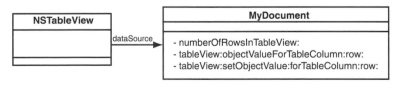

Figure 5.2   NSTableView's dataSource

```
// Data source methods
- (int)numberOfRowsInTableView:(NSTableView *)aTableView;
- (id)tableView:(NSTableView *)aTableView
    objectValueForTableColumn:(NSTableColumn *)aTableColumn
    row:(int)rowIndex;
- (void)tableView:(NSTableView *)aTableView
    setObjectValue:(id)anObject
    forTableColumn:(NSTableColumn *)aTableColumn
    row:(int)rowIndex;

// Private methods
- (void)updateUI;
- (void)createNewEmployee;
@end
```

After editing it, save the file.

Lay Out the User Interface

Open `MyDocument.nib`. You are going to edit the window to look like Figure 5.3.

First, delete the box and the text fields that displayed the person's name and expected raise. Also delete the labels for those text fields. Delete the buttons labeled Previous Record and Next Record. Drag an **NSTableView** onto the window (Figure 5.4).

Double-click on the headers of the columns to change the titles to Name and Expected Raise.

Interface Builder needs to be informed of all the changes that you made in `MyDocument.h`. Last time, you used the Read file... under the Classes menu. It is actually easier to simply drag `MyDocument.h` from Project Builder into your nib's document window (Figure 5.5).

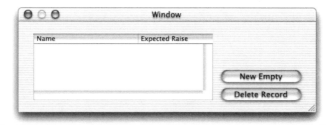

Figure 5.3   Completed Interface

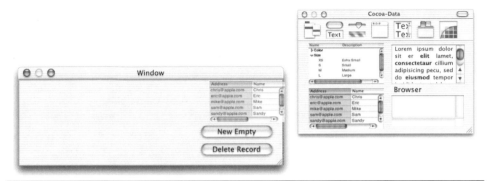

Figure 5.4   Drop a Table View on the Window

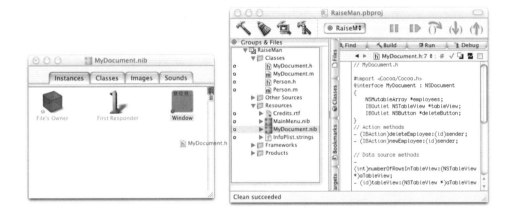

Figure 5.5   Parse MyDocument.h

You will get an alert panel informing you that the new class definition has deleted some outlets that are set in the nib. Choose to replace the old version with the new one by clicking the Replace button. If you look at the **MyDocument** class under the Classes tab, you should see the new outlets and actions from your MyDocument.h file.

Now drop a number formatter on the column to display the expected raise (Figure 5.6). Select the column (this involves clicking several times inside the column until the header turns blue) and look at the info panel. There should be a page for formatter. (If there is no formatter page, make sure you are looking at the **NSTableColumn** info. If there is still no formatter page, the column did not accept your formatter; try dropping another.)

Figure 5.6   Drop a Formatter on the Expected Raise Column

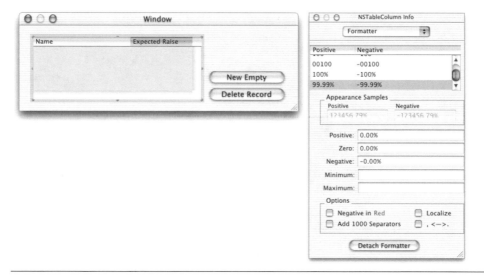

Figure 5.7   Inspect the Formatter

Select the format that shows the numbers as percentages with two decimal places (Figure 5.7).

We need an easy way to tell one column from the other in our code. Each **NSTableViewColumn** has an instance variable called the `identifier`. The identifier is a string, and you can set it in the inspector on the Attributes page. Set the `identifier` to match the name of the instance variable the column represents. For example, the column entitled Name should have the identifier personName (Figure 5.8). The column entitled Expected Raise should have the identifier expectedRaise. Note that these identifiers match the names of the instance variables that the columns will be displaying.

Figure 5.8   Inspect Each Column

Make Connections

Now make the connections. Figure 5.9 shows the object diagram.

First, you will set the dataSource outlet of the **NSTableView** to be your instance of **MyDocument**. Select the **NSTableView**. Control-drag from the table view to the File's Owner. In the connection page of the info panel, choose dataSource and click the Connect button. If you do not see dataSource in the inspector, you have selected the **NSScrollView**, not the **NSTableView** inside it.

The scroll view is the object that takes care of scrolling and the scroll bars. You will learn more about scroll views in Chapter 12. For now, just double-click in the interior of the table view until you see dataSource among the possible outlets (Figure 5.10).

Next, you will connect your **MyDocument** object's tableView outlet to the table view. Control-drag from File's Owner to the middle of the table view. In the info panel, connect to the tableView outlet (Figure 5.11).

Save the nib file and close it.

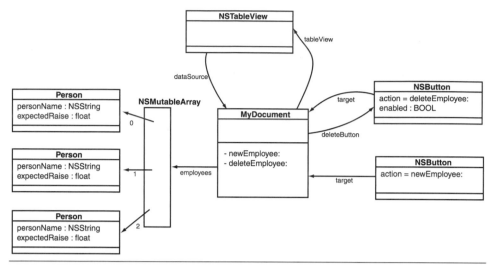

Figure 5.9 Object Diagram

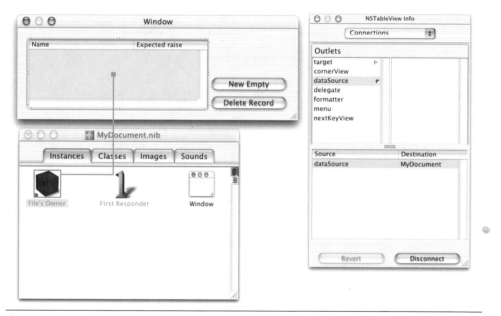

Figure 5.10 Set the tableView's dataSource Outlet

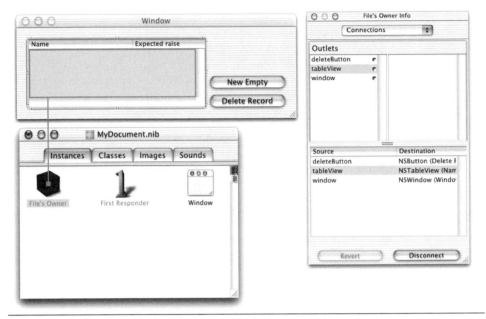

Figure 5.11   Set the MyDocument Object's tableView Outlet

Edit MyDocument.m

You no longer need the action methods for the two buttons that were removed, so delete **nextEmployee:** and **previousEmployee:** from MyDocument.m. Also, the table view will make calls to update the employee's data when the user edits the table, so you should also delete **updateEmployee**.

Now you have to implement the methods that you declared in MyDocument.h This is how your MyDocument.m file should look.

```
#import "MyDocument.h"
#import "Person.h"

@implementation MyDocument

- (id)init
{
    if (self = [super init]) {
      employees = [[NSMutableArray alloc] init];
      [self createNewEmployee];
    }
    return self;
}
```

```
- (void)createNewEmployee
{
    Person *newEmployee = [[Person alloc] init];
    [employees addObject:newEmployee];
    [newEmployee release];
}
- (IBAction)newEmployee:(id)sender
{
    [self createNewEmployee];
    [self updateUI];
}

- (IBAction)deleteEmployee:(id)sender
{
    // Which row is selected?
    int row = [tableView selectedRow];
    // Is there a selected row?
    if (row != -1) {
        // Remove the selected person
        [employees removeObjectAtIndex:row];
        [self updateUI];
    } else {
        NSBeep();
    }
}
- (void)updateUI
{
    // Tell the table to reload its data
    [tableView reloadData];
    [deleteButton setEnabled: ([employees count] > 1)];
}
- (int)numberOfRowsInTableView:(NSTableView *)aTableView
{
    return [employees count];
}
- (id)tableView:(NSTableView *)aTableView
      objectValueForTableColumn:(NSTableColumn *)aTableColumn
      row:(int)rowIndex
{
    // What is the identifier for the column?
    NSString *identifier = [aTableColumn identifier];
    // What person?
    Person *person = [employees objectAtIndex:rowIndex];
    // What is the value of the attribute named identifier?
    // See Key-value code discussion below
    return [person valueForKey:identifier];
}
- (void)tableView:(NSTableView *)aTableView
    setObjectValue:(id)anObject
    forTableColumn:(NSTableColumn *)aTableColumn
    row:(int)rowIndex
{
```

```
        NSString *identifier = [aTableColumn identifier];
        Person *person = [employees objectAtIndex:rowIndex];
        // Set the value for the attribute named identifier
        // See Key-value code discussion below
        [person takeValue:anObject forKey:identifier];
}

- (NSString *)windowNibName
{
    return @"MyDocument";
}
- (void)windowControllerDidLoadNib:(NSWindowController *) aController
{
    [super windowControllerDidLoadNib:aController];
    [self updateUI];
}
- (NSData *)dataRepresentationOfType:(NSString *)aType
{
    return nil;
}
- (BOOL)loadDataRepresentation:(NSData *)data ofType:(NSString *)aType
{
    return YES;
}
- (void)dealloc
{
    [employees release];
    [super dealloc];
}
@end
```

Key-value Coding

Notice the two strange lines from MyDocument.m:

- `return [person valueForKey:identifier];`
- `[person takeValue:anObject forKey:identifier];`

How does this work? Every object has methods for reading and setting variables by name:

```
- (id)valueForKey:(NSString *)attrName;
- (void)takeValue:(id)newValue forKey:(NSString *)attrName;
```

valueForKey: allows you to read the value of a variable by name. Of course, there may be an accessor method for the variable. So you will want the accessor used if it exists. If there is no accessor method, you will want the variable read directly.

Suppose that **valueForKey:** is passed a string like @"foo". If the object has a method **foo**, it is executed and the result is returned. If there is no method **foo**, it looks for an instance variable called foo. If the variable exists, the value of foo is returned. If there is neither a method nor a variable, you get an error.

takeValue:forKey: allows you to set the value of a variable by name. Once again, the accessor method (**setFoo:**, for instance) gets used if it exists. Otherwise it sets the variable directly. If there is neither a method nor a variable, you get an error.

This mechanism is called *key-value coding*. It is a powerful thing because otherwise you would have to have long sequences of if-statements like this:

```
if ([identifier isEqual: @"foo"]) {
    return [employee foo];
}
if ([identifier isEqual:@"bar"]){
    return [employee bar];
}
.... And so on for all the possibilities.....
```

This code, besides being annoying to create initially, would be very hard to maintain as columns are added and removed from the user interface.

This explains why you set the identifier of the table column to be the same as the name of the variable being displayed in the column. Using the identifier and the key-value coding methods made your methods very short and simple.

Notice that the key-value coding methods will automatically coerce the type for you. For example, when the user types in a new expected raise, the formatter creates an instance of **NSDecimalNumber**. The key-value coding method **takeValue:forKey:** automatically converts that into a float before calling **setExpectedRaise:**. This is extremely convenient.

There is, however, a problem with converting an NSDecimalNumber * into a float: pointers can be nil, floats cannot. If **takeValue:forKey:** is passed a nil value that needs to be converted into a nonpointer type, it will call **unableToSetNilForKey:** on itself. Just in case, you should override this method in your **Person** class. Add this method to Person.m:

```
- (void)unableToSetNilForKey:(NSString *)key
{
    if ([key isEqual:@"expectedRaise"]) {
        [self setExpectedRaise:0.0];
    } else {
        [super unableToSetNilForKey:key];
    }
}
```

Notice **unableToSetNilForKey:** usually sets the instance variable to a default value. (In this case, expectedRaise gets set to 0.0.)

Build and run your app. The table view made your interface much more elegant.

Delegates

This year, only even-numbered employees will get raises. How can you prevent users from selecting and editing the odd-numbered employees? Table views have another outlet that can be attached to another helper object. That outlet is called delegate. Lots of objects in the Cocoa frameworks have delegate outlets. The table view asks its delegate for permission to change the selection. You will create a method that gives permission only if the new row index is even (Figure 5.12).

In **MyDocument**, you are going to implement the delegate method:

```
- (BOOL)tableView:(NSTableView *)aTableView shouldSelectRow:(int)rowIndex
```

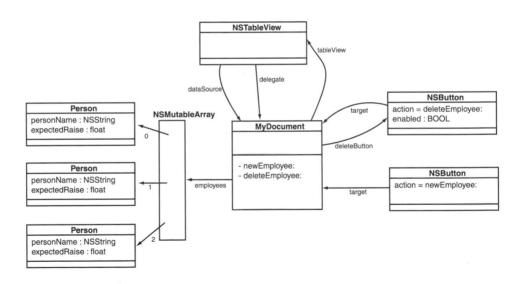

Figure 5.12 The Delegate

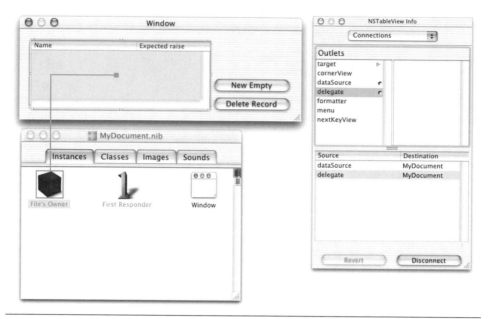

Figure 5.13   Set the TableView's Delegate Outlet

Declare it in the MyDocument.h file, and then implement it in the MyDocument.m file like this:

```
- (BOOL)tableView:(NSTableView *)aTableView shouldSelectRow:(int)rowIndex
{
    return ((rowIndex % 2) == 0);
}
```

Note that this method will return YES if the rowIndex is even.

Now open MyDocument.nib and connect the delegate outlet of the table view to File's Owner (Figure 5.13).

Compile and run your application. You should be unable to select odd-numbered rows. Note that the first row (being the zero row) is even.

How would you know about this method? The documentation for **NSTableView** includes all the messages that it might send to the delegate. Here they are.

- **tableView:shouldSelectRow:**
- **tableView:didClickTableColumn:**
- **tableView:didDragTableColumn:**

```
- tableView:mouseDownInHeaderOfTableColumn:
- tableView:shouldEditTableColumn:row:
- tableView:shouldSelectTableColumn:
- tableView:willDisplayCell:forTableColumn:row:
- tableViewColumnDidMove:
- tableViewColumnDidResize:
- tableViewSelectionDidChange:
- tableViewSelectionIsChanging:
```

Whew! That would be lot of methods if you were required to implement all of them, but you aren't. In your delegate, you just implement the ones you care about. Before an object sends a message to its delegate, it first checks to see if the delegate implements the method.

Common Errors in Implementing a Delegate

There are two very common errors people make when implementing a delegate.

- *Misspelling the name of the method.* The method will not get called and you will get no error or warning from the compiler. The best way to avoid this is to copy and paste the declaration of the method from the documentation.
- *Forgetting to set the delegate outlet.* Once again, you will get no error or warning from the compiler.

Which Objects Have Delegates?

Here is a list of the classes in the AppKit framework that have delegates.

```
NSApplication
NSBrowser
NSDrawer
NSFontManager
NSImage
NSLayoutManager
NSMatrix
NSSavePanel
NSSound
NSSplitView
NSTabView
NSTableView
NSText
NSTextField
NSTextStorage
NSTextView
NSWindow
```

Honestly, that is a pretty silly "enhancement" we just did. Delete the `tableView:shouldSelectRow:` method from MyDocument.h and MyDocument.m before you go on to the next chapter.

Retain Cycles

Notice that there is a problem with retain counts: If object A retains object B, and B retains A, they will never be deallocated. This is known as a *retain cycle*. A retain cycle can allow large islands of garbage to accumulate in your application's memory space.

To prevent retain cycles, the standard Cocoa objects do not retain their delegates, data sources, or targets.

For the More Curious: How Delegates Work

The delegate doesn't have to implement all the methods, but if the object does implement a delegate method it will get called. In many langauges, this sort of thing would impossible. How is it achieved in Objective-C?

NSObject has a method:

- (BOOL)**respondsToSelector:**(SEL)aSelector

Because every object inherits (directly or indirectly) from **NSObject**, every object has this method. It returns YES if the object has a method called aSelector. Notice that aSelector is an SEL not an **NSString**.

Imagine for a moment that you are the engineer who has to write **NSTableView**. You are writing the code that will change the selection from one row to another. You think to yourself, "I should check with the delegate." So you add a snippet of code that looks like this:

```
// about to change to row "rowIndex"
BOOL ok;
SEL theSelector = @selector(tableView:shouldSelectRow:);
ok = YES;
if ([delegate respondsToSelector:theSelector])
{
    ok = [delegate tableView:self shouldSelectRow:rowIndex];
}
```

```
if (ok)
{
    ....actually change the selection...
}
```

Notice that the delegate gets sent the message only if it has implemented the method. If the delegate doesn't implement the message, the default behavior happens.

(In reality, the result from **respondsToSelector:** is cached by the object with the delegate outlet. This makes performance considerably faster than would be implied by the foregoing code.)

After writing this method, you would carefully make note of its existence in the documentation for your class.

If you wanted to see the checks for the existence of the delegate methods, you could override **respondsToSelector:** in your delegate object like this:

```
- (BOOL)respondsToSelector:(SEL)aSelector
{
    NSString *methodName = NSStringFromSelector(aSelector);
    NSLog(@"respondsToSelector:%@", methodName);
    return [super respondsToSelector:aSelector];
}
```

Challenge 1

Using a delegate method in **NSTableView**, disable the delete button if no rows are selected. Here is the signature of the delegate method:

```
- (void)tableViewSelectionDidChange:(NSNotification *)n;
```

You can ignore the argument. We will discuss notifications in Chapter 9.

Challenge 2

Add the ability to select and delete multiple rows from your application. You will have to use an **NSEnumerator** in **deleteEmployee:**

```
NSNumber *anIndex;
int aRow;
NSEnumerator *e = [tableView selectedRowEnumerator];
```

```
while (anIndex = [e nextObject]) {
    aRow = [anIndex intValue];
    ...
}
```

This is trickier than it seems because when an object is removed from the array, the other objects shift to fill the space. So, for example, when you delete the object at index 1, the object at index 4 is moved to index 3.

Chapter 6
ARCHIVING

As an object-oriented program is running, a complex graph of objects is being created. It is often necessary to represent this graph of objects as a stream of bytes. This is called *archiving* (Figure 6.1). The stream of bytes can then be sent across a network connection or written into a file. For example, when you save a nib file, Interface Builder is archiving objects into a file.

When you need to recreate the graph of objects from the stream of bytes, you will *unarchive*. For example, when your application starts up, it unarchives the objects from the nib file created by Interface Builder.

Instead of "archiving," a Java programmer would call this "serialization."

Note that although objects have both instance variables and methods, only the instance variables and the name of the class go into the archive. In other words, only data goes into the archive, not code. As a result if one application archives an object and another application unarchives it, both applications must have the code for the class linked in. In the nib file, for example, you have used classes like **NSWindow** and **NSButton** from the AppKit framework. If you do not link your application against the AppKit framework, it will be unable to create the instances of **NSWindow** and **NSButton** that it finds in the archive.

There was once a shampoo ad that said, "I told two friends, and they told two friends, and they told two friends, and so on and so on and so on." The implication being that as long as you told your friends about the shampoo, everyone that matters would eventually be using the shampoo. Object archiving is like that. You archive a root object, it archives the objects that it is attached to, they archive the objects that they are attached to, and so on and so on and so on. Eventually every object that matters will be in the archive.

There are two parts to archiving. First, you need to teach your objects how to archive themselves. Then, you need to cause the archiving to occur.

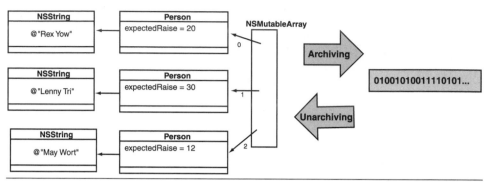

Figure 6.1   Archiving

The Objective-C language has a construct called a *protocol*. A protocol is identical to the Java construct called an *interface*. That is, a protocol is a list of method declarations. When you create a class that implements a protocol, it promises to implement all the methods declared in the protocol.

NSCoder and NSCoding

There is a protocol called **NSCoding**. If your class implements **NSCoding**, it promises to implement the following methods:

```
- (id)initWithCoder:(NSCoder *)coder;
- (void)encodeWithCoder:(NSCoder *)coder;
```

An **NSCoder** is an abstraction of a stream of bytes. You can write your data to a coder or read your data from a coder. The **initWithCoder:** method in your object will read data from the coder and save that data to its instance variables. The **encodeWithCoder:** method in your object will read its instance variables and write those values to the coder. In this chapter, you will be implementing both methods in your **Person** class.

NSCoder is actually an *abstract class*. You won't ever create instances of an abstract class. Instead, an abstract class has some capabilities that are intended to be inherited by subclasses. You will create instances of the concrete subclasses. You will use **NSUnarchiver** to read objects from a stream of data. You will use **NSArchiver** to write objects to the stream of data.

Encoding

NSCoder has many methods, but most programmers find themselves using just a few of them repeatedly. These two are commonly used when you are encoding data onto the coder:

> - (void)**encodeObject:**(id)aObject

Writes an object to the coder. This will cause anObject's **encodeWithCoder:** method to be called (and they told two friends, and they told two friends...).

> - (void)**encodeValueOfObjCType:**(const char *)typeString
>   **at:**(const void *)address

You will use this method to write C primitive types (like int and float) to the coder. The typeString is a C string that describes the type of the data you are trying to encode. "i," for example, represents an int. address and would then be a pointer to an int. Most people, however, can't remember what the typeString should be, so they use the @encode compiler directive. Instead of "i," you can use @encode(int). The compiler will do the appropriate substitution at compile time.

To add encoding to your **Person** class, add this method to Person.m:

```
- (void)encodeWithCoder:(NSCoder *)coder
{
    [coder encodeObject:personName];
    [coder encodeValueOfObjCType:@encode(float) at:&expectedRaise];
}
```

If you looked at the documentation for **NSString**, you would see that it implements the **NSCoding** protocol. Thus, the personName knows how to encode itself.

All the commonly used AppKit and Foundation classes implement the **NSCoding** protocol, with the notable exception of **NSObject**. Because **Person** inherits from **NSObject**, it doesn't call [super encodeWithCoder:coder]. If **Person**'s superclass *had* implemented the **NSCoding** protocol, the method would have looked like this:

```
- (void)encodeWithCoder:(NSCoder *)coder
{
    [super encodeWithCoder:coder];
    [coder encodeObject:personName];
    [coder encodeValueOfObjCType:@encode(float) at:&expectedRaise];
}
```

The call to the superclass's **encodeWithCoder:** method would give the superclass a chance to write its variables onto the coder. Thus, each class in the hierarchy writes only its instance variables (and not its superclass's instance variables) onto the coder.

Decoding

When decoding data from the coder, you will use the analogous decoding methods:

```
- (id)decodeObject
```

Reads an object from the coder.

```
- (void)decodeValueOfObjCType:(const char *)typeString
                            at:(void *)data
```

Reads C primitive types from the coder. Once again, use @encode to find the typeString.

To add decoding to your **Person** class, add this method to your Person.m file:

```
- (id)initWithCoder:(NSCoder *)coder
{
    if (self = [super init]) {
        [self setPersonName:[coder decodeObject]];
        [coder decodeValueOfObjCType:@encode(float) at:&expectedRaise];
    }
    return self;
}
```

Note that you must read the instance variables in the same order that you wrote them in the **encodeWithCoder:** method.

Once again, you did not call the superclass's implementation of **initWithCoder:**, because **NSObject** doesn't have one. If **Person**'s superclass *had* implemented the **NSCoding** protocol, the method would have looked like this:

```
- (id)initWithCoder:(NSCoder *)coder
{
    if (self = [super initWithCoder:coder]) {
        [self setPersonName:[coder decodeObject]];
        [coder decodeValueOfObjCType:@encode(float) at:&expectedRaise];
    }
    return self;
}
```

The attentive reader may now be saying, "Chapter 3 said that the designated initializer does all the work and calls the superclass's designated initializer. It said that all other initializers call the designated initializer. But **Person** has an **init** method, which is its designed initializer, and this new initializer doesn't call it." You are right: **initWithCoder:** is an exception to initializer rules.

You have now implemented the methods in the **NSCoding** protocol. To declare your **Person** class as implementing the **NSCoding** protocol, you will edit the Person.h file. Change the declaration of your class look to like this:

```
@interface Person : NSObject <NSCoding> {
```

Try to compile the project. Fix any errors. You could run it at this point, but, although you have taught **Person** objects to encode themselves, you haven't asked them to do so. Thus, you will see no change in the behavior of your application.

The Document Architecture

Applications that deal with multiple documents have a lot in common. All of them can create new documents, open existing documents, save or print open documents, and remind the user to save edited documents when she or he tries to close a window or quit the application. Apple supplies you with three classes that take care of most of the details for you: **NSDocumentController**, **NSDocument**, and **NSWindowController**. Together, these three classes comprise what is known as the *document architecture*.

The purpose of the document architecture relates back to the Model-View-Controller design pattern discussed in Chapter 4. Your subclass of **NSDocument** is the controller. It will have a pointer to the model objects, and will be responsible for:

- Saving that model data to a file
- Loading the model data from a file
- Displaying the model data in the views
- Taking user input from the views and updating the model

Info.plist and NSDocumentController

When Project Builder builds an application, it creates a file called Info.plist. (Later in this chapter, you will change Info.plist.) As the application launches, it reads from Info.plist, which tells it what type of files it works with. If it finds that it is a document-based application, it creates an instance of **NSDocumentController** (Figure 6.2). You will seldom have to deal with the document controller; it lurks in the background

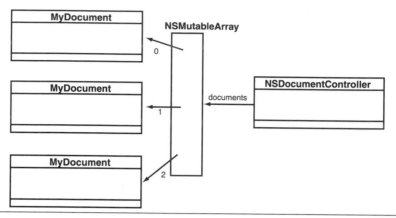

Figure 6.2   Document Controller

and takes care of a bunch of details for you. For example, when you choose the New or Save All menu item, the document controller handles the request. If you needed to send messages to the document controller, you could get to it like this:

```
NSDocumentController *dc = [NSDocumentController sharedDocumentController];
```

The document controller has an array of document objects: one for each document that you have open.

NSDocument

The document objects are instances of a subclass of **NSDocument**. In your RaiseMan application, for example, the document objects are instances of **MyDocument**. For many applications, you can simply extend **NSDocument** to do what you want; you don't have to worry about **NSDocumentController** or **NSWindowController** at all.

Saving

The menu items Save, Save As..., Save All, and Close are all different, but all deal with the same problem: getting the model into a file or file wrapper. (A file wrapper is a directory that looks like a file to the user.) To handle all these menu items, your **NSDocument** subclass must implement just one of the following methods.

    - (NSData *)**dataRepresentationOfType:**(NSString *)aType

Your document object supplies the model to go into the file as an **NSData** object. **NSData** is essentially a buffer of bytes. This is the easiest and most popular way to implement saving in a document-based application. Return nil if you are unable to create the data object and the user will get an alert sheet indicating that the save failed. Notice that you are passed the type. This allows you to save the document in one of several possible formats. For example, if you wrote a graphics program, you might allow the user to save the image as a gif or a jpg. When you are creating the data object, aType indicates the format that the user has requested that the document be saved as. If you are only dealing with one type of data, you may simply ignore aType.

- (NSFileWrapper *)**fileWrapperRepresentationOfType:**(NSString *)aType

Your document object returns the model as an **NSFileWrapper** object. It will be written to the file system in the location chosen by the user.

- (BOOL)**writeToFile:**(NSString *)filename **ofType:**(NSString *)type

Your document object is given the filename and the type. It is responsible for getting the model into the file. Return YES if the save is successful, NO if the save fails.

Loading

Likewise, the Open......, Open Recent, and Revert To Saved menu items, although different, deal with the same basic problem: Get the model from a file or file wrapper. To handle all these menu items, your **NSDocument** subclass must implement just one of the following methods.

- (BOOL)**loadDataRepresentation:**(NSData *)docData **ofType:**(NSString *)docType

Your document is passed an **NSData** object that is filled with contents of the file the user is trying to open. Return YES if you successfully create a model from the data. If you return NO, the user will get an alert panel telling him or her that the application was unable to read the file.

- (BOOL)**loadFileWrapperRepresentation:**(NSFileWrapper *)wrapper
                                 ofType:(NSString *)docType

Your document reads the data from an **NSFileWrapper** object.

- (BOOL)**readFromFile:**(NSString *)filename **ofType:**(NSString *)docType

Your document object is passed the path. The document reads the data from the file.

After implementing one save method and one load method, your document will know how to read from and write to files. When opening a file, the document will read the document file *before* reading the nib file. Note that this means that you will not be able to send messages to the UI objects immediately after loading the file (because they won't exist yet). To solve this problem, after the nib file is read, your document object is sent:

```
- (void)windowControllerDidLoadNib:(NSWindowController *)aController;
```

In your **NSDocument** subclass, you will implement this method to update the user interface objects as you did in Chapter 4.

If the user chooses Revert To Saved from the menu, the model is loaded, but **windowControllerDidLoadNib:** does not get called. So you will also have to update the user interface objects in the method that loads the data, just in case it was a revert. Note that this means that most of the time your update methods get called twice. (If the nib file is not loaded, the outlets are `nil`, so remember that sending messages to `nil` is OK.)

NSWindowController

The final class in the document architecture to discuss would be **NSWindowController**, but you will not initially need to worry about it. For each window that a document opens, it will typically create an instance of **NSWindowController**. Since most applications have only one window per document, the default behavior of the window controller is usually perfect. Here are some reasons that you might want to create a custom subclass of **NSWindowController**.

- You need to have more than one window on the same document. For example, in a CAD program you might have a window of text that describes the solid and another window that shows a rendering of the solid.
- You want to put the UI controller logic and model controller logic into separate classes.
- You want to create a window without a corresponding **NSDocument** object. You will do this in Chapter 7.

Saving and NSArchiver

Now that you have taught your object to encode and decode itself, you will use it to add saving and loading to your application. When it is time to save your people to a file, your **MyDocument** class will be asked to create an instance of **NSData**. Once your object has created and returned **NSData** object, it will be automatically written to a file.

To create an **NSData** object, you will use the **NSArchiver** class. **NSArchiver** has a class method:

```
+ (NSData *)archivedDataWithRootObject:(id)rootObject
```

This method archives the objects into the **NSData**'s buffer of bytes.

Once again, we return to the idea of "I told two friends, and they told two friends." By encoding an object, it will encode its objects and they will encode their objects and so on and so on and so on. What you will encode, then, is the employees array. It will encode the **Person** objects that it has references to. And each **Person** object (because you implemented **encodeWithCoder:**) will encode the personName string and the expectedRaise float.

To add saving to your application, edit the method **dataRepresentationOfType:** so that it looks like this:

```
- (NSData *)dataRepresentationOfType:(NSString *)aType {
    // End editing in table view
    // The argument of this action method is ignored, so we
    // are passing nil.
    [tableView deselectAll:nil];
    // Create an NSData object from the employees array
    return [NSArchiver archivedDataWithRootObject:employees];
}
```

Loading and NSUnarchiver

Now you will add the loading of files to your application. Once again, **NSDocument** has taken care of most of the details for you.

To do the unarchiving, you will use **NSUnarchiver**. **NSUnarchiver** has the following handy method:

```
+ (id)unarchiveObjectWithData:(NSData *)data
```

In your **MyDocument** class, edit your **loadDataRepresentation:ofType:** method to look like this:

```
- (BOOL)loadDataRepresentation:(NSData *)data ofType:(NSString *)aType {
    // Release the old array
    [employees release];
    // Read the array from the data object
```

```
    employees = [[NSUnarchiver unarchiveObjectWithData:data] retain];
    // Update UI in case this is a revert
    [self updateUI];
    return YES;
}
```

You will update the user interface after the nib file is loaded. This method needs no changing.

```
- (void)windowControllerDidLoadNib:(NSWindowController *)aController
{
    [super windowControllerDidLoadNib:aController];
    // Update UI in case this is *not* a revert
    [self updateUI];
}
```

Note that your document is asked which nib file to load when a document is opened or created. This method also needs no changing.

```
- (NSString *)windowNibName
{
    return @"MyDocument";
}
```

Informing the Document That It Has Been Edited

Finally, you need to inform the document that it has been edited so that the user will be reminded to save the changes before closing the window. **NSDocument** (from which **MyDocument** inherits) has a method called **updateChangeCount:**. Call it when the person objects are changed, added, or deleted. Here is how those methods should look.

```
- (IBAction)deleteEmployee:(id)sender
{
    // Which row is selected?
    int row = [tableView selectedRow];
    // Is there a selected row?
    if (row != -1) {
        // Remove the selected person
        [employees removeObjectAtIndex: row];
        [self updateChangeCount:NSChangeDone];
        [self updateUI];
    } else {
        NSBeep();
    }
}
```

```
- (IBAction)newEmployee:(id)sender
{
    [self createNewEmployee];
    [self updateChangeCount:NSChangeDone];
    [self updateUI];
}

- (void)tableView:(NSTableView *)aTableView
    setObjectValue:(id)anObject
    forTableColumn:(NSTableColumn *)aTableColumn
    row:(int)rowIndex
{
    NSString *identifier = [aTableColumn identifier];
    Person *person = [employees objectAtIndex:rowIndex];
    // Set the value for the attribute named identifier
    [person takeValue:anObject forKey:identifier];
    [self updateChangeCount:NSChangeDone];
}
```

Now when you make changes to a document, the window will look edited (a dot will appear in the close button) and if the user closes the window before saving, an alert sheet will appear.

At this point, your application can read and write to files. Compile your application and try it out. Everything should work fine, but all your files will have the extension "????". You need to define an extension for your application in the Info.plist.

Setting the Extension and Icon for the File Type

RaiseMan files will have the extension .rsmn and there will be an icon for .rsmn files. First, find a .icns file and copy it into your project. There is a fine icon at /Developer/Examples/AppKit/CompositeLab/BBall.icns. Drag it from the Finder into the Groups and Files view of Project Builder. Drop it in the Resources group (Figure 6.3).

Project Builder will bring up a sheet. Make sure that you check Copy items into destination group's folder (Figure 6.4). This will copy the icon file into your project directory.

To set the document-type information, choose Edit Active Target in the Project menu. Under the Application Settings tab, choose Simple. Scroll to the bottom to see the Type Information. It will have ???? as the Extensions and the OS types. Select the row,

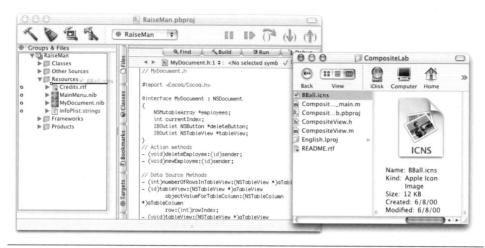

Figure 6.3   Drag Icon into Project

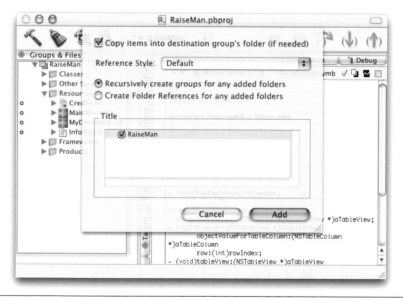

Figure 6.4   Make It a Copy

and change both to rsmn in the text fields below. Also change the Icon file to be BBall.icns. Click the Change button. Also, set the icon for the application to be BBall.icns (Figure 6.5).

Note that Project Builder does incremental builds: Only edited files are recompiled. To do this, it keeps many intermediate files around between builds. To remove these intermediate files, you can clean the project. To clean a project, click on the button with the picture of the whisk broom. In my experience, the changes that you have just made don't seem to take unless the project is cleaned and rebuilt.

Clean, build, and run your application. You should be able to save data to a file and read it in again. For the file icons to work right, you will need to move the application from the `Raiseman/build` directory to `/Applications`. Log out and log back in. In Finder, the `BBall.icns` icon will be used as the icon for your `.rsmn` files.

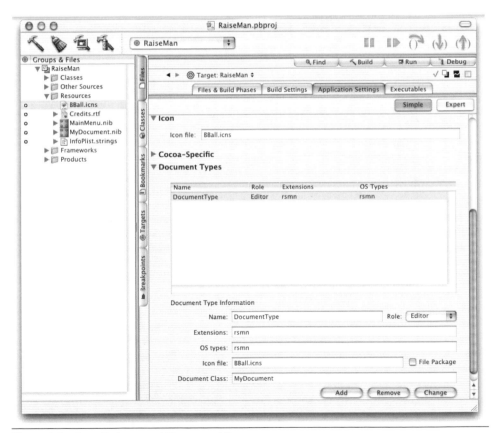

Figure 6.5 Specify Icon and Document Types

An application is actually a directory. The directory contains the nib files, images, sounds, and executable code for the application. In Terminal, try the following:

```
> cd /Applications/TextEdit.app/Contents
> ls
```

You will see three interesting things.

- The `Info.plist` file, which includes the information about the application, its filetypes, and associated icons. Finder uses this information.
- The `MacOS/` directory, which contains the executable code.
- The `Resources/` directory, which has the images, sounds, and nib files that the application uses. You will see localized resources for several different languages.

For the More Curious: Preventing Infinite Loops

The astute reader may have started wondering: "If object A causes object B to be encoded and object B causes object C to be encoded and then object C causes object A to be encoded again, couldn't it just go around and around in an infinite loop?" It would, but the **NSArchiver** was designed with this in mind.

When an object is encoded, a unique token is also put onto the stream. Once archived, the object is also added to the table of encoded objects under that token. When the **NSArchiver** is told to encode the same object again, it simply puts a token in the stream.

When the **NSUnarchiver** decodes an object from the stream, it puts the object and its token in a table. The unarchiver finds a token with no associated data, so it knows to look the object up in the table instead of creating a new instance.

This idea led to the method in **NSCoder** that often confuses developers when they read the documentation:

```
- (void)encodeConditionalObject:(id)object
```

This method is used when object A has a pointer to object B, but object A doesn't really care if B is archived. However, if *another* object *has* archived B, object A would like the token for B put into the stream. If no other object has archived B, it will be treated like nil.

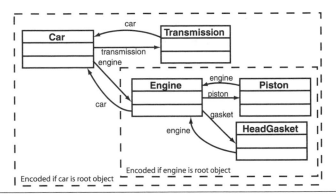

Figure 6.6   Conditional Encoding Example

For example, if you were writing an **encodeWithCoder:** method for an **Engine** object (Figure 6.6), it might have an instance variable called car that is a pointer to the **Car** object that it is part of. If you are just archiving the **Engine**, you wouldn't want the entire **Car** archived. But if you were archiving the entire **Car**, you would want the car pointer set. In this case, you would make the **Engine** object encode the car pointer conditionally.

For the More Curious: Versioning

As your application evolves, instance variables may be added and removed from your classes. A stream created by one version of your application may not be the same as a stream created by another. How will you deal with this?

When an object is encoded, the name of the class and its version is also added to the stream. To enable the developer to access this information, **NSCoder** has the following method:

```
- (unsigned)versionForClassName:(NSString *)className
```

Imagine that version 2 of the class **Person** had an instance variable called phone of type **NSString** but that version 1 did not. You could create a method like this:

```
- (id)initWithCoder:(NSCoder *)coder
{
    int version;
    if (self = [super init]) {
        version = [coder versionForClassName:@"Person"];
        [self setPersonName:[coder decodeObject]];
```

```
        [coder decodeValueOfObjCType:@encode(float) at:&;expectedRaise];
        if (version > 1)
            [self setPhone: [coder decodeObject]];
    }
    return self;
}
```

How do you set the version of your class before it is encoded? **NSObject** declares the class method:

```
+ (void)setVersion:(int)theVersion
```

By default, the version is 0.

If you are using versioning, be sure to call **setVersion:** before any instances get encoded. One easy way to do this is in the class's **initialize** method. Just as **init** is sent to an instance to make sure that it is prepared for use, **initialize** is sent to a class to make sure that it is prepared for use. Before a class is used, it is automatically sent the message **initialize**.

A subclass inherits this method from its superclass, so if you want the code executed only for this class (and not its subclasses), you will prefix it with an if statement, like this:

```
+ (void)initialize
{
    // Am I the Person class?
    if (self == [Person class]) {
        [self setVersion:2];
    }
}
```

For the More Curious: Creating a Protocol

Creating your own protocol is very simple. Here is a protocol with two methods. It would typically be in a file called Foo.h.

```
@protocol Foo
- (void)bar:(int)x;
- (float)baz;
@end
```

If you had a class that wanted to implement the **Foo** protocol and the **NSCoding** protocol, it would look like this:

```
#import "Rex.h"
#import "Foo.h"

@interface Fido:Rex<Foo,NSCoding>
...etc...
@end
```

A class doesn't have to redeclare any method it inherits from its superclass. Nor does it have to redeclare any of the methods from the protocols it implements. Thus in our example, the interface file for the class **Fido** is not required to list any of the methods in **Rex** or **Foo** or **NSCoding**.

Chapter 7
NIB FILES AND NSWINDOWCONTROLLER

In RaiseMan, you are already using two nib files: MainMenu.nib and MyDocument.nib. MainMenu.nib is automatically loaded for you by **NSApplication** when the application first launches. MyDocument.nib is automatically loaded for you each time an instance of **MyDocument** is created. In this section, you will learn how to load nibs using **NSWindowController**.

Why would you want to load a nib? Most commonly, your application will have several windows (like a find panel and a preferences panel) that are used only occasionally. By putting off loading the nib until the window is needed, your application will launch faster. Furthermore, if the user never needs the window, your program will use less memory.

NSPanel

In this chapter, you are going to create a preferences panel. The panel will be an instance of **NSPanel**, which is a subclass of **NSWindow**. There really are not that many differences between a panel and a general window, but because a panel is meant to be auxiliary, as opposed to a document window, it acts a little differently.

- Panels become the key window, but not the main window. For example, when the user brings up a print panel, he or she can type into it (it is key), but the document the user was looking at is still the main window (that is what will be printed). **NSApplication** has a mainWindow outlet and a keyWindow outlet. Both outlets point at the same window, unless a panel is involved; panels do not become the main window.
- If it has a close button, you can close a panel by pressing escape.
- Panels do not appear in the window list in the Window menu. After all, if the user is looking for a window, the user is probably looking for a document, not a panel.

All windows have a boolean variable called hidesOnDeactivate. If this is set to YES, the window will hide itself when the application is not active. Most document windows have this set to NO. Most auxilary panels have it set to YES. This mechanism reduces screen clutter. You can set hidesOnDeactivate using the window inspector in Interface Builder.

Adding a Panel to the Application

The preferences panel that you are going to add will not do anything but appear for now. But in the next chapter you will learn about user defaults. In that chapter, you will make the preferences panel actually do something.

The preferences panel will be in its own nib file. You will create a subclass of **NSWindowController** called **PreferenceController**. An instance of **Preference-Controller** will act as the controller for the preferences panel. When creating an auxiliary panel, it is important to remember that you may want to reuse it in the next application. Creating a class to act just as a controller and a nib that contains only the panel makes it easier to reuse the panel in another application. The hip programmers would say, "By making the application more modular, we can maximize reuse." The modularity also makes it easier to divide tasks among several programmers. A manager can say, "Rex, you are in charge of the preferences panel. Only you may edit the nib file and the preference controller class."

The objects on the preferences panel will be connected to the preference controller. In particular, the preference controller will be the target of a color well and the checkbox. The preference panel will appear when the user clicks on the Preferences... menu item. When running it will look like Figure 7.1.

Figure 7.2 presents a diagram of the objects that you will create and which nib file they will be in.

MainMenu.nib

Open your project and create a new Objective-C class named **AppController**. Edit AppController.h to look like this:

```
#import <Foundation/Foundation.h>
@class PreferenceController;

@interface AppController : NSObject {
```

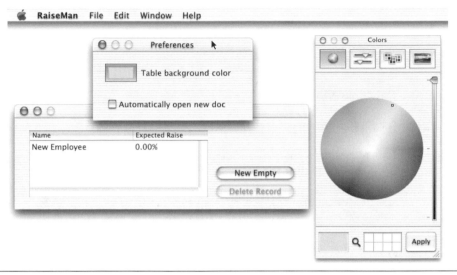

Figure 7.1   Completed Application

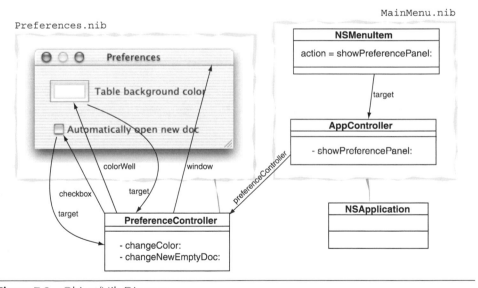

Figure 7.2   Object/Nib Diagram

```
    PreferenceController *preferenceController;
}
- (IBAction)showPreferencePanel:(id)sender;

@end
```

Notice the Objective-C syntax:

```
@class PreferenceController;
```

This tells the compiler that there is a class **PreferenceController**. This enables you to do the declaration

```
    PreferenceController *preferenceController;
```

without importing the header file for **PreferenceController**. You could replace @class PreferenceController; with #import "PreferenceController.h". This would import the header, and the compiler would learn that **PreferenceController** was a class. Because the import requires the compiler to parse more files, @class will often result in faster builds.

Note that you must always import the superclass's header file. This is because the compiler needs to know what instance variables are declared in the superclass. In this case, NSObject.h is imported by <Foundation/Foundation.h>.

Setting Up the Menu Item

Save AppController.h and drag it from Project Builder into MainMenu.nib in Interface Builder (Figure 7.3).

Then you will see the **AppController** class in the nib's class browser (Figure 7.4).

Use the Classes menu to instantiate an instance of **AppController** (Figure 7.5).

Control-drag from the Preferences...... menu item to the **AppController**. Make it the target and set the action to **showPreferencePanel:** (Figure 7.6).

Close the nib file.

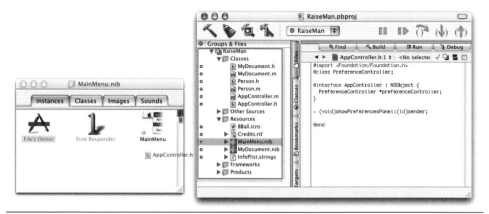

Figure 7.3   Parse AppController.h

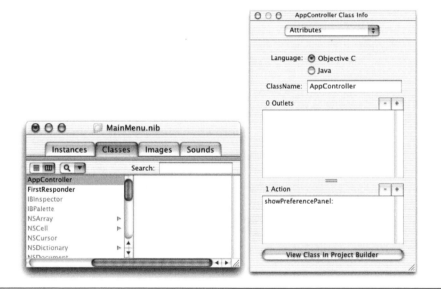

Figure 7.4   Outlets and Actions of AppController

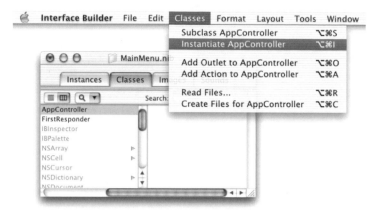

Figure 7.5   Instantiate an Instance of AppController

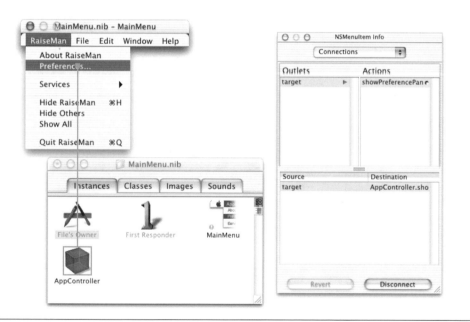

Figure 7.6   Set the Target of the Menu Item

AppController.m

Now you need to write the code for AppController. Make the contents of AppController.m look like this:

```
#import "AppController.h"
#import "PreferenceController.h"

@implementation AppController

- (IBAction)showPreferencePanel:(id)sender
{
    // Is preferenceController nil?
    if (!preferenceController) {
        preferenceController = [[PreferenceController alloc] init];
    }
    [preferenceController showWindow:self];
}
- (void)dealloc
{
    [preferenceController release];
    [super dealloc];
}
@end
```

Notice that it creates the instance of **PreferenceController** only once. If the preferenceController variable is non-nil, it simply sends the message **showWindow:** to the existing instance.

Preferences.nib

In Project Builder, choose New File... from the File menu, and create a new Objective-C NSWindowController subclass. Name it **PreferenceController** (Figure 7.7).

Edit the PreferenceController.h to look like this:

```
#import <AppKit/AppKit.h>

@interface PreferenceController : NSWindowController {
    IBOutlet NSColorWell *colorWell;
    IBOutlet NSButton *checkbox;
}
- (IBAction)changeColor:(id)sender;
- (IBAction)changeNewEmptyDoc:(id)sender;
@end
```

In Interface Builder, create a new nib file. Choose Empty as the starting point (Figure 7.8).

Save the new nib into your project directory as Preferences.nib. When asked, insert the new nib into the project (Figure 7.9).

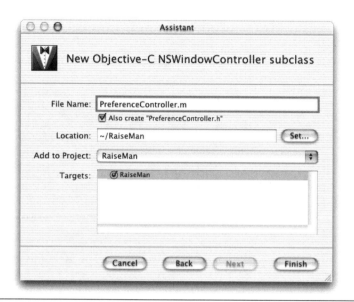

Figure 7.7 Create Files for Preference Controller

Figure 7.8 Create a New Nib File

Drag the `PreferenceController.h` file into the empty nib file (Figure 7.10).

Bring up the info panel, select File's Owner, and set its class to **PreferenceController** (Figure 7.11).

File's Owner

When a nib file is loaded into an application that has been running for a while, the objects that already exist need to establish some connection to the objects read from the nib file. File's Owner provides this connection. File's Owner is a placeholder in a

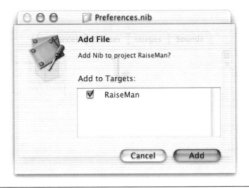

Figure 7.9   Add the Nib to the Project

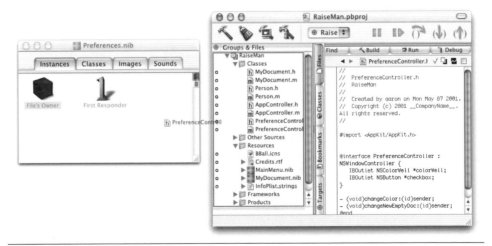

Figure 7.10   Parse PreferenceController.h

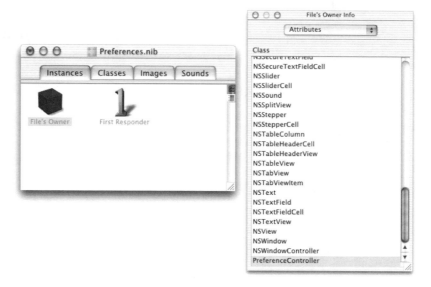

Figure 7.11   Set File's Owner to an Instance of Preference Controller

nib file for an object that will already exist when the nib file is loaded. An object loading a nib file will provide the owner object. The owner is put into the place that File's Owner represents. In this particular application, the owner will be the instance of **PreferenceController** that was created by the **AppController**.

The use of File's Owner is confusing to many people. You will *not* instantiate **PreferenceController** in the nib file. Instead, you have just informed the nib file that the owner (which will be provided when the nib file is loaded) is a **Preference-Controller**.

Lay Out the User Interface

Create a new panel by dragging a panel from the palette window and dropping it anywhere on the screen (Figure 7.12).

Make the panel smaller and drop a color well and a checkbox on it. Label them as shown in Figure 7.13.

Set the target of the color well to be File's Owner (your preference controller) and set the action to be **changeColor:** (Figure 7.14).

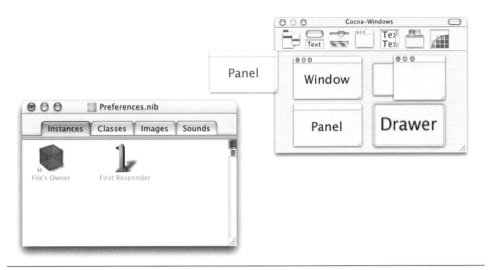

Figure 7.12   Create an Instance of NSPanel

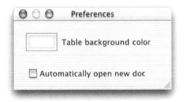

Figure 7.13   Complete Interface

Also make your preference controller the target of the checkbox and set the action to be **changeNewEmptyDoc:**.

Set the colorWell outlet of File's Owner to the color well object. Set the checkbox outlet of File's Owner to the checkbox object. Set the window outlet of File's Owner to the panel (Figure 7.15).

Open the size inspector for the panel. Disable resizing.

Save the nib file. Change the title on the window to "Preferences."

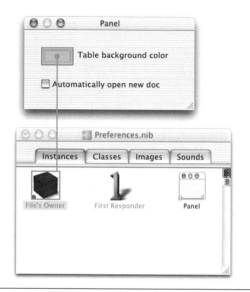
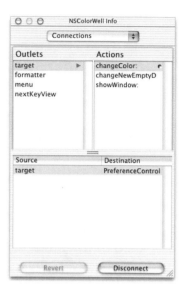

Figure 7.14   Set the Target of the Color Well

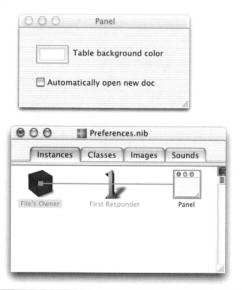

Figure 7.15   Set the Window Outlet of the File's Owner

PreferenceController.m

In Project Builder, edit the `PreferenceController.m` to look like this:

```
#import "PreferenceController.h"

@implementation PreferenceController

- (id)init {
    self = [super initWithWindowNibName:@"Preferences"];
    return self;
}

- (void)windowDidLoad {
    NSLog(@"Nib file is loaded");
}

- (IBAction)changeColor:(id)sender {
    NSLog(@"Color changed: %@", [sender color]);
}

- (IBAction)changeNewEmptyDoc:(id)sender {
    NSLog(@"Checkbox changed %d", [sender state]);
}

@end
```

Note that you set the name of the nib file to be loaded in the **init** method. This nib file will be loaded automatically when it is needed. The instance of **Preference-Controller** will be substituted in for the File's Owner in the nib file.

After the nib file is loaded, the **PreferenceController** will be sent **windowDidLoad**. This is an opportunity (like **awakeFromNib** or **windowControllerDidLoadNib:**) for the controller object to initialize the UI objects that have been read from the nib file.

When sent **showWindow:** for the first time, the **NSWindowController** automatically loads the nib file and moves the window on screen and to the front. The nib file is loaded only once. When the user closes your preference panel, it is moved off screen but not deallocated. The next time the user asks for the preference panel, it is simply moved on screen.

The **colorChanged:** and **checkboxChanged:** methods are pretty boring right now. They simply print out a message. In the next chapter, you will change them to update the user's defaults database.

Build and run the application. You should get the new panel to appear, and altering the checkbox or color well should result in a message in the console (Figure 7.16).

The first time a user encounters a color well is sometimes confusing. If you click on the edge of the color well, the edge becomes highlighted, the color panel appears, and the well is in "active" mode.

For the More Curious: NSBundle

A *bundle* is a directory of resources that may be used by an application. These resources are things like images, sounds, compiled code, and nib files. The class **NSBundle** is a very elegant way of dealing with bundles.

Notice that your application is a bundle. In Finder, an application looks to the user like any other file, but it is really a directory filled with nib files, compiled code, and other resources. We call this directory the *main bundle* of your application.

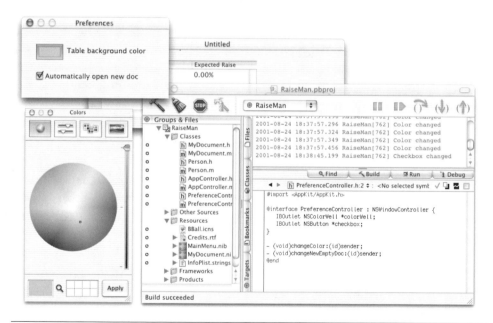

Figure 7.16   Completed Application

Some resources in a bundle can be localized. For example, you could have two different versions of foo.nib, one for English speakers and one for French speakers. The bundle would have two subdirectories: English.lproj and French.lproj. You would put an appropriate version of foo.nib in each. When your application asks the bundle to load foo.nib, if the user has set the preferred language to French, the bundle will automatically load the French version of foo.nib. We will cover localization in Chapter 11.

To get the main bundle of an application:

```
NSBundle *myBundle = [NSBundle mainBundle];
```

This is the most commonly used bundle. But if you need to access resources in another directory, you could ask for the bundle at a certain path:

```
NSBundle *goodBundle = [NSBundle bundleWithPath:@"~/.myApp/Good.bundle"];
```

Once you have an **NSBundle** object you can ask it for its resources:

```
// Extension is optional
NSString *path = [goodBundle pathForImageResource:@"Mom"];
NSImage *momPhoto = [[NSImage alloc] initWithContentsOfFile:path];
```

A bundle may have a library of code. By asking for a class from the bundle, the bundle will link in the library and search for a class by that name:

```
Class newClass = [goodBundle classNamed:@"Rover"];
id newInstance = [[newClass alloc] init];
```

If you do not know the name of any classes in the bundle, you can simply ask for the principal class:

```
Class aClass = [goodBundle principalClass];
id anInstance = [[aClass alloc] init];
```

You can see that **NSBundle** is handy in many ways. In this section, the **NSBundle** was actually responsible (behind the scenes) for loading the nib file. If you wished to load a nib file without an **NSWindowController**, you could do it like this:

```
BOOL successful = [NSBundle loadNibNamed:@"FindPanel" owner:someObject];
```

Note that you would supply the object that will act as the File's Owner.

Challenge 1

Delete your color well and checkbox. Drop an **NSTabView** on the preferences panel. Put the color well under one tab, put the checkbox under the other. Be sure to reconnect them.

Challenge 2

Create another nib file for a custom about panel. Use **NSBundle** to load it explicitly. To bring the window forward (and onscreen if necessary), send it the message **makeKeyAndOrderFront:**.

Chapter 8
USER DEFAULTS

M any applications have preferences panels that allow the user to choose a preferred appearance or behavior. The user's choices go into the user defaults database in the user's home directory. Note that only the choices that vary from the factory defaults are saved in the user defaults database. If you go to ~/Library/Preferences, you can see your user defaults database. The files are in XML format; you can browse through them with a text editor.

The **NSUserDefaults** class allows your application to register the factory defaults, save the user's preferences, and read previously saved user preferences.

The color well that you dropped into the preferences window will determine the background color of the table view. When the user changes his or her preference, your application will write the new preference to the user defaults database. When your application creates a new document window, it will read from the user defaults database. Notice that this means that only windows created after the change will be affected (Figure 8.1).

Also, have you noticed how every time you start the app, it brings up an untitled document? The Automatically open new doc checkbox will allow the user to choose whether or not the untitled document will appear.

NSDictionary and NSMutableDictionary

Before you do anything with user defaults, we need to discuss the classes **NSDictionary** (Figure 8.2) and **NSMutableDictionary**. A dictionary is a collection of keyvalue pairs. The keys are strings, and the values are pointers to objects.

A string can be a key only once in a dictionary. When you want to know which value a key is bound to, you will use the method **objectForKey:**.

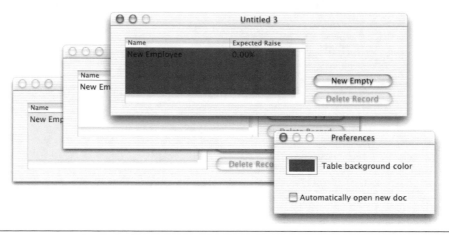

Figure 8.1 Completed Application

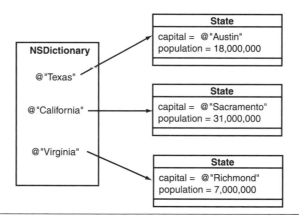

Figure 8.2 An Instance of NSDictionary

```
anObject = [myDictionary objectForKey:@"foo"];
```

If the key is not in the dictionary, it will return nil.

NSMutableDictionary is a subclass of **NSDictionary**. An instance of **NSDictionary** is created with all the keys and values it will ever have. You can query the object, but you cannot change it. **NSMutableDictionary**, on the other hand, allows you to add and remove keys and values.

NSDictionary

A dictionary is implemented as a hash table. Looking up keys is very fast. Here are a few of the most commonly used methods in the class **NSDictionary**.

- (NSArray *)**allKeys**

Returns a new array containing the keys in the dictionary.

- (unsigned)**count**

Returns the number of key/value pairs in the dictionary.

- (id)**objectForKey:**(NSString *)aKey

Returns the value associated with aKey, or returns nil if no value is associated with aKey.

- (NSEnumerator *)**keyEnumerator**

Enumerators are also known as *iterators* or *enumerations*. You can use them to step through all the members of a collection. This method returns an enumerator that steps through all the keys in the dictionary. Here is how you would use one to list out all the keys in a dictionary:

```
NSString *s;
NSEnumerator *e = [myDict keyEnumerator];
while (s = [e nextObject]) {
    NSLog(@"Key is %@", s);
}
```

The class **NSArray** can also create enumerators. It has a method **objectEnumerator**, which returns an enumerator that steps through the elements in the array.

- (NSEnumerator *)**objectEnumerator**

Returns an enumerator that steps through all the values in the dictionary.

NSMutableDictionary

+ (id)**dictionary**

This class method creates an empty dictionary.

- (void)**removeObjectForKey:**(NSString *)aKey

Removes aKey and its associated value object from the dictionary.

- (void)**setObject:**(id)anObject **forKey:**(NSString *)aKey

Adds an entry to the dictionary, consisting of aKey and its corresponding value object anObject. The value object receives a **retain** message before being added to the dictionary. If aKey already exists in the receiver, the receiver's previous value object for that key is sent a **release** message and anObject takes its place.

NSUserDefaults

Every application comes with a set of defaults "from the factory." When a user edits her or his defaults, only the differences between the user's wishes and the factory defaults are stored in the user's defaults database. So every time the application starts up, you need to remind it what the factory defaults are. This is called *registering defaults*.

After registering, you will use the user defaults object to determine how the user wants his or her app to behave. This is *reading and using the defaults*. The data from the user's defaults database will be automatically read from the file system.

You will also create a preferences panel that will allow the user to set the defaults. The changes to the defaults object will be automatically written to the file system. This is known as *setting the defaults* (Figure 8.3).

Here are some commonly used methods that are implemented in **NSUserDefaults**.

+ (NSUserDefaults *)**standardUserDefaults**

Returns the shared defaults object.

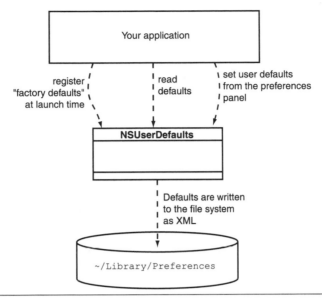

Figure 8.3   NSUserDefaults and the File System

```
- (void)registerDefaults:(NSDictionary *)dictionary
```

Registers the factory defaults for the application.

```
- (void)setBool:(BOOL)value    forKey:(NSString *)defaultName
- (void)setFloat:(float)value forKey:(NSString *)defaultName
- (void)setInteger:(int)value forKey:(NSString *)defaultName
- (void)setObject:(id)value forKey:(NSString *)defaultName
```

Methods for changing and saving a user's wishes.

```
- (BOOL)boolForKey:(NSString *)defaultName
- (float)floatForKey:(NSString *)defaultName
- (int)integerForKey:(NSString *)defaultName
- (id)objectForKey:(NSString *)defaultName
```

Methods for reading the defaults. If the user hasn't changed them, the factory defaults are returned.

```
- (void)removeObjectForKey:(NSString *)defaultName
```

Removes the user's preference. This means that the application will return to using the factory defaults.

Precedence of Different Types of Defaults

We have talked about two levels of precedence: What the user writes to his defaults database overrides the factory defaults. Actually, there are several more levels of precedence. Here they are, in order of priority.

Arguments: Passed on the command line. Most people start their applications by double-clicking on an icon instead of from the command line, so this feature is seldom used in a production app.

Application: What comes from the user's defaults database.

Global: What the user has set for his entire system.

Language: What is set based upon the user's preferred language.

Registered defaults: The factory defaults for your app.

Creating Keys for the Names of the Defaults

You will be registering, reading, and setting defaults in several different classes in your application. To make sure that you are always using the same name, you should declare those strings in a single file and then simply #import that file into any file where you use them.

There are several ways to do this (for example, you could use the C preprocessor's #define command), but most Cocoa programers would use global variables. Add this to your PreferenceController.h file after the #import statement:

```
extern NSString *BNRTableBgColorKey;
extern NSString *BNREmptyDocKey;
```

Now actually define these variables in PreferenceController.m. Put them after the #import lines and before @implementation :

```
NSString *BNRTableBgColorKey = @"Table Background Color";
NSString *BNREmptyDocKey = @"Empty Document Flag";
```

Why would we declare global variables that simply contain a constant string? After all, you could simply remember what the string was and type it in whenever you need it. The problem is that you might misspell the string. If the string is in quotes, the compiler will accept the misspelled string. If you misspell the name of a global variable, the compiler will catch your error.

To keep the global variables from conflicting with another company's global variables, you will prefix them with "BNR" (for Big Nerd Ranch). Global variables from Cocoa are prefixed with "NS." These prefixes are important only when you start using classes and frameworks developed by third parties. (Note that class names are also global. You might also prefix all the class names with "BNR" to keep them from conflicting with anyone else's classes.)

Registering Defaults

As mentioned in Chapter 6, each class gets sent the message **initialize** before any other message. To ensure that your defaults are registered early, you are going to override **initialize** in AppController.m:

```
+ (void)initialize {
    // Create a dictionary
    NSMutableDictionary *defaultValues = [NSMutableDictionary dictionary];
    // Archive the color object
    NSData *colorAsData = [NSArchiver archivedDataWithRootObject:
                    [NSColor yellowColor]];
    // Put defaults in the dictionary
    [defaultValues setObject:colorAsData forKey:BNRTableBgColorKey];
    [defaultValues setObject:[NSNumber numberWithBool:YES]
                    forKey:BNREmptyDocKey];
    // Register the dictionary of defaults
    [[NSUserDefaults standardUserDefaults] registerDefaults: defaultValues];
    NSLog(@"registered defaults: %@", defaultValues);
}
```

(Notice also that we had to store the color as a data object. **NSColor** objects do not know how to write themselves out as XML, so we pack them into a data object that does. Hopefully, this will not be necessary in later versions of Mac OS.)

Let the User Edit the Defaults

Now you are going to alter the **PreferenceController** class so that the preferences panel will actually cause the defaults database to get updated. Make your PreferenceController.m file look like this:

```
#import "PreferenceController.h"

NSString *BNRTableBgColorKey = @"Table Background Color";
NSString *BNREmptyDocKey = @"Empty Document Flag";
```

```
@implementation PreferenceController

- (id)init {
    self = [super initWithWindowNibName:@"Preferences"];
    return self;
}

- (void)windowDidLoad
{
    NSUserDefaults *defaults;
    NSData *colorAsData;

    defaults = [NSUserDefaults standardUserDefaults];
    colorAsData = [defaults objectForKey: BNRTableBgColorKey];
    [colorWell setColor:[NSUnarchiver unarchiveObjectWithData:colorAsData]];
    [checkbox setState:[defaults boolForKey:BNREmptyDocKey]];
}

- (IBAction)changeColor:(id)sender
{
    NSColor *color = [sender color];
    NSData *colorAsData = [NSArchiver archivedDataWithRootObject:color];
    [[NSUserDefaults standardUserDefaults] setObject:colorAsData
                    forKey: BNRTableBgColorKey];
}

- (IBAction)changeNewEmptyDoc:(id)sender
{
    [[NSUserDefaults standardUserDefaults] setBool:[sender state]
            forKey: BNREmptyDocKey];
}

@end
```

Note that in the **windowDidLoad** method, you are reading the defaults and making the color well and checkbox reflect the current settings. In **changeColor:** and **changeNewEmptyDoc:** you are updating the defaults database.

You should now be able to build and run your application. It will read and write to the defaults database, so the preferences panel will display the last color you chose and whether the checkbox was on or off. You have not, however, actually done anything with this information yet, so the untitled document will continue to appear and the background of the table view will continue to be white.

Using the Defaults

Now you are going to use the defaults. First, you are going to make your **AppController** a delegate of the **NSApplication** object and suppress the creation of an untitled document, depending on the user defaults. Then, in **MyDocument**, you will set the background color of the table view from the user defaults.

Suppressing the Creation of Untitled Documents

As before, there are two parts to creating a delegate: implementing the delegate method and setting the delegate outlet to point to the object (Figure 8.4).

Before automatically creating a new untitled document, the **NSApplication** object will send the message **applicationShouldOpenUntitledFile:** to its delegate. In AppController.m, add the following method:

```
- (BOOL)applicationShouldOpenUntitledFile:(NSApplication *)sender
{
    NSLog(@"applicationShouldOpenUntitledFile:");
    return [[NSUserDefaults standardUserDefaults]
      boolForKey:BNREmptyDocKey];
}
```

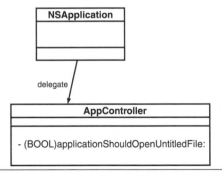

Figure 8.4   Delegate Suppresses Creation of Untitled Documents

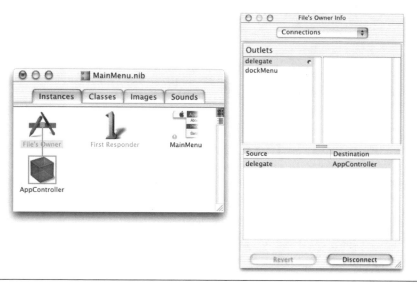

Figure 8.5   Select the Delegate Outlet

To make your **AppController** the delegate of the **NSApplication** object, open your MainMenu.nib file, and control-drag from the File's Owner (which represents the **NSApplication** object) to your **AppController**. Set the delegate outlet (Figure 8.5).

Setting the Background Color on the Table View

After the nib file for a new document window has been successfully unarchived, your **MyDocument** object gets sent the message **windowControllerDidLoadNib:**. That is the moment when you can update the background color of the table view. You should already have this method in MyDocument.m; just edit it to look like this:

```
- (void)windowControllerDidLoadNib:(NSWindowController *) aController
{
    NSData *colorAsData;
    [super windowControllerDidLoadNib:aController];
    colorAsData = [[NSUserDefaults standardUserDefaults]
            objectForKey:BNRTableBgColorKey];
    [tableView setBackgroundColor:
            [NSUnarchiver unarchiveObjectWithData:colorAsData]];
    [self updateUI];
}
```

Also, make sure that you import `PreferenceController.h` at the beginning of `MyDocument.m` so that you can use the global variables that are declared there.

Build and run your application.

Saving the Frame of a Window

When a user moves or resizes a window, a kind application will store the new frame in the defaults database. When the window is created again, it will use the stored frame. Thus the window will appear with the user's preferred size and location.

Because this is such a common situation, the clever engineers at Apple have made it easy. If you set a window's frame autosave name, when the user moves or resizes the window, its frame will be saved to the defaults. If you have an **NSWindowController**, you can set this name using its **setWindowFrameAutosaveName:**. Add this line to the **init** method in `PreferenceController.m`:

```
- (id)init {
    if (self = [super initWithWindowNibName:@"Preferences"]) {
        [self setWindowFrameAutosaveName:@"PrefWindow"];
    }
    return self;
}
```

Build and run your app. Open the preferences panel and move it. Quit the app and run it again. Note that the preferences panel opens in the location you moved it to.

For the More Curious: Reading and Writing Defaults from the Command Line

The user defaults database is in `~/Library/Preferences/`. To edit it from the command line, you will use a tool called *defaults*. For example, to see your defaults for Project Builder, you can bring up the terminal and enter the command

```
defaults read com.apple.ProjectBuilder
```

You should see all your defaults for Project Builder. Mine look like this:

```
{
    NSDefaultOpenDirectory = /Users/aaron/RaiseMan;
    NSRecentDocuments = (
```

```
                /Users/aaron/TypingTutor/TypingTutor.pbproj/,
                /Users/aaron/CounterJava/CounterJava.pbproj/,
                /Users/aaron/DocBooker/DocBooker.pbproj/,
                /Users/aaron/ImageFun/ImageFun.pbproj/,
                /Users/aaron/BigLetter/BigLetter.pbproj/,
                /Users/aaron/RaiseMan/RaiseMan.pbproj/
            );
    "NSWindow Frame PBXAddFilesOptionsPanel" = "404 358 400 273 0 56 1024 690 ";
    "NSWindow Frame PBXSaveMultiplePanel" = "300 365 423 302 0 56 1024 690 ";
    "NSWindow Frame PBXSimpleFinder" = "388 453 545 236 0 4 1024 742 ";
    PBXFindIgnoreCase = NO;
    PBXFindWholeWordOnly = NO;
    PBXReplaceSelectionOnly = NO;
    PBXReuseNavigators = YES;
    PBXSyntaxColoringUseSeparateFonts = NO;
}
```

You can also write to the defaults database. To set Project Builder's default directory in the **NSOpenPanel** to the /Users directory, you could enter this:

```
defaults write com.apple.ProjectBuilder NSDefaultOpenDirectory /Users
```

Try

```
defaults read RaiseMan
```

Challenge

Add a button to the preferences panel that will remove all the user's defaults. Label the button Reset Preferences.

Chapter 9
USING NOTIFICATIONS

A user may have several RaiseMan documents open when deciding that it is hard to read with a purple background. The user opens the preferences panel, changes the background color, and then is disappointed when the color of existing windows doesn't change. When the user sends you e-mail, you reply, "The defaults are read only when the document window is created. Just save the document, close it, and open it again." Then the user sends you a mean e-mail. It would be better to update all the existing windows. But how many are there? Will you have to keep a list of all the open documents?

What Notifications Are

It is actually much easier than that. There is an instance of **NSNotificationCenter** in every running application. The **NSNotificationCenter** works like a bulletin board. Objects register as interested in certain notifications ("Please write me if anyone finds a lost dog"). We call the registered object an *observer*. Other objects can then post notifications to the center ("I have found a lost dog"). That notification gets forwarded to all the objects that are registered as interested. We call the object that posted the notification a *poster*.

Lots of standard Cocoa classes post notifications: Windows send notifications that they have changed size. When the selection of a table view changes, the table view sends a notification. The notifications sent by standard Cocoa objects are listed in the online documentation.

In our example, you are going to register all of your **MyDocument** objects as observers. Your preference controller will post a notification when the user chooses a new color. When sent the notification, the **MyDocument** objects will change the background color.

Before the **MyDocument** object is deallocated, you must remove it from the notification center's list of observers. Typically, this is done in the **dealloc** method.

When sending the notification, you can attach an object to it. This is how you can send extra information to all the observers. The object attached can be any object, but it is usually the poster of the notification.

What Notifications Are Not

When programmers first hear about the notification center, they sometimes think it is a form of interprocess communications. They think, "I will create an observer in one application and post notifications from an object in another." This doesn't work: A notification center allows objects in an application to send notifications to other objects *in that same application*. Notifications do not travel between applications.

There is, however, a class that does handle notifications between applications. It is **NSDistributedNotificationCenter**. Refer to the documentation for details.

NSNotification

Notification objects are very simple. A notification is like an envelope into which the poster will place information for the observers. It has two important instance variables: name and object. Nearly always, object is a pointer to the object that posted the notification. (This is analogous to a return address.)

The two interesting methods on the notification then are

```
- (NSString *)name
- (id)object
```

NSNotificationCenter

The **NSNotificationCenter** is the brains of the operation. It allows you to do three things:

- Register observer objects.
- Post notifications.
- Unregister observers.

Here are some commonly used methods implemented by **NSNotificationCenter**.

```
+ (NSNotificationCenter *)defaultCenter
```

Returns the notification center.

```
- (void)addObserver:(id)anObserver
            selector:(SEL)aSelector
                name:(NSString *)notificationName
              object:(id)anObject
```

Registers anObserver to receive notifications with the name notification-Name and containing anObject (Figure 9.1). When a notification of name notificationName containing the object anObject is posted, anObserver gets sent an aSelector message with this notification as the argument:

If notificationName is nil, the notification center sends the observer all notifications with an object matching anObject.

If anObject is nil, the notification center sends the observer all notifications with the name notificationName.

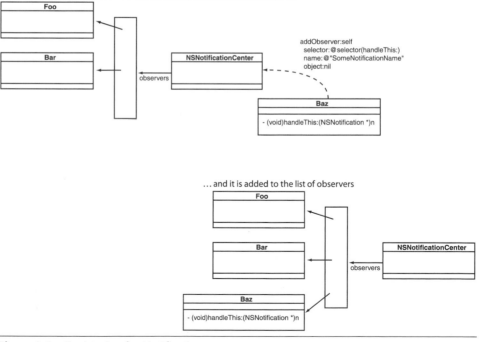

Figure 9.1   Registering for Notifications

The observer is *not* retained by the notification center. Notice that the method takes a selector.

- (void)**postNotification:**(NSNotification *)notification

Posts notification to the notification center (Figure 9.2).

- (void)**postNotificationName:**(NSString *)aName **object:**(id)anObject

Creates and posts a notification.

- (void)**removeObserver:**(id)observer

Removes observer from the list of observers.

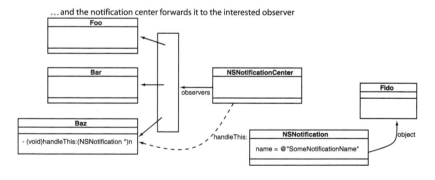

Figure 9.2 Posting a Notification

Posting a Notification

Posting a notification is the easiest part, so you will start there. When your **PreferenceController** object gets sent a **colorChanged:** message, it will post a notification with the new color. Name the notification @"BNRColorChanged". (Experienced programmers put a prefix on the notification so that it doesn't conflict with other notifications that may be flying around the application.) Make your **colorChanged:** method in PreferenceController.m look like this:

```
- (IBAction)changeColor:(id)sender
{
    NSNotificationCenter *nc;
    NSColor *color = [sender color];
    NSData *colorAsData = [NSArchiver archivedDataWithRootObject:color];
    [[NSUserDefaults standardUserDefaults] setObject:colorAsData
            forKey:BNRTableBgColorKey];
    nc = [NSNotificationCenter defaultCenter];
    [nc postNotificationName:@"BNRColorChanged" object:color];
    NSLog(@"Sent notification BNRColorChanged");
}
```

Notice that you are sending the color as the object instead of as the poster. Some Cocoa programmers would argue that this is not very stylish. They would say that the notification's object should always be the poster. In this case, the poster would always be the same object, and the color is what the receiver is really interested in, so I decided to send the color instead. My apologies to the purists.

Registering As an Observer

To register as an observer, you must supply several things: the object that is the observer, the name of the notifications it is interested in, and the message that you want sent when an interesting notification arrives. You can also specify that you are interested only in notifications with a certain object attached to them. (Remember that this is often the object that posted the notification. Thus, when you specify that you want resize notifications with a certain window attached, you are saying that you are interested only in the resizing of that particular window.) In this case, you are interested in the notification regardless of what color is attached to it.

Edit your **MyDocument** class's **init** method:

```
- (id)init
{
    NSNotificationCenter *nc;
    if (self = [super init]) {
        employees = [[NSMutableArray alloc] init];
        [self createNewEmployee];
        nc = [NSNotificationCenter defaultCenter];
        [nc addObserver:self
            selector:@selector(handleColorChange:)
                name:@"BNRColorChanged"
              object:nil];
        NSLog(@"Registered with notification center");
    }
    return self;
}
```

Unregistering the Observer

Remember to remove your document from the notification center if it is closed. Edit the **dealloc** method in MyDocument.m:

```
- (void)dealloc
{
    NSNotificationCenter *nc;
    nc = [NSNotificationCenter defaultCenter];
    [nc removeObserver:self];
    NSLog(@"Unregistered with notification center: %@", [self fileName]);
    [employees release];
    [super dealloc];
}
```

Handling the Notification When It Arrives

When the notification arrives, the method **handleColorChange:** will get called. Add this method to your MyDocument.m file.

```
- (void)handleColorChange:(NSNotification *)note
{
    NSColor *color = [note object];
    NSLog(@"Got notification: %@", note);
    [tableView setBackgroundColor:color];
    [self updateUI];
}
```

Build and run the application. Open several windows and change the preferred background color. Note that all of them receive the notification and change color immediately.

For the More Curious: Delegates and Notifications

If an object has made itself the delegate of some standard Cocoa object, it is probably interested in receiving notifications from that object as well. For example, if you have implemented a delegate to handle the **windowShouldClose:** delegate method for a window, that same object is likely to be interested in the NSWindowDidResize-Notification from that same window.

If a standard Cocoa object has a delegate and posts notifications, the delegate is automatically registered as an observer for the methods it implements. If you are implementing such a delegate, how would you know what to call the method?

The rule is simple: Start with the name of the notification. Remove the "NS" from the beginning and make the first letter lowercase. Remove the "Notification" from the end. Add a colon. For example, to be notified that the window has posted an NSWindowDidResizeNotification, the delegate would implement the following method:

- (void)**windowDidResize:**(NSNotification *)aNotification

This method will be called automatically after the window resizes. You can also find this method listed in the documentation and header files for the class **NSWindow**.

For the More Curious: The userInfo Dictionary

If you wanted to include more than just the poster with the notification, you would use the user info dictionary. Every notification has a variable called userInfo that can be attached to an **NSDictionary** filled with other information that you wanted to pass to the observers:

```
NSDictionary *d = [NSDictionary withObject:@"867-5309"
                                    forKey:@"phoneNumber"];
NSNotification *n = [NSNotification notificationWithName:@"BNRFoo"
                                                 object:self
                                               userInfo:d];
[[NSNotificationCenter defaultCenter] postNotification:n];
```

On the other end, the receiver of the notification can use the data in the `userInfo` dictionary:

```
- (void)myMethod:(NSNotification *)note
{
    NSString *thePhoneNumber;
    thePhoneNumber = [[note userInfo] objectForKey:@"phoneNumber"];
}
```

Just as you defined global variables to hold onto constant strings in Chapter 8 so that the compiler would catch your misspellings, most programmers define global variables for the names of their notifications and the keys in their user info dictionary.

Challenge

Make your application beep when it gives up its active status. **NSApplication** posts an NSApplicationDidResignActiveNotification notification. Your **AppController** is a delegate of **NSApplication**. **NSBeep()** will cause a system beep.

Chapter 10
USING ALERT PANELS

Occasionally you will want to warn the user about something by means of an alert panel. Alert panels are easy to create. While most things in Cocoa are object-oriented, showing an alert panel and getting the user's feedback is done with a C function: **NSRunAlertPanel()**.

Here is the declaration:

```
int NSRunAlertPanel(NSString *title, NSString *msg,
    NSString *defaultButton, NSString *alternateButton,
    NSString *otherButton, ...);
```

If you run the function like this:

```
int choice = NSRunAlertPanel(@"Fido", @"Rover",
                          @"Rex", @"Spot", @"Fluffy");
```

it will look like Figure 10.1.

The second and third buttons are optional. To prevent them from appearing, replace the label with nil. (Note that the icon on the panel will be the icon for the responsible application.)

NSRunAlertPanel() returns an int which indicates which button the user clicked. There are global variables for these constants: NSAlertDefaultReturn, NSAlert-AlternateReturn, and NSAlertOtherReturn.

Note also that **NSRunAlertPanel()** takes a variable number of arguments. The first two strings may include printf-like tokens. Values supplied after the otherButton label will be substituted in. So the code

```
int choice = NSRunAlertPanel(@"Fido", @"Rover is %d",
                          @"Rex", @"Spot", nil, 8);
```

Figure 10.1   Example Alert Panel

Figure 10.2   Another Example Alert Panel

would result in the alert panel in Figure 10.2.

Alert panels run *modally*; that is, other windows in the application don't receive events until the alert panel has been dismissed.

Make the User Confirm the Delete

If the user clicks the delete button, an alert panel should display before the records are deleted (Figure 10.3).

First, open MyDocument.nib, select the table view, and open the inspector. Allow the user to make multiple selections (Figure 10.4).

Figure 10.3   Completed Application

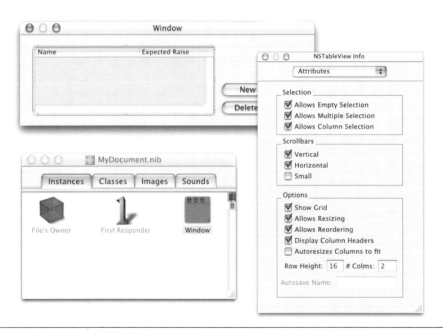

Figure 10.4   Inspect TableView

In Project Builder, open the MyDocument.m and change **deleteEmployee:**. The new version will iterate through the selected rows, show the alert panel, and delete the rows:

```
- (IBAction)deleteEmployee:(id)sender
{
    Person *currentPerson;
    NSNumber *index;
    int choice;

    // Create an autoreleased mutable array
    NSMutableArray *peopleToRemove = [NSMutableArray array];

    // Get an enumerator for the selected rows
    NSEnumerator *e = [tableView selectedRowEnumerator];

    // Interate over the selected rows
    while (index = [e nextObject])
    {
        // Look up the person in the selected row
        currentPerson = [employees objectAtIndex:[index intValue]];

        // Add the person to the array
        [peopleToRemove addObject:currentPerson];
    }

    // Run an alert panel
    choice = NSRunAlertPanel(@"Delete",
            @"Do you really want to delete %d records?",
            @"Yes", @"No", nil, [peopleToRemove count]);

    // If the user chose Yes, delete the people
    if (choice == NSAlertDefaultReturn) {
        [employees removeObjectsInArray:peopleToRemove];
        // Note that the document has been changed
        [self updateChangeCount: NSChangeDone];
        // Update the UI
        [self updateUI];
    }
}
```

Build it and run it.

Challenge

Add another button to the alert panel, one that says "Keep, but no raise." Instead of deleting the employees, this button will simply set the raises of the selected employees to zero.

Chapter 11
LOCALIZATION

If the application you create is useful, you will want to share it with all the people of the world. Unfortunately, we don't all speak the same language. Suppose you wish to make your RaiseMan application available to French speakers. We would say, "You are going to *localize* RaiseMan for French speakers."

If you are creating an application for the world, you should plan on localizing for at least the following languages: English, French, Spanish, German, Dutch, Italian, and Japanese. Clearly, you do not want to have to rewrite the whole app for each language. In fact, our goal is to make it so that you don't have to rewrite any Objective-C code for each language. That way all the nations of the world can use a single executable in peace and harmony.

Instead of creating multiple executables, you will localize resources and create string tables. Inside your project directory there is an English.lproj directory. This holds all the resources for English speakers: Nib files, images, and sounds. To localize the app for French speakers, you will add a French.lproj directory. The nibs, images, and sounds in this directory will be appropriate for French speakers. At runtime, the app will automatically use the version of the resource appropriate to the user's language preference.

What about the places in your application where you use the language programmatically? For example, in MyDocument.m, you have the following line of code:

```
choice = NSRunAlertPanel(@"Delete",
    @"Do you really want to delete %d records?",
    @"Yes", @"No", nil, [peopleToRemove count]);
```

That alert panel is not going to bring about world peace. For each language, you will have a table of strings. You will ask **NSBundle** to look up the string, and it will automatically use the version appropriate to the user's language preference (Figure 11.1).

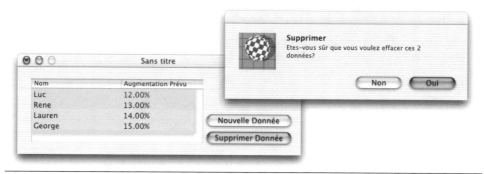

Figure 11.1   Completed Application

Localizing a Nib File

In Project Builder, select the English version of MyDocument.nib and bring up the info panel. (It is not enough to select MyDocument.nib. You must select the word English under MyDocument.nib.) Choose Add Localized Variant... from the Localization & Platforms pop-up (Figure 11.2).

You will be prompted for a locale; choose French.

If you look in the Finder, a copy of English.lproj/MyDocument.nib has been created in French.lproj. You will francophize the copy. In Project Builder, under the Resources group, you will have two versions of MyDocument.nib: English and French. Double-click on the French version to open it in Interface Builder.

Make your window look like Figure 11.3.

To type in characters with accents, you will need to use the option key. For example, to type é, type the "e" while holding down the option key, and then type "e" again. There is an application that will help you figure out the keystrokes for such characters: /Applications/Utilities/KeyCaps.

You have created a localized resource. Notice that if you make a lot of changes to your program, you may need to update both nib files (the French version and the English version). It is a good idea to wait until the application is completed and tested before localizing it.

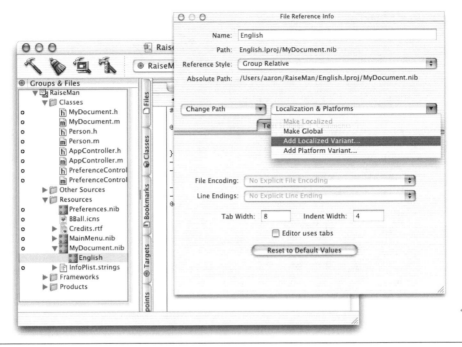

Figure 11.2   Create a French Version of MyDocument.nib

Figure 11.3   Completed Interface

Build your app. Before running it, bring up the International page of the System Preferences application. Set Francais as your preferred language. Now run your application. Note that the French version of the nib is used automatically.

Your keyboard will act French if you leave the preferred language French in the System Preference panel, so return it to English before continuing.

String Tables

For each language, you can create several string tables. Each string table is a file with the extension .strings. For example, if you had a find panel, you might create a Find.strings file for each language. This file would have the phrases used by the find panel, like "None found."

The file is just a collection of key-value pairs. The key and the value are strings in quotes and the pair is terminated with a semicolon:

```
"Key1" = "Value1";
"Key2" = "Value2";
```

To find a value for a given key, you will use **NSBundle**:

```
NSBundle *main;
NSString *aString;

main = [NSBundle mainBundle];
aString = [main localizedStringForKey:@"Key1"
                        value:@"DefaultValue1"
                        table:@"Find"];
```

This would search for the value for "Key1" from the Find.strings file. If it is not found in the user's preferred language, the second-favorite language is searched, and so on. If the key is not found in any of the user's languages, "DefaultValue1" is returned. If you do not supply the name of the table, Localizable is used. Most simple applications just have one string table for each language: Localizable.strings.

Creating String Tables

To create a Localizable.strings file for English speakers, choose the New File… menu item in Project Builder. Create an empty file, and name it Localizable.strings. Save it in the English.lproj directory (Figure 11.4).

Edit the new file to have the following text:

```
"Delete" = "Delete";
"SureDelete" = "Are you sure you want to delete %d records?";
"Yes" = "Yes";
"No" = "No";
```

Save it.

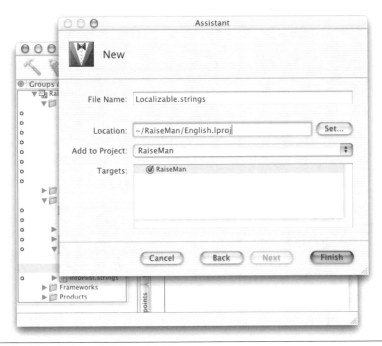

Figure 11.4   Create an English String Table

Now create a localized version of that file for French. Select the English version of the `Localizable.strings` file in Project Builder, bring up the info panel, and create a Localized variant (Figure 11.5).

Edit the file to look like this:

```
"Delete" = "Supprimer";
"SureDelete" = "Etes-vous sûr que vous voulez effacer ces %d données?";
"Yes" = "Oui";
"No" = "Non";
```

(To create the "u" with the circumflex, type "i" while holding down the option key. Then type "u." To type é, type the "e" while holding down the option key, and then type "e" again.)

When saving a file with unusual characters, you should use the Unicode file encoding. While the French `Localizable.strings` file is active in Project Builder, choose Unicode from the File Encodings in the Format menu (Figure 11.6).

Save the file.

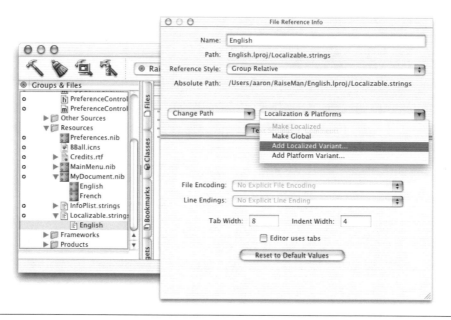

Figure 11.5   Create a French String Table

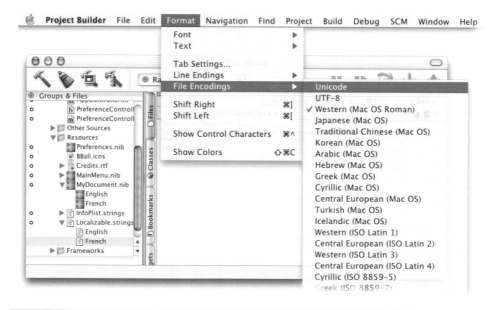

Figure 11.6   Change the File Encoding

Using the String Table

In an app with just one string table, you would probably do this:

```
NSString *deleteString;
deleteString = [[NSBundle mainBundle]
                    localizedStringForKey:@"Delete"
                                    value:@"Delete?"
                                    table:nil];
```

Fortunately, there is a macro defined in `NSBundle.h`:

```
#define NSLocalizedString(key, comment)
        [[NSBundle mainBundle] localizedStringForKey:(key)
                                    value:@""
                                    table:nil]
```

(Notice that the comment is completely ignored.)

In `MyDocument.m`, find the place where you run the alert panel. Replace that line with this one:

```
choice = NSRunAlertPanel(NSLocalizedString(@"Delete", nil),
    NSLocalizedString(@"SureDelete", nil),
    NSLocalizedString(@"Yes", nil),
    NSLocalizedString(@"No", nil),
    nil,
    [peopleToRemove count]);
```

Build the app. Change your preferred language to French, and run the app. When you delete a row from the table, you should get an alert panel in French.

For the More Curious: nibtool

Clearly, as you develop and localize many applications, you will develop a set of common translations. It would be handy to know an automated way to get the translated strings into a nib file. This is one of several uses for `nibtool`.

`nibtool` is a command that is run from the terminal. It can list the classes or objects that are in a nib file. It can also dump the localizable strings into a plist. Here is how you would dump the localizable strings from the `English.lproj/MyDocument.nib` file into a file named `Doc.strings`:

```
> cd RaiseMan/English.lproj
> nibtool -L MyDocument.nib > Doc.strings
```

This would result in a Doc.strings file that would look something like this:

```
/* NSButton (Delete Record) : <title:Delete Record> (oid:24) */
"Delete Record" = "Delete Record";

/* NSTableColumn : <title:Expected Raise> (oid:53) */
"Expected Raise" = "Expected Raise";

/* NSTableColumn : <title:Name> (oid:54) */
"Name" = "Name";

/* NSButton (New Empty) : <title:New Empty> (oid:23) */
"New Empty" = "New Empty";

/* NSWindow (Window) : <title:Window> (oid:5) */
"Window" = "Window";
```

To create a Spanish dictionary for this nib file, you could edit the file to look like this:

```
/* NSButton (Delete Record) : <title:Delete Record> (oid:24) */
"Delete Record" = "Borre Árchivo";

/* NSTableColumn : <title:Expected Raise> (oid:53) */
"Expected Raise" = "Aumento Esperado";

/* NSTableColumn : <title:Name> (oid:54) */
"Name" = "Nombre";

/* NSButton (New Empty) : <title:New Empty> (oid:23) */
"New Empty" = "Crea Nuevo Árchivo";

/* NSWindow (Window) : <title:Window> (oid:5) */
"Window" = "Window";
```

To substitute the strings in a nib file with their Spanish equivalents from this dictionary, you could create a new nib file like this:

```
> mkdir ../Spanish.lproj
> nibtool -d Doc.strings -w ../Spanish.lproj/MyDocument.nib MyDocument.nib
```

To learn more about nibtool, use Unix's man command:

```
> man nibtool
```

Challenge

For RaiseMan to be truly localized, you would also need a French version of Main-Menu.nib. The application menu and the file menu to get you started are shown in Figures 11.7 and 11.8, respectively.

Figure 11.7   The Main Menu in French

Figure 11.8   The File Menu in French

Chapter 12
CUSTOM VIEWS

All the visible objects in an application are either windows or views. In this chapter, you will create a subclass of **NSView**. From time to time, you will create a custom view to do custom drawing or event handling. Even if you do not plan to do custom drawing or event handling, by learning how to create a new view class, you will learn a lot about how Cocoa works.

Windows are instances of the class **NSWindow**. Each window has a collection of views. Each view is responsible for a rectangle of the window. The view draws inside that rectangle and handles mouse events that occur there. A view may also handle keyboard events. You have worked with several subclasses of **NSView** already: **NSButton**, **NSTextField**, **NSTableView**, and **NSColorWell** are all views. (Note that a window is not a subclass of **NSView**.)

The View Hierarchy

Views are arranged in a hierarchy (Figure 12.1). The window has a content view that completely fills its interior. The content view usually has several subviews. Each subview may have subviews of its own. Every view knows its superview, its subviews, and the window it lives on.

Here are the relevant methods:

```
- (NSView *)superview;
- (NSArray *)subviews;
- (NSWindow *)window;
```

Any view can have subviews, but most don't. Here are five views that commonly have subviews.

- The content view of a window.
- **NSBox**. The contents of a box are its subviews.

- **NSScrollView**. If a view appears in a scroll view, it is a subview of the scroll view. The scroll bars are also subviews of the scroll view.
- **NSSplitView**. Each view in a split view is a subview (Figure 12.2).
- **NSTabView**. As the user chooses different tabs, different subviews are swapped in and out (Figure 12.3).

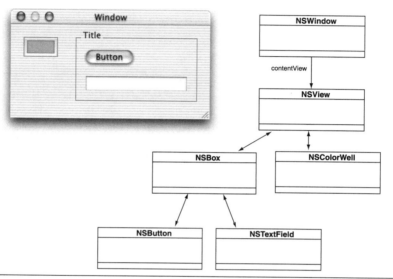

Figure 12.1   Views Are in a Hierarchy

Figure 12.2   A Scroll View in a Split View

Figure 12.3   A Tab View

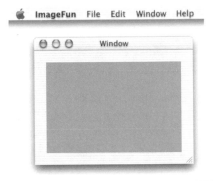

Figure 12.4   Completed Application

Get a View to Draw Itself

In this section, you are going to create a very simple view. It will simply appear and paint itself green. It will look like Figure 12.4.

Create a new project of type Cocoa Application (Figure 12.5).

Name it ImageFun.

After the new project is created, open MainMenu.nib, and select **NSView** in the classes browser (Figure 12.6).

Press return to create a subclass, and name it **StretchView** (Figure 12.7).

Create the files for **StretchView** (Figure 12.8).

Save the files in the project directory.

Figure 12.5   Choose Project Type

Figure 12.6   Select NSView

Figure 12.7   Create the StretchView Class

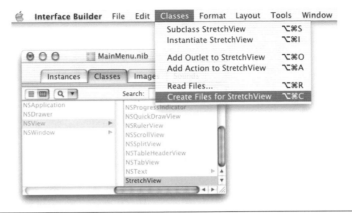

Figure 12.8 Create the Files for the StretchView Class

Create an Instance of a View Subclass

Now create an instance of your class by dragging out a CustomView placeholder and dropping it on the window (Figure 12.9).

Resize the view to fill most of the window. Open the info panel and set the class of the view to be **StretchView** (Figure 12.10).

Notice that creating an instance of a view is different from creating an instance of a controller object like **AppController**. To create an instance of **AppController** in Chapter 7, you used the Instantiate menu item. When creating a view, it is important that you attach it to a window and give it a size and location in that window.

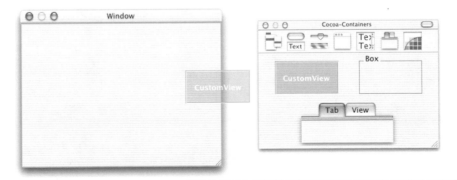

Figure 12.9 Drop a View on Your Window

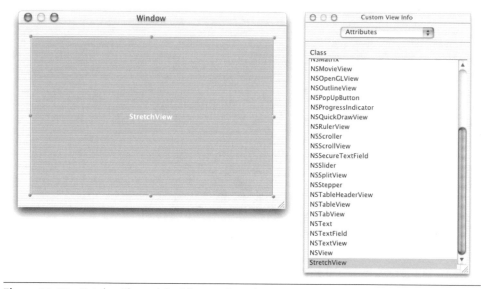

Figure 12.10   Set the Class of the View to StretchView

Size Info

Your **StretchView** object is a subview of the window's content view. An interesting question is: What happens to the view when the superview resizes? There is a page in the info panel that allows you to set that behavior. Open the size info panel, and set it as shown in Figure 12.11. This means that it will grow and shrink as necessary to keep the distance from its edges to the edges of its superview constant.

If you wanted the view to stay the same size, you could let the distance between the edges of the view and the edges of the superview grow and shrink. In this exercise, you do not want this behavior. But in a parallel universe where you did, the inspector would look like this (Figure 12.12).

Save and close the nib file.

drawRect:

When a view needs to draw itself, it is sent the message **drawRect:** with the rectangle that needs to be drawn or redrawn. This method is called automatically, and you will

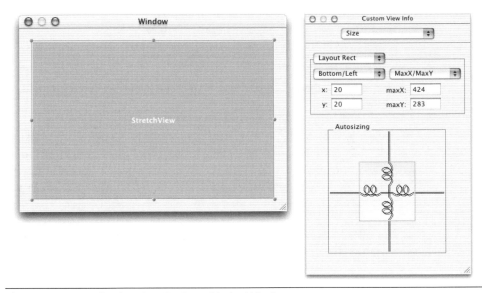

Figure 12.11   Make the View Resize with the Window

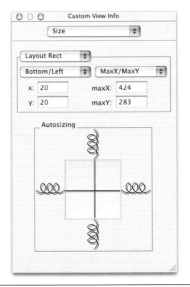

Figure 12.12   Not This!

never need to call it directly. Instead, if you know that a view needs redrawing, you will send the view the message **setNeedsDisplay:**:

```
[myView setNeedsDisplay:YES];
```

This informs myView that it is "dirty." After the event has been handled, the view will be redrawn.

Before it is redrawn, the system *locks focus* upon it. Each view has its own graphics context. The graphics context includes things like the view's coordinate system, its current color, its current font, and the clipping rectangle. When the focus is locked on a view, the view's graphics context is active. When the focus is unlocked, the graphics context is no longer active.

You can use **NSBezierPath** to draw lines, circles, curves, and rectangles. You can use **NSImage** to composite images onto the view. In this example, you will fill the entire view with a green rectangle.

Open StretchView.m and add this method:

```
- (void)drawRect:(NSRect)rect
{
    NSRect bounds = [self bounds];
    [[NSColor greenColor] set];
    [NSBezierPath fillRect:bounds];
}
```

As shown in Figure 12.13, an NSRect is a struct with two members: origin, which is an NSPoint, and size, which is an NSSize.

An NSSize is a struct with two members: width and height are both floats.

An NSPoint is a struct with two members: x and y are both floats.

Notice that your view knows its location as an NSRect called bounds. In this method, you fetched the bounds rectangle, set the current color to green, and filled the entire bounds rectangle with the current color.

The NSRect that is passed as an argument to the view is the region that is "dirty" and needs redrawing. This may be less than the entire view. If you are doing very time-consuming drawing, you should be careful to redraw only the dirty rectangle. This may speed up your application considerably.

Notice that **setNeedsDisplay:** will trigger the entire visible region of the view to be redrawn. If you wish to be more precise about which part of the view needs redrawing, you should use **setNeedsDisplayInRect:** instead:

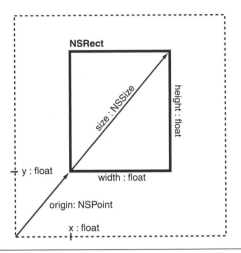

Figure 12.13   NSRect, NSSize, and NSPoint

```
NSRect dirtyRect;
dirtyRect = NSMakeRect(0, 0, 50, 50);
[myView setNeedsDisplayInRect:dirtyRect];
```

Build and run your app. Try resizing the window.

Drawing with NSBezierPath

If you want to draw lines, ovals, curves, or polygons, you will use **NSBezierPath**. In this chapter, you already used the **NSBezierPath**'s **fillRect:** class method to color your view. In this section, you will use **NSBezierPath** to draw lines connecting random points (Figure 12.14).

The first thing you will need is an instance variable to hold on to the instance of **NSBezierPath**. You are also going to create an instance method that returns a random point in the view. Open StretchView.h and make it look like this:

```
#import <Cocoa/Cocoa.h>

@interface StretchView : NSView
{
    NSBezierPath *path;
}
- (NSPoint)randomPoint;

@end
```

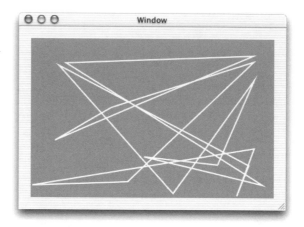

Figure 12.14   Completed Application

Now in StretchView.m, you are going to override **initWithFrame:**. **initWithFrame:** is the designated initializer for views, and it will get called automatically when an instance of your view is created. In your version of **initWithFrame:**, you are going to create the path object and fill it with lines to random points. Make StretchView.m look like this:

```
#import "StretchView.h"

@implementation StretchView

- (id)initWithFrame:(NSRect)rect
{
    int i;
    NSPoint p;

    if (self = [super initWithFrame: rect]) {
      // Seed the the random number generator
      srandom(time(NULL));

      // Create a path object
      path = [[NSBezierPath alloc] init];
      [path setLineWidth: 2.3];
      p = [self randomPoint];
      [path moveToPoint: p];
      for (i = 0; i < 15; i++) {
          p = [self randomPoint];
          [path lineToPoint: p];
      }
      [path closePath];
    }
```

```objc
        return self;
}

// randomPoint returns a random point inside the view
- (NSPoint)randomPoint
{
    NSPoint result;
    NSRect r;
    int width, height;
    r = [self bounds];
    width = round(r.size.width);
    height = round (r.size.height);
    result.x = (random() % width) + r.origin.x;
    result.y = (random() % height) + r.origin.y;
    return result;
}

- (void)drawRect:(NSRect)rect
{
    NSRect r = [self bounds];

    // Fill view with green
    [[NSColor greenColor] set];
    [NSBezierPath fillRect: r];

    // Draw the path in white
    [[NSColor whiteColor] set];
    [path stroke];
}

- (void)dealloc
{
    [path release];
    [super dealloc];
}
@end
```

Build and run your app.

NSScrollView

In the world of art, a larger work is typically more expensive than a small one of equal quality. Your beautiful view is lovely, but it would be more valuable if it were larger. How can it be larger yet still fit inside that tiny window? You are going to put it in a scroll view (Figure 12.15).

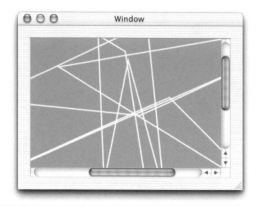

Figure 12.15 Completed Application

A scroll view has three parts: the document view, the content view, and the scroll bars. In this example, your view will become the document view. It will be displayed in the content view, which is an instance of **NSClipView**.

It looks tricky, but it is actually very simple to do. In fact, it requires no code at all. Open up MainMenu.nib in Interface Builder. Select the view, and choose Group In Scroll View from the Layout menu (Figure 12.16).

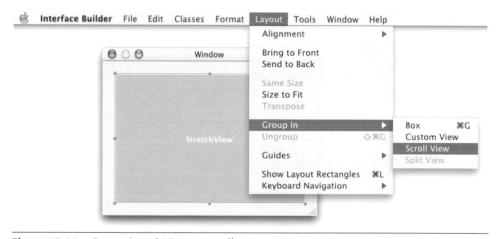

Figure 12.16 Group StretchView in ScrollView

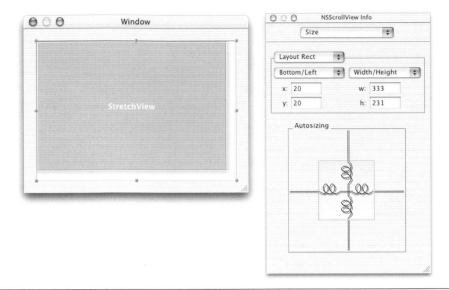

Figure 12.17   Make ScrollView Resize With Window

As the window resizes, you want the scroll view to resize, but you do not want your document to resize. So open the Info Panel, select the scroll view, and set the size inspector so that it resizes (Figure 12.17).

Also, note the width and height of the view.

To select the document view, double-click inside the scroll view. You should see the title of the Info Panel change to StretchView (Custom) Info. Make the view about twice as wide and twice as tall as the scroll view. Set the size inspector so that the view will not resize (Figure 12.18). Build it and run it.

For the More Curious: Cells

NSControl inherits from **NSView**. **NSView** is a relatively large and expensive object to create. When the **NSButton** class was first created, the first thing someone did was to create a calculator with 10 rows and 10 columns of buttons. The performance was less than it could have been because of the 100 tiny views. So someone had the clever idea of moving the brains of the button into another object (not a view) and creating

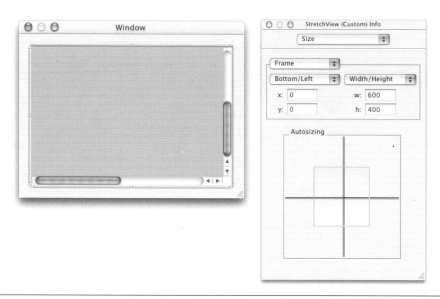

Figure 12.18   Make StretchView Larger and Non-resizing

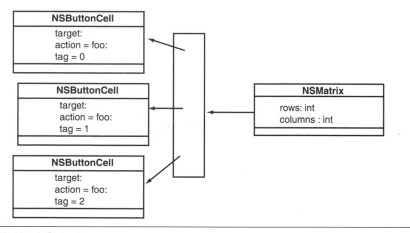

Figure 12.19   NSMatrix

one big view (called an **NSMatrix**) that would act as the view for all 100 button brains. The class for the button brains was **NSButtonCell** (Figure 12.19).

NSButton became just a view that had an **NSButtonCell**. The button cell does everything, and **NSButton** simply claims a space in the window (Figure 12.20).

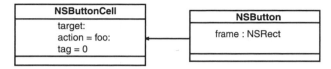

Figure 12.20 NSButton and NSButtonCell

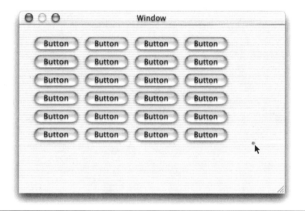

Figure 12.21 A Matrix of Buttons

Likewise, **NSSlider** is simply a view with an **NSSliderCell**, and **NSTextField** is a view with an **NSTextFieldCell**. **NSColorWell**, on the other hand, has no cell.

To create an instance of **NSMatrix** in Interface Builder, you drop a control with a cell onto the window and option-drag as if resizing until the matrix has the correct number of rows and columns (Figure 12.21).

An **NSMatrix** has a target and an action. A cell may also have a target and an action. If the cell is activated, the cell's target and action get used. If the target and action of the selected cell are not set, the matrix's target and action will be used.

When dealing with matrices, it is common to ask which cell was activated. Cells can also be given a tag.

```
- (IBAction)myAction:(id)sender {
    id theCell = [sender selectedCell];
    int theTag = [theCell tag];
    ...
}
```

The cell's tag can be set in Interface Builder.

Cells are used in several other types of objects. The **NSTableView**, for example, is filled with cells.

Challenge

NSBezierPath can also draw Bezier curves. Replace the straight lines with randomly curved ones. Hint: Look in NSBezierPath.h.

Chapter 13
IMAGES AND MOUSE EVENTS

In the last chapter, you drew lines connecting random points. A more interesting application would have been to write some sort of a drawing application. To write this sort of application, you will need to be able to get and handle mouse events.

NSResponder

NSView inherits from **NSResponder**. All the event-handling methods are declared in **NSResponder**. We will discuss keyboard events in Chapter 14. For now, we are only interested in mouse events. **NSResponder** declares these methods:

```
- (void)mouseDown:(NSEvent *)theEvent;
- (void)rightMouseDown:(NSEvent *)theEvent;
- (void)otherMouseDown:(NSEvent *)theEvent;
- (void)mouseUp:(NSEvent *)theEvent;
- (void)rightMouseUp:(NSEvent *)theEvent;
- (void)otherMouseUp:(NSEvent *)theEvent;
- (void)mouseMoved:(NSEvent *)theEvent;
- (void)mouseDragged:(NSEvent *)theEvent;
- (void)scrollWheel:(NSEvent *)theEvent;
- (void)rightMouseDragged:(NSEvent *)theEvent;
- (void)otherMouseDragged:(NSEvent *)theEvent;
- (void)mouseEntered:(NSEvent *)theEvent;
- (void)mouseExited:(NSEvent *)theEvent;
```

Notice that the argument is always an **NSEvent** object.

NSEvent

An event object has all the information about what the user did to trigger the event. When you are dealing with mouse events, you might be interested in the following methods.

```
- (NSPoint)locationInWindow
```

Returns the location of the mouse event.

```
- (unsigned int)modifierFlags
```

The integer tells you which modifier keys the user is holding down on the keyboard. This enables the programmer to tell a control-click from a shift-click, for example. The code would look like this:

```
- (void)mouseDown:(NSEvent *)e
{
    unsigned int flags;
    flags = [e modifierFlags];
    if (flags & NSControlKeyMask) {
        ...handle control click...
    }
    if (flags & NSShiftKeyMask) {
        ...handle shift click...
    }
}
```

Here are the constants that you will AND (&) against the modifier flags:

NSAlphaShiftKeyMask

NSShiftKeyMask

NSControlKeyMask

NSAlternateKeyMask

NSCommandKeyMask

NSNumericPadKeyMask

NSHelpKeyMask

NSFunctionKeyMask

```
- (NSTimeInterval)timestamp
```

The time interval in seconds between the time the machine booted and the time of the event. NSTimeInterval is a double.

```
- (NSWindow *)window
```

The window associated with the event.

```
- (int)clickCount
```

Was it a single-, double-, or triple-click?

```
- (float)pressure
```

If the user is using an input device that gives pressure (a tablet, for example), this method returns the pressure. It is between 0 and 1.

```
- (float)deltaX;
- (float)deltaY;
- (float)deltaZ;
```

These methods give the change in the position of the scroll wheel.

Getting Mouse Events

To get mouse events, you simply need to override the mouse event methods in StretchView.m:

```
- (void)mouseDown:(NSEvent *)event
{
    NSLog(@"mouseDown: %d", [event clickCount]);
}
- (void)mouseDragged:(NSEvent *)event
{
    NSLog(@"mouseDragged:");
}
- (void)mouseUp:(NSEvent *)event
{
    NSLog(@"mouseUp:");
}
```

Build and run your application. Try double-clicking, and check the click count. Note that the first click is sent and then the second. The first click has a click count of 1. The second has a click count of 2.

Using NSOpenPanel

It would be fun to composite an image onto the view, but first you need to create a controller object that will read the image data from a file. This is a good opportunity to learn how to use **NSOpenPanel**. Note that the RaiseMan application used the

Figure 13.1   NSOpenPanel

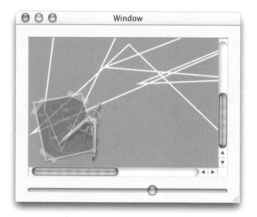

Figure 13.2   Completed Application

NSOpenPanel, but it was done automatically by the **NSDocument** class. Here you will use the **NSOpenPanel** explicitly. Figure 13.1 shows what your application will look like while the open panel is active. Figure 13.2 shows what it will look like once the user has chosen an image. The slider at the bottom of the window will control how opaque the image is.

Figure 13.3 shows the object diagram.

Change the Nib File

Open the nib file and create a new subclass of **NSObject** called **AppController**. Create two outlets called stretchView and slider. Create two actions: **open:** and **fade:** (Figure 13.4). Create files for the **AppController** class.

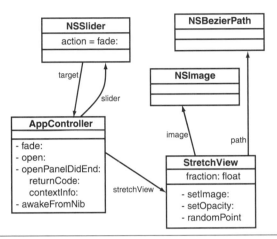

Figure 13.3   Object Diagram

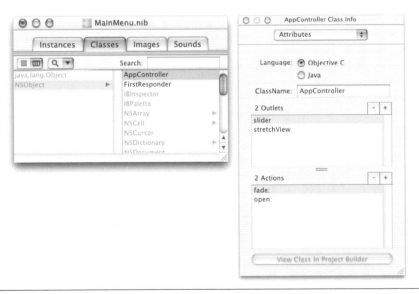

Figure 13.4   Create AppController Class

In the classes menu, use the Instantiate AppController to create an instance of your new class (Figure 13.5).

Control-drag from the **AppController** to the **StretchView** and connect the stretchView outlet (Figure 13.6).

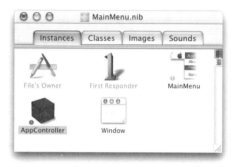

Figure 13.5   Create an Instance of AppController

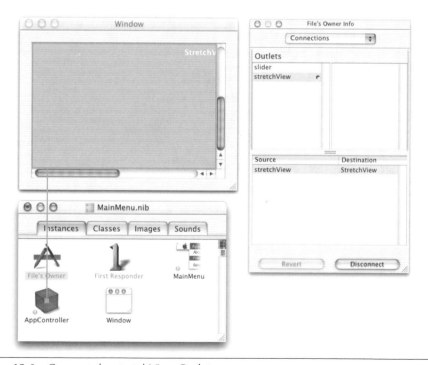

Figure 13.6   Connect the stretchView Outlet

Drop a slider on the window. Set its range from 0 to 1. This slider will control how opaque the image is (Figure 13.7).

Connect the `slider` outlet to the instance of **NSSlider** (Figure 13.8).

Set the target of the slider to be the **AppController**. Its action will be **fade:** (Figure 13.9).

Look at the main menu in your nib. Open the File menu and delete all the menu items except Open. Control-drag to connect the menu item to the **AppController**'s **open:** action (Figure 13.10). Save the file.

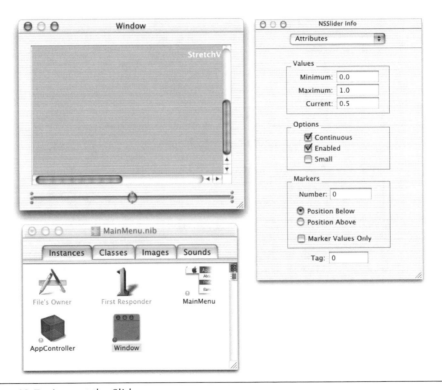

Figure 13.7   Inspect the Slider

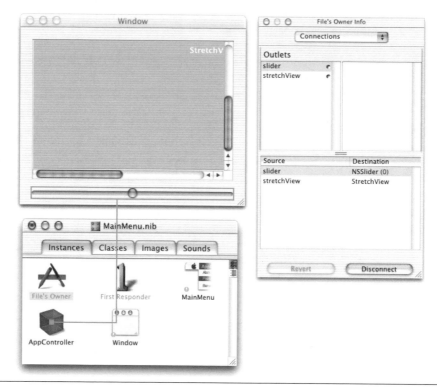

Figure 13.8   Connect the Slider Outlet

awakeFromNib Versus init

When your nib file is loaded, these three things will happen (in this order) to your **AppController** object (and any other object in the nib file):

- It will be allocated and sent the message **init**. (Views will be sent **initWithFrame:**.)
- Its outlets will be set.
- It will be sent **awakeFromNib** .

Note that **init** gets sent before the outlets of the object get set. Thus, you cannot send messages to any of the other objects from the nib file in the **init** method. You can, however, send them messages in the **awakeFromNib** method.

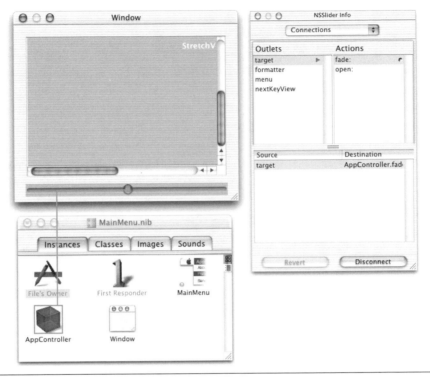

Figure 13.9   Set the Action of the Slider

Edit the Code

Edit AppController.m:

```
#import "AppController.h"
#import "StretchView.h"
#import <Cocoa/Cocoa.h>

@implementation AppController

- (void)awakeFromNib
{
    // Make sure the slider and the stretch view
    // agree on the initial opacity
    [slider setFloatValue:0.5];
    [stretchView setOpacity:0.5];
}
```

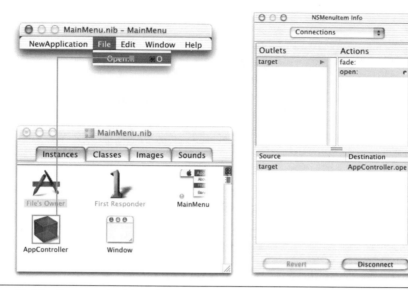

Figure 13.10   Connect the Menu Item

```
- (IBAction)fade:(id)sender
{
    // The sender is the slider
    [stretchView setOpacity:[sender floatValue]];
}

- (void)openPanelDidEnd:(NSOpenPanel *)openPanel
        returnCode:(int)returnCode
        contextInfo:(void *)x
{
    NSString *path;
    NSImage *image;

    // Did they choose "Open"?
    if (returnCode == NSOKButton) {
        path = [openPanel filename];
        image = [[NSImage alloc] initWithContentsOfFile:path];
        [stretchView setImage:image];
        [image release];
    }
}

- (IBAction)open:(id)sender
{
    NSOpenPanel *panel = [NSOpenPanel openPanel];
```

```
    // Run the open panel
    [panel beginSheetForDirectory:nil
            file:nil
            types:[NSImage imageFileTypes]
            modalForWindow:[stretchView window]
            modalDelegate:self
            didEndSelector:
                @selector(openPanelDidEnd:returnCode:contextInfo:)
            contextInfo:nil];
}

@end
```

Notice the line where you start the sheet. This is a very handy method:

```
- (void)beginSheetForDirectory:(NSString *)path
                          file:(NSString *)name
                modalForWindow:(NSWindow *)docWindow
                 modalDelegate:(id)delegate
                didEndSelector:(SEL)didEndSelector
                   contextInfo:(void *)contextInfo
```

This method brings up an open panel as a sheet. If docWindow is nil, the open panel is standalone; otherwise it slides down as a sheet on the docWindow. The didEndSelector should have the following signature:

```
- (void)openPanelDidEnd:(NSWindow *)sheet
            returnCode:(int)returnCode
           contextInfo:(void *)contextInfo;
```

And it should be implemented in the delegate. The path is the place where the file browser will open initially. The name is the name of the file that will be chosen initially. Both the path and the name may be nil.

Composite an Image Onto Your View

You will also need to change **StretchView** so that it uses the opacity and image. First, declare variables and methods in your StretchView.h file:

```
#import <Cocoa/Cocoa.h>

@interface StretchView : NSView
{
    NSBezierPath *path;
    NSImage *image;
    float opacity;
}
```

```
- (void)setImage:(NSImage *)x;
- (void)setOpacity:(float)x;
- (NSPoint)randomPoint;
```

@end

Now implement these methods in your `StretchView.m` file:

```
- (void)setImage:(NSImage *)newImage
{
    [newImage retain];
    [image release];
    image = newImage;
    [self setNeedsDisplay:YES];
}
- (void)setOpacity:(float)x
{
    opacity = x;
    [self setNeedsDisplay:YES];
}
```

Note at the end of each of the methods, you inform the view that it needs to redraw itself.

Also in `StretchView.m`, you need to add compositing of the image to the **drawRect:** method:

```
- (void)drawRect:(NSRect)rect
{
    NSRect r = [self bounds];
    NSPoint p = r.origin;
    [[NSColor greenColor] set];
    [NSBezierPath fillRect:r];
    [[NSColor whiteColor] set];
    [path stroke];
    if (image) {
        [image dissolveToPoint:p fraction:opacity];
    }
}
```

Notice that the **dissolveToPoint:fraction:** method composites the image onto the view. The fraction determines the image's opacity.

In the name of tidiness, be sure to release the image in your view's **dealloc** method:

```
- (void)dealloc
{
    [image release];
    [path release];
    [super dealloc];
}
```

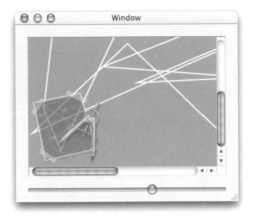

Figure 13.11   Completed Application

Build and run your application. You will find a few images in `/Developer/Examples` `/AppKit/Sketch` . When you open an image it will appear in the lower left corner of your **StretchView** object (Figure 13.11).

The View's Coordinate System

So the final bit of fun is to be able to choose the location and dimensions of the image based on the user's dragging. The mouse down will indicate one corner of the rectangle where the image will appear, and the mouse up will indicate the opposite corner. The final app will look something like Figure 13.12.

Each view has its own coordinate system. By default, (0,0) is in the lower left corner. This is consistent with PDF and PostScript. You can change the coordinate system of the view if you wish. You can move the origin, change the scale, or rotate the coordinates. The window also has a coordinate system.

If you have two views, a and b, and you need to translate an NSPoint p from b's coordinate system to a's, it would look like this:

```
NSPoint q = [a convertPoint:p fromView:b];
```

If b is nil, the point is converted from the window's coordinate system.

Mouse events have their location in the window's coordinate system, so you will nearly always have to convert the point to the local coordinate system. You are going

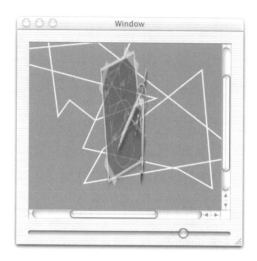

Figure 13.12   Completed Application

to create variables to hold onto the corners of the rectangle where the image will be drawn

Add these instance variables to StretchView.h:

```
NSPoint downPoint;
NSPoint currentPoint;
```

downPoint will be the location of the mouseDown. currentPoint will be updated by **mouseDragged:** and **mouseUp:** .

Edit the mouse event-handling methods to update downPoint and currentPoint:

```
- (void)mouseDown:(NSEvent *)event
{
    NSPoint p = [event locationInWindow];
    downPoint = [self convertPoint:p fromView:nil];
    currentPoint = downPoint;
    [self setNeedsDisplay:YES];
}
- (void)mouseDragged:(NSEvent *)event
{
    NSPoint p = [event locationInWindow];
    currentPoint = [self convertPoint:p fromView:nil];
    [self setNeedsDisplay:YES];
}
```

```
- (void)mouseUp:(NSEvent *)event
{
    NSPoint p = [event locationInWindow];
    currentPoint = [self convertPoint:p fromView:nil];
    [self setNeedsDisplay:YES];
}
```

Add a method to calculate the rectangle based on the two points:

```
- (NSRect)currentRect
{
    float minX = MIN(downPoint.x, currentPoint.x);
    float maxX = MAX(downPoint.x, currentPoint.x);
    float minY = MIN(downPoint.y, currentPoint.y);
    float maxY = MAX(downPoint.y, currentPoint.y);

    return NSMakeRect(minX, minY, maxX-minX, maxY-minY);
}
```

Also, declare the **currentRect** method in StretchView.h.

In the **drawRect:** method, composite the image inside the rectangle:

```
- (void)drawRect:(NSRect)rect
{
    [[NSColor greenColor] set];
    [NSBezierPath fillRect:[self bounds]];
    [[NSColor whiteColor] set];
    [path stroke];
    if (image) {
        NSRect imageRect;
        NSRect drawingRect;
        imageRect.size = [image size];
        drawingRect = [self currentRect];
        [image drawInRect:drawingRect
                fromRect:imageRect
                operation:NSCompositeSourceOver
                fraction:opacity];
    }
}
```

Build and run your application. Notice that the view doesn't scroll when you drag past the edge. It would be nice if the scroll view would move to allow the user to see where they have dragged to. This is known as *autoscrolling*. In the next section, you will add autoscrolling to your app.

Autoscrolling

To add autoscrolling to your application, you will simply send the message **auto-scroll:** to the clip view when the user drags. You will include the event as an argument. Open StretchView.m and add a line to the **mouseDragged:** method:

```
- (void)mouseDragged:(NSEvent *)event
{
    NSPoint p = [event locationInWindow];
    currentPoint = [self convertPoint:p fromView:nil];
    [[self superview] autoscroll:event];
    [self setNeedsDisplay:YES];
}
```

Build and run your application.

Notice that autoscrolling happens only as you drag. For smoother autoscrolling, most developers will create a timer that sends the view the **autoscroll:** method periodically while the user is dragging. We discuss timers in Chapter 19.

For the More Curious: NSImage

For most things, it is enough simply to read in an image, resize it, and composite it onto a view, as you did in this exercise.

An **NSImage** object has an array of representations. For example, your image might be a drawing of a cow. That drawing can be in PDF, a color bitmap, and a black-and-white bitmap. Each of these is an instance of a subclass of **NSImageRep**. You can add representations to and remove representations from your image. When you sit down to rewrite Adobe Photoshop™, you will be manipulating the image representations.

Here is a list of the subclasses of **NSImageRep**:

- NSBitmapImageRep
- NSEPSImageRep
- NSPICTImageRep
- NSCachedImageRep
- NSCustomImageRep
- NSPDFImageRep

Although there are only five subclasses of **NSImageRep**, it is important to note that **NSImage** knows how to read about two dozen types of image files. All the common formats are included in these: PICT, GIF, JPG, PNG, PDF, BMP, TIFF, etc.

Challenge

Create a new document-based application that allows the user to draw ovals in arbitrary locations and sizes. **NSBezierPath** has the method:

+ (NSBezierPath *)**bezierPathWithOvalInRect:**(NSRect)rect;

If you are feeling ambitious, add saving and reading files.

Chapter 14

RESPONDERS AND KEYBOARD EVENTS

When the user types, where do the corresponding events get sent? First, the window manager gets the event and forwards it on to the active application. The active application forwards the keyboard events on to the key window. The key window forwards the event on to the "active" view. Which view, then, is the active one? Each window has an outlet called firstResponder that points to one view of that window. That view is the "active" one for that window. For example, when you click on a text field, it becomes the firstResponder of that window (Figure 14.1).

When the user tries to change the firstResponder to another view (by the tabbing or clicking the other view) there is a ritual that the views go through before firstResponder outlet is changed. First, the view that may become the firstResponder gets asked if it accepts first-responder status. If it returns NO, that means the view is not interested in keyboard events. For example, you can't type into a slider, so it refuses to accept first-responder status. If the view does accept first-responder status, the view that is currently the first responder is asked if it resigns first-responder status. If the editing is not done, the view can refuse to give up first-responder status. For example, if the user had not typed in his or her entire phone number, the text field could refuse to resign first-responder status. Finally, the view is told that it is becoming first responder. Often, this triggers a change in its appearance (Figure 14.2).

Note that each window has its own first responder. There may be several windows open. Only the first responder of the key window gets the keyboard events.

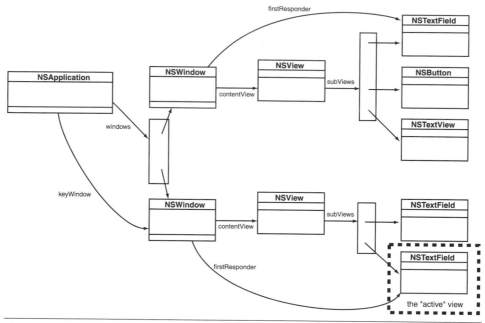

Figure 14 1   The First Responder of the Key Window is "Active"

NSResponder

Here, then, are the methods that are inherited from **NSResponder** that we are interested in.

- (BOOL)**acceptsFirstResponder**

Overridden by a subclass to return YES if it handles keyboard events.

- (BOOL)**resignFirstResponder**

Asks the receiver if it is willing to give up first-responder status.

- (BOOL)**becomeFirstResponder**

Notifies the receiver that it's about to become first responder in its **NSWindow**.

- (void)**keyDown:**(NSEvent *)theEvent

Informs the receiver that the user has pressed a key.

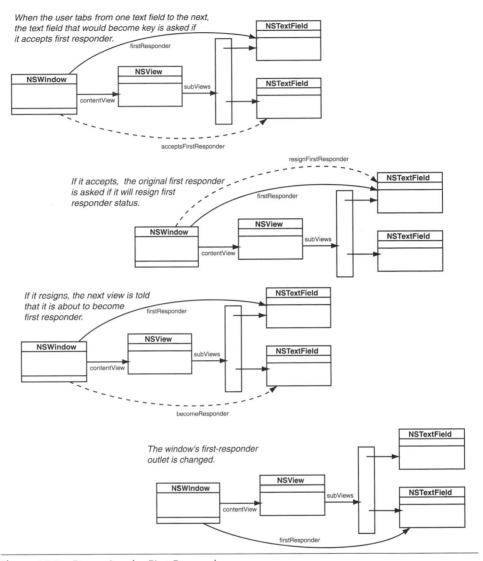

Figure 14.2   Becoming the First Responder

- (void)**keyUp:**(NSEvent *)theEvent

Informs the receiver that the user has released a key.

- (void)**flagsChanged:**(NSEvent *)theEvent

Informs the receiver that the user has pressed or released a modifier key (Shift, Control, or so on).

NSEvent

We discussed **NSEvent** in terms of mouse events in the last chapter. Here are some of the common methods used when getting information about a keyboard event.

- (NSString *)**characters**

Returns the characters created by the event.

- (BOOL)**isARepeat**

Returns YES if the key event is a repeat caused by the user's holding the key down, NO if the key event is new.

- (unsigned short)**keyCode**

Returns the code for the keyboard key that caused the event. Its value is hardware dependent.

- (unsigned int)**modifierFlags**

Returns an integer bit field indicating the modifier keys in effect for the receiver. For information about what the bits of the integer mean, refer to the discussion in Chapter 13.

Create a New Project with a Custom View

Create a new project of type Cocoa Application. Name it TypingTutor.

Edit the Nib File

Open MainMenu.nib. Select **NSView** in the classes browser (Figure 14.3).

Create a subclass, and name it **BigLetterView** (Figure 14.4).

Create the files for **BigLetterView** (Figure 14.5).

Save the files in the project directory (Figure 14.6).

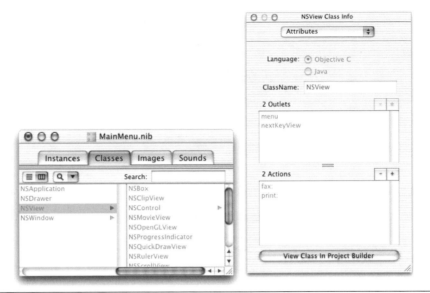

Figure 14.3   Select NSView

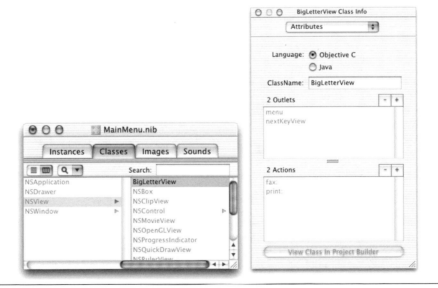

Figure 14.4   Create the Subclass BigLetterView

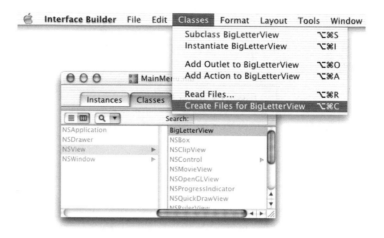

Figure 14.5   Create the Files for BigLetterView

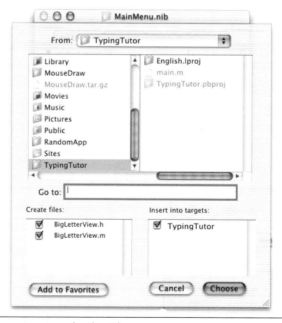

Figure 14.6   Choose a Location for the Files

Lay Out the Interface

Now create an instance of your class by dragging out a CustomView placeholder and dropping it on the window (Figure 14.7).

Open the inspector and set the class of the view to be **BigLetterView** (Figure 14.8).

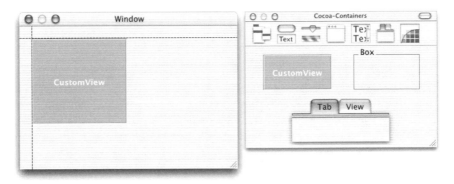

Figure 14.7   Drop a View on the Window

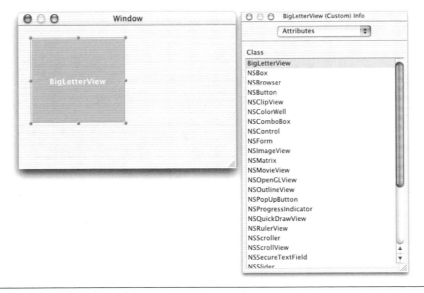

Figure 14.8   Set the Class of the View to BigLetterView

Size Info

Select the new view and open the size info panel, and set it as shown in Figure 14.9. This means that it will keep constant its distance from the upper left corner of its superview. It will grow and shrink with the superview.

Really small windows will mess up your nice resizing, so open the size info panel for the window. In particular, click the Current button in the Min Size box. That will prevent the user from making the window any smaller.

Drop two text fields on the window (Figure 14.10).

Make Connections

Now you need to create the loop of key views for your window. That is, you are setting the order in which the views will be selected as the user tabs from one to the next. The order will be the text field on the left, the text field on the right, and the **BigLetterView** and back to the text field on the left.

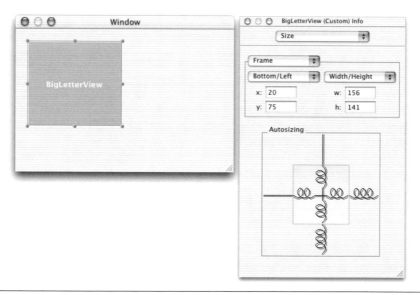

Figure 14.9 Set Size Info

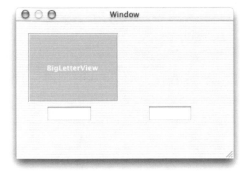

Figure 14.10   Completed Interface

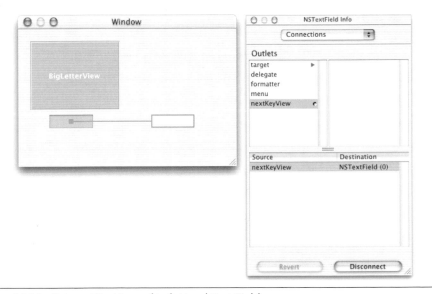

Figure 14.11   Set nextKeyView of Left-Hand Text Field

Set the left-hand text field's nextKeyView to be the right-hand text field (Figure 14.11).

Set the right-hand text field's nextKeyView to be the **BigLetterView** (Figure 14.12).

Finally, set the nextKeyView of the **BigLetterView** to be the left-hand text field. This will enable the user to tab between the three views. Shift-tabbing will move the selection in the opposite direction.

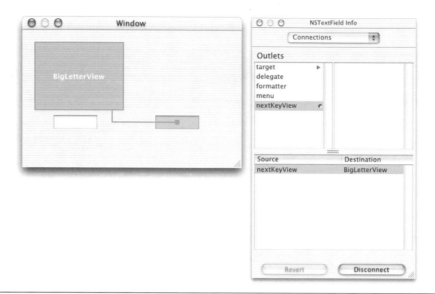

Figure 14.12 Set nextKeyView of Right-Hand Text Field

Which view, then, should be the firstResponder when the window first appears? Let's make the left-hand text field the initialFirstResponder of the window. Drag from the window to the text field and set the initialFirstResponder outlet (Figure 14.13).

Save and close the nib file.

Writing the Code

In this section, you are going to make your **BigLetterView** respond to key events. You are also going to make it accept first-responder status. The characters typed by the user will appear in the console. The completed application will look like Figure 14.14.

In BigLetterView.h

Your **BigLetterView** will have two instance variables and accessor methods for those variables. bgColor will be the background color of the view, and it will be an **NSColor** object. string will hold on to the letter that the user most recently typed, and it will be an **NSString** object.

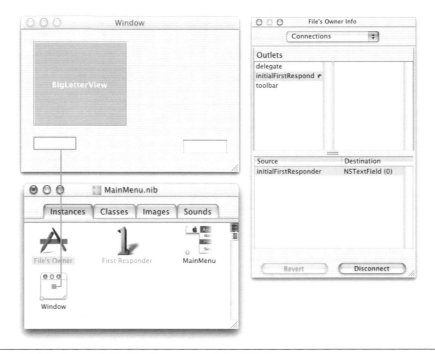

Figure 14.13   Set the initialFirstResponder of the Window

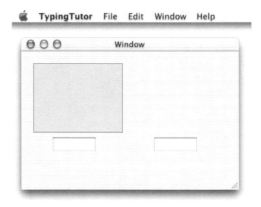

Figure 14.14   Completed Application

```
#import <Cocoa/Cocoa.h>

@interface BigLetterView : NSView
{
    NSColor *bgColor;
    NSString *string;
}
- (void)setBgColor:(NSColor *)c;
- (NSColor *)bgColor;
- (void)setString:(NSString *)c;
- (NSString *)string;

@end
```

In BigLetterView.m

The designated initializer for a view is **initWithFrame:**. In this method, you will call the superclass's **initWithFrame:** method and initialize bgColor and string to default values. Add the following method to BigLetterView.m:

```
- initWithFrame:(NSRect)rect
{
    if (self = [super initWithFrame:rect]) {
      NSLog(@"initializing view");
      [self setBgColor:[NSColor yellowColor]];
      [self setString:@" "];
    }
    return self;
}
```

Create accessor methods for bgColor and string:

```
- (void)setBgColor:(NSColor *)c
{
    [c retain];
    [bgColor release];
    bgColor = c;
    [self setNeedsDisplay: YES];
}

- (NSColor *)bgColor
{
    return bgColor;
}

- (void)setString:(NSString *)c
{
    [c retain];
    [string release];
    string = c;
    NSLog(@"The string is now %@", string);
}
```

```
- (NSString *)string
{
    return string;
}
```

Create the **drawRect:** method. This will fill the view with bgColor. If the view is the window's firstResponder, it will stroke a black rectangle around its bounds:

```
- (void)drawRect:(NSRect)rect
{
    NSRect bounds = [self bounds];
    [bgColor set];
    [NSBezierPath fillRect:bounds];

    // Am I the window's first responder?
    if ([[self window] firstResponder] == self) {
        [[NSColor blackColor] set];
        [NSBezierPath strokeRect:bounds];
    }
}
```

Then the methods to become firstResponder are

```
- (BOOL)acceptsFirstResponder {
    NSLog(@"Accepting");
    return YES;
}

- (BOOL)resignFirstResponder {
    NSLog(@"Resigning");
    [self setNeedsDisplay: YES];
    return YES;
}

- (BOOL)becomeFirstResponder {
    NSLog(@"Becoming");
    [self setNeedsDisplay: YES];
    return YES;
}
```

Once the view is first responder, it will handle key events. For most keyDowns, the view will simply change string to be whatever the user typed. If, however, the user presses tab or shift-tab, the view will ask the window to change the first responder.

```
- (void)keyDown: (NSEvent *) event {
    NSString *input = [event characters];
    // Is it a tab?
    if ([input isEqual: @"\t"]){
        [[self window] selectNextKeyView: nil];
        return;
    }
    // Is it a shift-tab?
    if ([input isEqual: @"\031"]){
```

```
        [[self window] selectPreviousKeyView: nil];
        return;
    }
    // Set string to be what the user typed
    [self setString:input];
}
```

Of course, you want to be a tidy programmer, so you will be sure to release your instance variables when the view is deallocated:

```
// release instance variables
- (void)dealloc
{
    [string release];
    [bgColor release];
    [super dealloc];
}
@end
```

Build your program and run it. You should see that your view becomes the first responder and takes key events. Also, note that you can tab and shift-tab between the views (Figure 14.15).

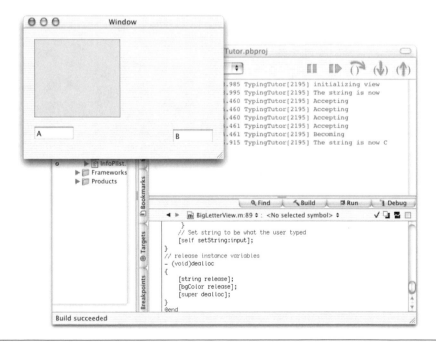

Figure 14.15   Completed Application

Chapter 15

WORKING WITH FONTS AND NSSTRING

The next step is to get the string to appear in our view. At the end of the chapter, your application will look like Figure 15.1. The character being displayed will change as you type.

NSFont

Overall, the class **NSFont** has basically only two types of methods:

- Class methods for getting the font you want
- Methods for getting metrics on the font like letter height

Commonly Used Methods in NSFont

+ (NSFont *)**fontWithName:**(NSString *)fontName **size:**(float)fontSize

Returns a font object. fontName is a family-face name, such as "Helvetica-BoldOblique" or "Times-Roman." If you use a fontSize of 0.0, this method uses the default User Font size.

+ (NSFont *)**userFixedPitchFontOfSize:**(float)fontSize
+ (NSFont *)**userFontOfSize:**(float)fontSize
+ (NSFont *)**messageFontOfSize:**(float)fontSize
+ (NSFont *)**toolTipsFontOfSize:**(float)fontSize
+ (NSFont *)**titleBarFontOfSize:**(float)fontSize

These return the user's default font for the corresponding string types. Once again, a size of 0.0 will get a font of default size.

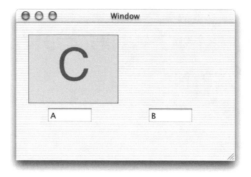

Figure 15.1   Completed Application

- (float)**descender**

Returns the *y*-coordinate of the bottom of the longest descender.

- (float)**ascender**

Returns the *y*-coordinate of the top of the tallest ascender.

NSAttributedString

Sometimes it is necessary for a string that you want to display to have certain attributes for a range of characters. For example, let's say you want to display the string "Big Nerd Ranch," and you want the letters 0 through 2 to be underlined, letters 0 through 7 should be green, and letters 9 through 13 should be subscript.

When dealing with a range of numbers, Cocoa uses the struct NSRange. NSRange has two members: location and length are both integers. The location is the index of the first item, and the length is the number of items in the range. You can use the function **NSMakeRange()** to create an NSRange.

To create strings with attributes that are in effect over a range of characters, Cocoa has **NSAttributedString** and **NSMutableAttributedString**. Here is how you could create the **NSAttributedString** just described:

```
NSMutableAttributedString *s;
s = [[NSMutableAttributedString alloc]
        initWithString:@"Big Nerd Ranch"];
```

```
[s addAttribute:NSFontAttributeName
        value:[NSFont userFontOfSize:22]
        range:NSMakeRange(0, 14)];

[s addAttribute:NSUnderlineStyleAttributeName
        value:[NSNumber numberWithInt:1]
        range:NSMakeRange(0,3)];

[s addAttribute:NSForegroundColorAttributeName
        value:[NSColor greenColor]
        range:NSMakeRange(0, 8)];

[s addAttribute:NSSuperscriptAttributeName
        value:[NSNumber numberWithInt:-1]
        range:NSMakeRange(9,5)];
```

Once you have an attributed string, you can do lots of stuff with it.

```
[s drawInRect:[self bounds]];

// Put it in a text field
[textField setAttributedStringValue:s];

// Put it on a button
[button setAttributedTitle:s];
```

Figure 15.2 shows what the result would be.

Here are the names of the global variables for the most commonly used attributes and what they mean.

NSFontAttributeName   A font object. By default, Helvetica 12-point.

NSForegroundColorAttributeName   A color. By default, black.

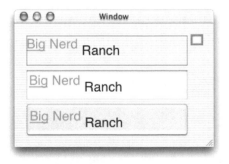

Figure 15.2   Using the Attributed String

NSBackgroundColorAttributeName   A color. By default, no background drawn.

NSUnderlineStyleAttributeName   A number. By default, 0 (which means no underline).

NSSuperscriptAttributeName   A number. By default, 0 (which means no super or subscripting).

A list of all the attribute names can be found in <AppKit/NSAttributedString.h>

Drawing Strings and Attributed Strings

Both **NSString** and **NSAttributedString** have methods that cause them to be drawn onto a view. **NSAttributedString** has the following methods.

- (void)**drawAtPoint:**(NSPoint)aPoint

Draws the receiver. aPoint is the lower left corner of the string.

- (void)**drawInRect:**(NSRect)rect

Draws the receiver. All drawing occurs inside rect. If rect is too small for the string to fit, the drawing is clipped to fit inside rect.

- (NSSize)**size**

Returns the size that the receiver would be if drawn.

NSString has analogous methods. With **NSString**, you need to supply a dictionary of attributes to be applied for the entire string.

- (void)**drawAtPoint:**(NSPoint)aPoint
    withAttributes:(NSDictionary *)attribs

Draws the receiver with the attributes in attribs.

- (void)**drawInRect:**(NSRect)aRect
    withAttributes:(NSDictionary *)attribs

Draws the receiver with the attributes in attribs.

- (NSSize)**sizeWithAttributes:**(NSDictionary *)attribs

Returns the size that the receiver would be if drawn with atttibutes in attribs.

Making Letters Appear

Open `BigLetterView.h`. Add an instance variable to hold onto the attributes dictionary. Declare the methods that you are about to implement:

```
#import <Cocoa/Cocoa.h>

@interface BigLetterView : NSView
{
    NSColor *bgColor;
    NSString *string;
    NSMutableDictionary *attributes;
}
- (void)prepareAttributes;
- (void)drawStringCenteredIn:(NSRect)bounds;
- (void)setBgColor:(NSColor *)c;
- (void)setString:(NSString *)c;
- (NSString *)string;

@end
```

Open `BigLetterView.m`. Create a method that creates the `attributes` dictionary with a font and a foreground color.

```
- (void)prepareAttributes
{
 attributes = [[NSMutableDictionary alloc] init];

 [attributes setObject:
        [NSFont fontWithName: @"Helvetica"
                        size: 75]
              forKey: NSFontAttributeName];

 [attributes setObject: [NSColor redColor]
              forKey: NSForegroundColorAttributeName];
}
```

In the **initWithFrame:** method, call the new method.

```
- initWithFrame:(NSRect)rect
{
    if (self = [super initWithFrame:rect]) {
      NSLog(@"initializing view");
      [self prepareAttributes];
      [self setBgColor:[NSColor yellowColor]];
      [self setString:@" "];
    }
    return self;
}
```

In the **setString:** method, tell the view that it needs to redisplay itself.

```
- (void)setString:(NSString *)c
{
    [c retain];
    [string release];
    string = c;
    NSLog(@"The string: %@", string);
    [self setNeedsDisplay: YES];
}
```

Create a method that will display the string in the middle of a rectangle.

```
- (void)drawStringCenteredIn:(NSRect)r
{
    NSPoint stringOrigin;
    NSSize stringSize;

    stringSize = [string sizeWithAttributes:attributes];
    stringOrigin.x = r.origin.x + (r.size.width - stringSize.width)/2;
    stringOrigin.y = r.origin.y + (r.size.height - stringSize.height)/2;
    [string drawAtPoint:stringOrigin withAttributes:attributes];
}
```

Call that method from inside your **drawRect:** method.

```
- (void)drawRect:(NSRect)rect
{
    NSRect bounds = [self bounds];
    [bgColor set];
    [NSBezierPath fillRect:bounds];

    [self drawStringCenteredIn: bounds];
    if ([[self window] firstResponder] == self) {
        [[NSColor blackColor] set];
        [NSBezierPath strokeRect:bounds];
    }
}
```

Make sure you release the attributes dictionary in the **dealloc** method.

```
- (void)dealloc
{
    [string release];
    [attributes release];
    [bgColor release];
    [super dealloc];
}
```

Build and run the application. Note that keyboard events go to your view unless they trigger a menu item. Try Command-w. It should close the window.

Getting Your View to Generate PDF Data

All the drawing commands can be converted into PDF by the AppKit framework. The PDF data can be sent to a printer or to a file. Note that the PDF will always look as good as possible on any device, because it is device independent.

You have created a view that knows how to generate PDF to describe how it is supposed to look. Getting the PDF into a file is really pretty easy. **NSView** has the following method:

```
- (NSData *)dataWithPDFInsideRect:(NSRect)aRect
```

This method creates a data object and then calls **drawRect:**. The drawing commands that would usually go to the screen go into the data object. Once you have this data object, you simply save it to a file.

Open `BigLetterView.m` and add a method that will create a save panel as a sheet.

```
- (IBAction)savePDF:(id)sender
{
    NSSavePanel *panel = [NSSavePanel savePanel];
    [panel setRequiredFileType:@"pdf"];
    [panel beginSheetForDirectory: nil
                             file: nil
                    modalForWindow: [self window]
                     modalDelegate: self
                    didEndSelector:
                      @selector(didEnd:returnCode:contextInfo:)
                       contextInfo: nil];
}
```

Note that when the person has chosen the filename, the method **didEnd:returnCode:contextInfo:** will be called. Implement this method in `BigLetterView.m`.

```
- (void)didEnd:(NSSavePanel *)sheet
    returnCode:(int)code
    contextInfo:(void *)contextInfo
{
    NSRect r;
```

```
   NSData *data;

   if (code == NSOKButton) {
     r = [self bounds];
     data = [self dataWithPDFInsideRect: r];
     [data writeToFile: [sheet filename] atomically: YES];
   }
 }
}
```

Also, declare these methods in the BigLetterView.h file.

```
- (IBAction)savePDF:(id)sender;
- (void)didEnd:(NSSavePanel *)sheet
     returnCode:(int)code
  contextInfo:(void *)contextInfo;
```

Open the nib file. Drag in BigLetterView.h so that **savePDF:** will appear as one of the actions. Select the Save As... menu item to the File menu. Relabel it Save PDF.... (You may delete all of the other menu items from the menu, if you wish.) Make the Save PDF... menu item trigger the **BigLetterView**'s **savePDF:** method (Figure 15.3).

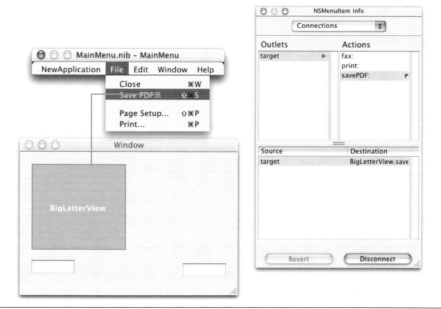

Figure 15.3   Connect Menu Item

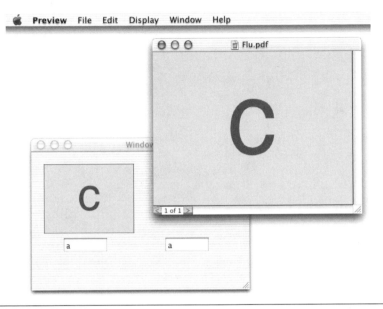

Figure 15.4 Completed Application

Save and build. You should be able to generate a PDF file and view it in Preview (Figure 15.4).

For the More Curious: NSFontManager

Sometimes you will have a font that is good and that would be perfect if it were bold or italicized or condensed. **NSFontManager** can be used to make this sort of conversion. You can also use a font manager to change the size of the font.

For example, imagine you have a font that you wanted another font to like, but bold. Here is the code:

```
fontManager = [NSFontManager sharedFontManager];
boldFont = [fontManager convertFont:aFont toHaveTrait:NSBoldFontMask];
```

Challenge 1

Make the letter appear underlined in your view.

Challenge 2

Add boolean variables: bold and italic to your **BigLetterView**. Add checkboxes that toggle these variables. If bold is YES, make the letter appear in boldface; if italic is YES, make the letter appear in italics.

Chapter 16

PASTEBOARDS AND NIL-TARGETED ACTIONS

There is a process running on your Mac called the pasteboard server (/System/Library/CoreServices/pbs). Applications use the **NSPasteboard** class to write data into that process and read data from that process. The pasteboard server makes things like copy, cut, and paste between applications possible.

An application can copy the same data onto the pasteboard in several formats. For example, an image could be copied onto the pasteboard as a PDF document and as a bitmapped image. Then the application that reads the data can choose the format that it likes most.

When putting data on the pasteboard, your application typically declares the types it will put on the pasteboard and then immediately copies those data to the pasteboard. The receiving application will first ask the pasteboard what types are available and then read the data in their preferred format.

You can also copy data to the pasteboard in a lazy manner. You simply declare all the types of data you could put on the pasteboard and then supply the data when they are needed. We will talk about lazy copying at the end of the chapter.

There are multiple pasteboards. There is a pasteboard for copy and paste and another for drag-and-drop. There is a pasteboard that stores the last string that the user searched for. There is a pasteboard for copying rulers and another for copying fonts.

In this section, you will add cut, copy, and paste to your **BigLetterView**. First, you will implement the methods that will read from and write to the pasteboard. Then we will discuss how those methods get called.

NSPasteboard

As mentioned before, the **NSPasteboard** class acts as an interface with the pasteboard server. The following are some of the commonly used methods of **NSPasteboard**.

+ (NSPasteboard *)**generalPasteboard**

Returns the general **NSPasteboard**. You will use this pasteboard to copy, cut, and paste.

+ (NSPasteboard *)**pasteboardWithName:**(NSString *)name

Returns the pasteboard by name. Here are the global variables that contain the names of the standard pasteboards:

NSGeneralPboard

NSFontPboard

NSRulerPboard

NSFindPboard

NSDragPboard

- (int)**declareTypes:**(NSArray *)types **owner:**(id)theOwner

Declares the types of data that theOwner will put on the pasteboard. Here are the global variables for the standard types:

NSColorPboardType

NSFileContentsPboardType

NSFilenamesPboardType

NSFontPboardType

NSPDFPboardType

NSPICTPboardType

NSPostScriptPboardType

NSRulerPboardType

NSRTFPboardType

NSRTFDPboardType

NSStringPboardType

NSTabularTextPboardType

NSTIFFPboardType

NSURLPboardType

You can also create your own pasteboard types.

```
- (BOOL)setData:(NSData *)aData forType:(NSString *)dataType
- (BOOL)setString:(NSString *)aString forType:(NSString *)dataType
```

These methods write data to the pasteboard.

```
- (NSArray *)types
```

Returns an array containing the types of data that are available to be read from the pasteboard.

```
- (NSString *)availableTypeFromArray:(NSArray *)types
```

types should be a list of all the types that you would be able to read. This method returns the first type found in types that is available for reading from the pasteboard.

```
- (NSData *)dataForType:(NSString *)dataType
- (NSString *)stringForType:(NSString *)dataType
```

These methods read data from the pasteboard.

Add Cut, Copy, and Paste to BigLetterView

You are going to create methods named **cut:**, **copy:**, and **paste:** in the **BigLetterView** class. To make these methods easier to write, you are first going to create methods for putting data onto and reading data off of a pasteboard. Add these methods to BigLetterView.m.

```
- (void)writeStringToPasteboard:(NSPasteboard *)pb {
    // Declare types
    [pb declareTypes:
        [NSArray arrayWithObject:NSStringPboardType]
            owner:self];
    // Copy data to the pasteboard
    [pb setString:string forType:NSStringPboardType];
}
```

```
- (BOOL)readStringFromPasteboard:(NSPasteboard *)pb {
    NSString *value;
    NSString *type;

    // Is there a string on the pasteboard?
    type = [pb availableTypeFromArray:
              [NSArray arrayWithObject:NSStringPboardType]];
    if (type) {
        // Read the string from the pasteboard
        value = [pb stringForType:NSStringPboardType];
        // Our view can only handle one letter
        if ([value length] == 1) {
            [self setString:value];
            return YES;
        }
    }
    return NO;
}
```

Add **cut:**, **copy:**, and **paste:** to BigLetterView.m:

```
- (IBAction)cut:(id)sender
{
    [self copy:sender];
    [self setString:@" "];
}

- (IBAction)copy:(id)sender
{
    NSPasteboard *pb = [NSPasteboard generalPasteboard];
    [self writeStringToPasteboard:pb];
}

- (IBAction)paste:(id)sender
{
    NSPasteboard *pb = [NSPasteboard generalPasteboard];
    if(![self readStringFromPasteboard:pb]) {
        NSBeep();
    }
}
```

Declare these methods in BigLetterView.h :

```
#import <Cocoa/Cocoa.h>

@interface BigLetterView : NSView
{
    NSColor *bgColor;
    NSString *string;
    NSMutableDictionary *attributes;
}
```

```
- (void)prepareAttributes;
- (IBAction)savePDF:(id)sender;
- (void)didEnd:(NSSavePanel *)sheet
    returnCode:(int)code
  contextInfo:(void *)contextInfo;
- (void)drawStringCenteredIn:(NSRect)bounds;
- (void)setBgColor:(NSColor *)c;
- (NSColor *)bgColor;
- (void)setString:(NSString *)c;
- (NSString *)string;
- (IBAction)cut:(id)sender;
- (IBAction)copy:(id)sender;
- (IBAction)paste:(id)sender;
- (void)writeStringToPasteboard:(NSPasteboard *)pb;
- (BOOL)readStringFromPasteboard:(NSPasteboard *)pb;

@end
```

Nil-Targeted Actions

The question, then, is how the right view gets sent the **cut:**, **copy:** or **paste:** message. After all, there are many, many views. If you select a text field, it is the one that should get the message. When you select another view and choose the Copy or Paste menu item, the message should go to the newly selected view.

To solve this problem, the clever engineers at NeXT came up with *nil-targeted actions*. If you set the target of a control to nil, the application will try to send the action message to several objects until one of them responds. The application first tries to send the message to the first responder of the key window. This is exactly the behavior that you want for Cut and Paste. You can have several windows and each can have several views. The active view on the active window gets sent the cut and paste messages.

The beauty of the nil-targeted actions doesn't end there. **NSView**, **NSApplication**, and **NSWindow** all inherit from **NSResponder**. **NSResponder** has an instance variable called nextResponder. If an object doesn't respond to a nil-targeted action, its nextResponder gets a chance. The nextResponder for a view is usually its super-view. The nextResponder of the content view of the window is the window. So the responders are linked together in what we call the *responder chain*.

Thus, for example, there is a menu item that closes the key window. That menu item has a target of nil. The action is **performClose:**. None of the standard objects respond to **performClose:** except **NSWindow**. So the selected text field, for example, refuses to respond to **performClose:**. Then the superview of the text field refuses, and on up the view hierarchy. Then the window (the key window) accepts the **performClose:** method. So, to the user, the "active" window is closed.

As was mentioned in Chapter 7, a panel can become the key window but not the main window. If the key window and main window are different, both windows get a chance to respond to the nil-targeted action.

Your question at this point should be: What is the order of all the objects that will be tested before a nil-targeted action is discarded?

- The firstResponder of the keyWindow and its responder chain. The responder chain would typically include the superviews and, finally, the key window.
- Then the delegate of the key window.
- Then, if it is a document-based application, the **NSWindowController** and then **NSDocument** object for the key window.
- If the main window is different from the key window, it then goes through the same ritual with the main window:
  The firstResponder of the main window and its responder chain (including the main window itself).
  Then the main window's delegate.
  Then the **NSWindowController** and then **NSDocument** object for the main window.
- Then the instance of **NSApplication**.
- Then the delegate of the **NSApplication**.
- Finally, the **NSDocumentController** is given a chance.

This series of objects is known as *the responder chain*. Figure 16.1 presents an example. The numbers indicate the order in which the objects would be asked if they respond to the nil-targeted action.

Note that in document-based applications (like RaiseMan), the **NSDocument** object gets a chance to respond to the nil-targeted action. This is how it gets sent the messages from the following menu items: Save, Save As…, Revert To Saved, Print…, and Page Layout….

Looking at the Nib File

Open the nib file and note that the cut, copy, and paste items are connected to the icon that is labeled First Responder. The First Responder icon represents nil. It gives you something to drag to when you want an object to have a nil target (Figure 16.2).

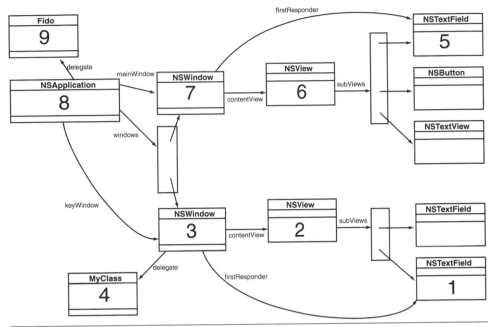

Figure 16.1   An Example of the Order in Which Responders Get a Chance to Respond

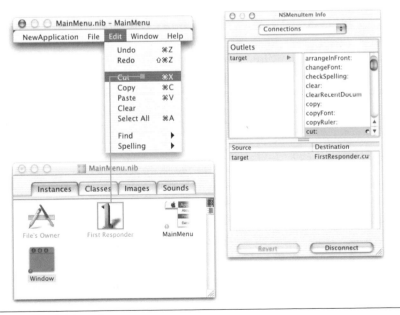

Figure 16.2   Check Menu Item

The actions that appear in the inspector when you drag to the First Responder are in the class browser in Interface Builder. If you want an action to appear there, simply add it in the class browser.

Build and run your application. Note that cut, copy, and paste now work with your view. Note that the keyboard equivalents also work. You can only copy strings that have one character into the **BigLetterView**.

For the More Curious: Which Object Really Sends the Action Message?

The target on the cut, copy, and paste menu items is nil. We know that sending a message to nil is not going to do anything. Actually, all target-action messages are handled by **NSApplication**. It has a method:

- (BOOL)**sendAction:**(SEL)anAction **to:**(id)aTarget **from:**(id)sender

When the target is nil, **NSApplication** knows to try to send messages to the objects in the responder chain.

For the More Curious: Lazy Copying

An application can implement copying to a pasteboard in a lazy manner. For example, imagine a graphics application that copies large images to the pasteboard in several formats: PICT, TIFF, PDF, etc. You can imagine that copying all these formats onto the pasteboard would be hard on the application and the pasteboard server. Such an application might do a lazy copy. That is, it will declare all the types that it could put on the pasteboard but will put off actually copying those data until another application asks for them.

Essentially, it puts an "IOU" (instead of the data) on the pasteboard and gives an object that will provide the data when they are needed. When another application actually asks for the data, the pasteboard server calls back for the data.

The declaration works the same as earlier:

- (int)**declareTypes:**(NSArray *)types **owner:**(id)theOwner

But `theOwner` must implement the following method:

- (void)**pasteboard:**(NSPasteboard *)sender **provideDataForType:**(NSString *)type

When another application needs the data, this method will be called. At that point, the application must copy the data it promised onto the supplied pasteboard.

As you can imagine, it would be a problem if the pasteboard server asked for the data after the application had terminated. When the application is terminating, if it has an "IOU" currently on the pasteboard, it will be asked to supply all the data that was promised before terminating. Thus, it is not uncommon that an "IOU" owner will get sent **pasteboard:provideDataForType:** several times while the application is in the process of terminating.

The trickiest part of a lazy copy is that when the user copies data to the pasteboard and later pastes it into another application, he doesn't want the most recent state of the data. He wants it *the way it was when he copied it*. Most developers when implementing a lazy copy will take some sort of a snapshot of the information when declaring the types. When providing the data, the developer will copy the snapshot, instead of the current state, onto the pasteboard.

Challenge

You are putting the string on the pasteboard. Create the PDF for the view and put that on the pasteboard, too. Now you will be able to copy the image of the letter into graphics programs.

Chapter 17
CATEGORIES

Although the engineers at Apple are very wise, one day you will think, "Golly, if only they had put that method on that class, my life would be so much easier." When this happens, you will want to create a *category*. A category is simply a collection of methods that you would like added to an existing class. The category concept is very useful, and I find it surprising that so few of the other object-oriented languages include this powerful idea.

Creating a category is easier than talking about them. In the previous chapter, you added pasting to your **BigLetterView**. Notice, however, that if the string on the pasteboard has more then one letter, the paste will fail. This is because **BigLetterView** is capable of displaying only one letter at a time. Let's extend the example to take just the first letter of the string instead of failing.

Add a Method to NSString

It would be nice if every **NSString** object had a method that returned its first letter. It does not, so you will use a category to add it.

Open your project and create a new file of type Objective-C class. You are not really creating a class, but this is a good starting place for the creation of a category (Figure 17.1).

Name the category **FirstLetter** (Figure 17.2).

Change FirstLetter.h to declare your category. Here is what it looks like:

```
#import <Foundation/Foundation.h>

@interface NSString (FirstLetter)
```

Figure 17.1   Choose File Type

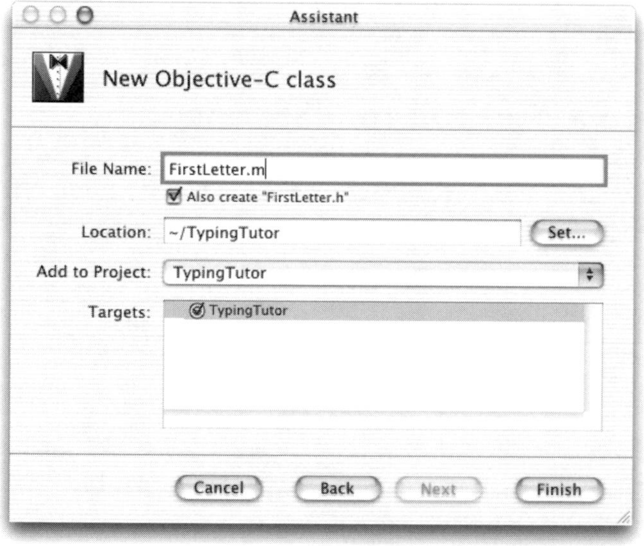

Figure 17.2   Name File

```
- (NSString *)firstLetter;

@end
```

Notice that this looks like you are declaring the class **NSString**, but you are not giving it any instance variables or a superclass. Instead, you are naming the category **FirstLetter** and declaring a method. A category cannot add instance variables to the class, only methods.

Now implement the method **firstLetter** in the file FirstLetter.m. Make the file look like this:

```
#import "FirstLetter.h"

@implementation NSString (FirstLetter)

- (NSString *)firstLetter
{
    NSRange r;
    if ([self length] < 2) {
        return self;
    }
    r.location = 0;
    r.length = 1;
    return [self substringWithRange:r];
}
@end
```

Now you can use this method as if it were part of **NSString**. In BigLetterView.m, change **readStringFromPasteboard:** to look like this:

```
- (BOOL)readStringFromPasteboard:(NSPasteboard *)pb
{
    NSString *value;
    NSString *type = [pb availableTypeFromArray:
                        [NSArray arrayWithObject:NSStringPboardType]];
    if (type) {
        value = [pb stringForType:NSStringPboardType];
        [self setString:[value firstLetter]];
        return YES;
    }
    return NO;
}
```

At the beginning of the BigLetterView.m, import FirstLetter.h.

Build and run your app. You will be able to copy strings with more than one letter into the **BigLetterView**. Only the first letter of the string will actually be copied.

In this example, you added only one method, but note that you can add as many methods to the class as you wish. Also, you used only the methods of the class, but you can also access its instance variables directly.

Warning: If you use a lot of categories, your code may become difficult for others to read and maintain. Some large teams discourage the use of categories for this reason.

Chapter 18
DRAG-AND-DROP

Drag-and-drop is little more than a flashy copy-and-paste. When the drag starts, data are copied onto the dragging pasteboard. When the drop occurs, the data are read off the dragging pasteboard. The only thing that makes it trickier than copy-and-paste is that the user needs feedback: an image that appears as they drag, the view that highlights when they drag into it, and maybe a big gulping sound when the user drops the image.

There are several different things that can happen when data are dragged from one application to another: nothing, a copy of the data can be created, or a link to the existing data can be created. There are constants that represent these operations:

```
NSDragOperationNone,
NSDragOperationCopy,
NSDragOperationLink
```

Both the source and the destination must agree on the operation that will occur when the user drops the image.

When you add drag-and-drop to a view, there are two distinct parts.

- Make it a drag source.
- Make it a drag destination.

Let's take these separately. First, you will make your view a drag source. When that is working, you will make it a drag destination.

Make BigLetterView a Drag Source

When you finish this section, you will be able to drag a letter off the **BigLetterView** and drop it into any text editor. It will look like Figure 18.1.

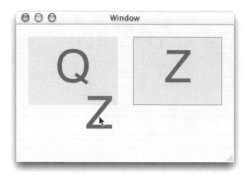

Figure 18.1 Completed Application

To be a drag source, your view must implement **draggingSourceOperationMask ForLocal:**. This method declares what operations the view is willing to participate in as a source. Add this method to your BigLetterView.m .

```
- (unsigned int)draggingSourceOperationMaskForLocal:(BOOL)flag
{
    return NSDragOperationCopy;
}
```

To start a drag operation, you will use a method on **NSView**.

```
- (void)dragImage:(NSImage *)anImage
               at:(NSPoint)imageLoc
           offset:(NSSize)mouseOffset
            event:(NSEvent *)theEvent
       pasteboard:(NSPasteboard *)pboard
           source:(id)sourceObject
        slideBack:(BOOL)slideBack
```

You will supply it with the image to be dragged and the point at which you want the drag to begin. The documentation says to include the mouseDown event, but a mouseDragged event works fine. The offset seems to be completely ignored. The pasteboard is usually the standard drag pasteboard. If the drop does not occur, you can choose whether the icon should slide back to the place from which it came.

You will also need to create an image to drag. You can draw on an image just like you can on a view. To make the drawing appear on the image instead of the screen, you must first lock focus on the image. When the drawing is done, you must unlock the focus.

Here is the whole method to add to `BigLetterView.m`:

```objc
- (void)mouseDragged:(NSEvent *)event
{
    NSRect imageBounds;
    NSPasteboard *pb;
    NSImage *anImage;
    NSSize s;
    NSPoint p;

    // Create the image that will be dragged
    anImage = [[NSImage alloc] init];

    // Get the size of the string
    s = [string sizeWithAttributes:attributes];

    // Create a rect in which you will draw the letter
    // in the image.
    imageBounds.origin = NSMakePoint(0,0);
    imageBounds.size = s;
    [anImage setSize:s];

    // Draw the letter on the image
    [anImage lockFocus];
    [self drawStringCenteredIn:imageBounds];
    [anImage unlockFocus];

    // Get the location of the drag event
    p = [self convertPoint:[event locationInWindow] fromView:nil];

    // Drag from the center of the image
    p.x = p.x - s.width/2;
    p.y = p.y - s.height/2;

    // Get the pasteboard
    pb = [NSPasteboard pasteboardWithName:NSDragPboard];

    // Put the string on the pasteboard
    [self writeStringToPasteboard:pb];

    // Start the drag
    [self dragImage:anImage
        at:p
        offset:NSMakeSize(0, 0)
        event:event
        pasteboard:pb
        source:self
        slideBack:YES];
    [anImage release];
}
```

That's it. Build it and run it. You should be able to drag a letter off the view and into any text editor. (Try dragging it into Project Builder.)

Make BigLetterView a Drag Destination

There are several parts to being a drag destination. First, you need to declare your view a destination for the dragging of certain types. **NSView** has a method for this:

```
- (void)registerForDraggedTypes:(NSArray *)pboardTypes
```

You typically call this method in your **initWithFrame:** method.

Then you need to implement six methods. (Yes, six!) All six methods have the same argument: an **NSDraggingInfo** object. It has the dragging pasteboard. The six methods are invoked as follows.

- As the image is dragged into the destination, the destination is sent a **draggingEntered:** message. Often, the destination view updates its appearance. For example, it might highlight itself.
- While the image remains within the destination, a series of **draggingUpdated:** messages are sent. Implementing **draggingUpdated:** is optional.
- If the image is dragged outside of the destination, **draggingExited:** is sent.
- If the image is released on the destination, either it slides back to its source (and breaks the sequence) or a **prepareForDragOperation:** message is sent to the destination, depending on the value returned by the most recent invocation of **draggingEntered:** (or **draggingUpdated:** if the view implemented it).
- If the **prepareForDragOperation:** message returns YES, a **performDragOperation:** message is sent. This is typically where the application actually reads data off the pasteboard.
- Finally, if **performDragOperation:** returned YES, **concludeDragOperation:** is sent. The appearance may change. This is where you might generate the big gulping sound that implies a successful drop.

registerForDraggedTypes:

Add **registerForDraggedTypes:** to **BigLetterView**'s **initWithFrame:** method in BigLetterView.m.

```
- initWithFrame:(NSRect)rect
{
```

```
        if (self = [super initWithFrame:rect]) {
          NSLog(@"initializing view");
          [self prepareAttributes];
          [self setBgColor:[NSColor yellowColor]];
          [self setString:@" "];
          [self registerForDraggedTypes:
              [NSArray arrayWithObject: NSStringPboardType]];
        }
        return self;
}
```

Add Highlighting

To signal the user that the drop is acceptable, your view will highlight itself. Add a highlighted instance variable to BigLetterView.h.

```
@interface BigLetterView : NSView
{
    NSColor *bgColor;
    NSString *string;
    NSMutableDictionary *attributes;
    BOOL highlighted;
}
...
```

Add highlighting to **drawRect:**.

```
- (void)drawRect:(NSRect)rect
{
    NSRect bounds = [self bounds];

    // Draw white background if highlighted
    if (highlighted) {
        [[NSColor whiteColor] set];
    } else {
        [bgColor set];
    }
    [NSBezierPath fillRect:bounds];

    // Draw the string
    [self drawStringCenteredIn: bounds];

    // Draw black rectangle if first responder
    if ([[self window] firstResponder] == self) {
        [[NSColor blackColor] set];
        [NSBezierPath strokeRect:bounds];
    }
}
```

Implement the Dragging Destination Methods

So far, we have seen two ways to declare a pointer to an object. If the pointer can refer to any type of object, we would declare it like this:

```
id foo;
```

If the pointer should refer to an instance of a particular class, we can declare it like this:

```
MyClass *foo;
```

Here is a third possibility. If we have a pointer that should refer to an object that conforms to a particular protocol, we can declare it like this:

```
id <MyProtocol> foo;
```

NSDraggingInfo is actually a protocol, not a class. All the dragging destination methods expect an object that conforms to the **NSDraggingInfo** protocol.

Add the following methods to BigLetterView.m.

```
- (unsigned int)draggingEntered:(id <NSDraggingInfo>)sender
{
    NSLog(@"draggingEntered:");
    if ([sender draggingSource] != self) {
        NSPasteboard *pb = [sender draggingPasteboard];
        NSString *type = [pb availableTypeFromArray:
                [NSArray arrayWithObject: NSStringPboardType]];
        if (type != nil) {
            highlighted = YES;
            [self setNeedsDisplay:YES];
            return NSDragOperationCopy;
        }
    }
    return NSDragOperationNone;
}

- (void)draggingExited:(id <NSDraggingInfo>)sender
{
    NSLog(@"draggingExited:");
    highlighted = NO;
    [self setNeedsDisplay:YES];
}

- (BOOL)prepareForDragOperation:(id <NSDraggingInfo>)sender
{
    return YES;
}
```

```
- (BOOL)performDragOperation:(id <NSDraggingInfo>)sender
{
    NSPasteboard *pb = [sender draggingPasteboard];
    if(![self readStringFromPasteboard:pb]) {
        NSLog(@"Error: Could not read from dragging pasteboard");
        return NO;
    }
    return YES;
}

- (void)concludeDragOperation:(id <NSDraggingInfo>)sender
{
    NSLog(@"concludeDragOperation:");
    highlighted = NO;
    [self setNeedsDisplay:YES];
}
```

Test It

Open the nib file, and add another **BigLetterView** to the window. Delete the text fields. Make sure to set the nextKeyView for each **BigLetterView** so that you can tab between them (Figure 18.2).

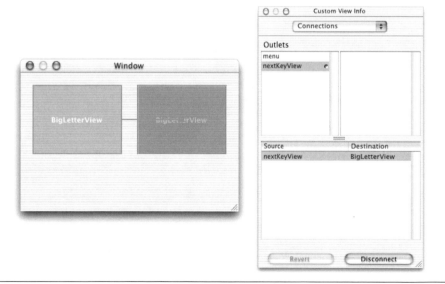

Figure 18.2   Set nextKeyView for Each BigLetterView

Build it and run it. Note that you can drag characters between the views and from other applications.

Challenge

It is easy to add drag-and-drop to a table view. The delegate of the table is responsible for dealing with the pasteboard. Add drag-and-drop to the RaiseMan application by implementing the following methods in MyDocument.m.

```
// Iterate through the rows with an enumerator
// Put the people for the rows in a new array
// Archive the new array into a data object
// Copy the data to the pasteboard, return YES
- (BOOL)tableView:(NSTableView *)tv
        writeRows:(NSArray *)rows
     toPasteboard:(NSPasteboard *)pboard;

// Check the type, if it is good, return NSDragOperationCopy
// If not return NSDragOperationNone
// Ignore the proposed drop operation
- (NSDragOperation)tableView:(NSTableView *)tv
                validateDrop:(id <NSDraggingInfo>)info
                 proposedRow:(int)row
        proposedDropOperation:(NSTableViewDropOperation)op;

// Check the type, if good, read data from pasteboard
// Recreate the array of people
// Add the people to the employees array
// Return YES
// Ignore the drop operation
- (BOOL)tableView:(NSTableView *)tv
        acceptDrop:(id <NSDraggingInfo>)info
               row:(int)row
     dropOperation:(NSTableViewDropOperation)op;
```

Notice that you will be creating your own drag type (instead of using one of the standard types, like NSStringPboardType). Make sure that you also send the message **registerForDraggedTypes:** to the table view.

Chapter 19
NSTimer

An instance of **NSButton** has a target and a selector (the action). When the button is clicked, the action message is sent to the target. Timers work in a similar way. A timer is an object that has a target, a selector, and a delay, in seconds (Figure 19.1). After the delay, the selector message is sent to the target. The timer sends itself as an argument to the message. The timer can also be set to send the message repeatedly.

To play with timers a bit, you are going to create a typing tutor application. The application will have two **BigLetterView** objects. One will display what the user should type, and the other will display what the user has typed (Figure 19.2). There will be an **NSProgressIndicator** that will display how much time is left. When 2 seconds has passed, the application will beep to indicate that the user took too long. Then the user is given 2 more seconds.

You will create an **AppController** class. When the user clicks the Go button, an instance of **NSTimer** will be created. The timer will send a message every 0.2 seconds. The method triggered will check to see if the two views match. If so, the user is given a new letter to type. Otherwise, the progress indicator is incremented. If the user pauses the application, the timer is invalidated.

Figure 19.3 shows the object diagram.

Lay Out the Interface

Go back to your TypingTutor project. Open the MainMenu.nib.

Create a new subclass of **NSObject** called **AppController**. Add three outlets to **AppController**: inLetterView, outLetterView, and progressView. Add one action: **stopGo:** (Figure 19.4).

Create the files for **AppController**. Create an instance of **AppController**.

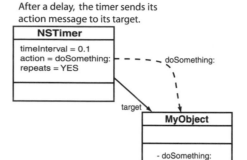

Figure 19.1   NSTimer

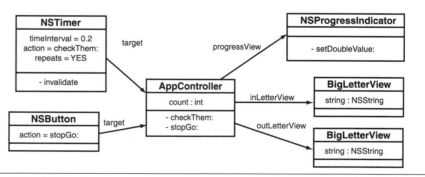

Figure 19.2   Completed Application

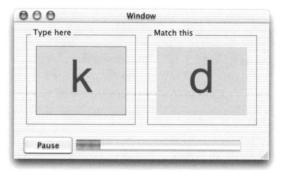

Figure 19.3   Object Diagram

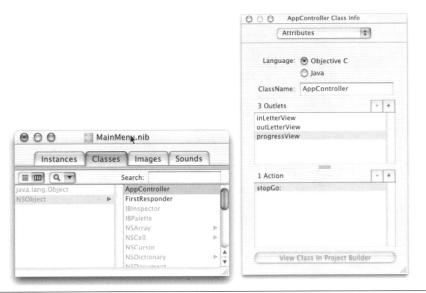

Figure 19.4   AppController's Actions and Outlets

Select the **BigLetterView** on the left. From the Layout menu, choose the Group in box menu item. Relabel the box "Type here." Group the other **BigLetterView** in a box, and relabel that box "Match this".

Drop an **NSProgressIndicator** on the window. Use the inspector to make it not indeterminate. Set its range to be 0 to 100 (Figure 19.5).

Put a button on the window. Using the inspector, set its title to Go and its alternate title to Pause. Make the button type Rounded Bevel Button and set its behavior to Toggle (Figure 19.6).

Make Connections

Control-drag from the button to the **AppController** object. Set the action to be **stopGo:** (Figure 19.7).

Control-drag from the **AppController** to the **NSProgressIndicator** and set the progressView outlet.

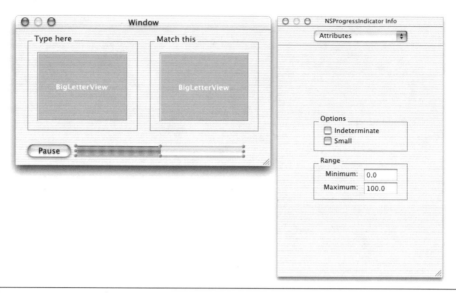

Figure 19.5   Inspect the Progress Indicator

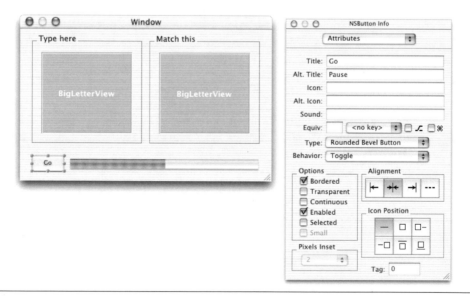

Figure 19.6   Inspect the Button

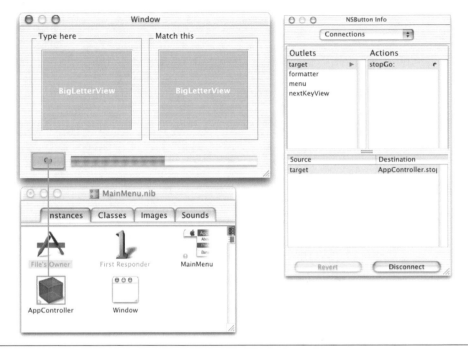

Figure 19.7   Connect the Button to the AppController

Control-drag from the **AppController** to the **BigLetterView** on the left and set the inLetterView outlet (Figure 19.8).

Control-drag from the **AppController** to the **BigLetterView** on the right and set the outLetterView outlet (Figure 19.9).

Adding Code to AppController

Add instance variables and methods to AppController.h.

```
#import <Cocoa/Cocoa.h>
@class BigLetterView;

@interface AppController : NSObject
{
    IBOutlet BigLetterView *inLetterView;
    IBOutlet BigLetterView *outLetterView;
    IBOutlet NSProgressIndicator *progressView;
```

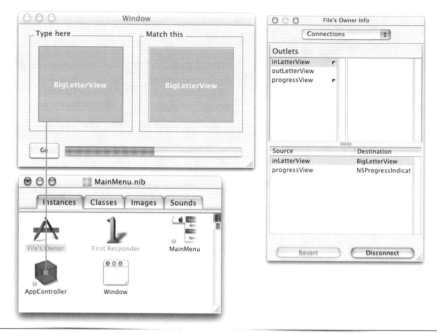

Figure 19.8   Connect the inLetterView Outlet

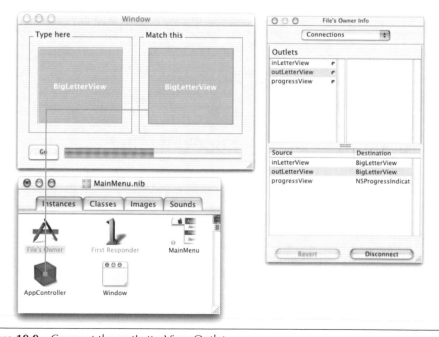

Figure 19.9   Connect the outLetterView Outlet

```
        int count;          // How many times has the timer gone off?
        NSTimer *timer;
        NSArray *letters;   // The array of letters that the user will type
        int lastIndex;      // The index in the array of the
                            // letter the user is trying to type
}
- (void)showAnotherLetter;
- (IBAction)stopGo:(id)sender;
@end
```

Implement the following methods in AppController.m.

```
#import "AppController.h"
#import "BigLetterView.h"

// Number of times the timer will fire
#define TICKS 10

@implementation AppController

- init
{
    if (self = [super init]) {

      // Create an array of letters
      letters = [[NSArray alloc] initWithObjects:@"a", @"s", @"d",@"f",
                                    @"j", @"k", @"l", @";",nil];
      lastIndex = 0;
    }
    // Seed the random number generator
    srandom(time(NULL));
    return self;
}

- (void)awakeFromNib
{
    [self showAnotherLetter];
}

- (void)showAnotherLetter
{
    int x;
    //Choose random numbers until you get a different number than last time
    x = lastIndex;
    while (x == lastIndex){
        x = random() % [letters count];
    }
    lastIndex = x;
    [outLetterView setString:[letters objectAtIndex:x]];

    [progressView setDoubleValue:0.0];
    count = 0;
```

```
}
- (IBAction)stopGo:(id)sender
{
    if ([sender state] == 1) {
        NSLog(@"Starting");

        // Create a timer
        timer = [[NSTimer scheduledTimerWithTimeInterval:0.2
                                        target:self
                                      selector:@selector(checkThem:)
                                      userInfo:nil
                                       repeats:YES] retain];
    } else {
        NSLog(@"Stopping");

        // Invalidate and release the timer
        [timer invalidate];
        [timer release];
    }
}

- (void)checkThem:(NSTimer *)aTimer
{
    if ([[inLetterView string] isEqual:[outLetterView string]]) {
        [self showAnotherLetter];
    }
    count++;
    if (count > TICKS){
        NSBeep();
        count = 0;
    }
    [progressView setDoubleValue:(100.0 * count) / TICKS];
}
@end
```

Build and run your application.

Note, once again, that we have separated our classes into views (**BigLetterView**) and controllers (**AppController**). If I were creating a full-featured application, I would probably also create model classes like **Lesson** and **Student**.

Challenge

Change your ImageFun application so that autoscrolling is timer driven. Delete your **mouseDragged:** method from **StretchView**. In **mouseDown:**, create a repeating timer that invokes a method in the view every tenth of a second. In the invoked method, autoscroll using the current event. To get the current event, use **NSApplication**'s **currentEvent** method:

```
NSEvent *e = [NSApp currentEvent];
```

(Remember that NSApp is a global variable that points to the instance of **NSApplication**.) Invalidate and release the timer in **mouseUp:**. Note that the auto-scrolling becomes much smoother and more predictable.

Chapter 20
SHEETS

A sheet is simply an instance of **NSWindow** that is attached to another window. The sheet comes down over the window, and the window stops getting events until the sheet is dismissed. Typically, you will compose a sheet as an off-screen window in your nib file.

NSApplication has the methods that make sheets possible.

```
// Start a sheet
- (void)beginSheet:(NSWindow *)sheet
    modalForWindow:(NSWindow *)docWindow
     modalDelegate:(id)modalDelegate
     didEndSelector:(SEL)didEndSelector
        contextInfo:(void *)contextInfo;

// End the sheet
- (void)endSheet:(NSWindow *)sheet returnCode:(int)returnCode;
```

Notice that besides the sheet window and the window it is attached to, you supply a modal delegate, a selector, and a pointer when you start the sheet. The modalDelegate will get sent the didEndSelector, and the sheet, its return code, and the contextInfo will get sent along as arguments. Thus, the method triggered by the didEndSelector should have have a signature like this:

```
- (void)rex:(NSWindow *)sheet
       fido:(int)returnCode
      rover:(void *)contextInfo;
```

The dog names are to indicate that you could name the method anything you wish. Most programmers name the method something more meaningful, like sheetDidEnd: returnCode:contextInfo:.

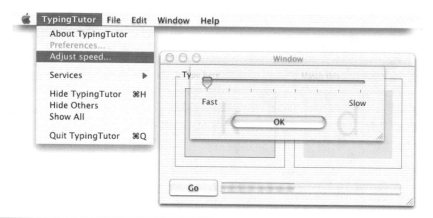

Figure 20.1   Completed Application

Adding a Sheet

You are going to add a sheet that will allow the user to adjust the speed of the TypingTutor application. You will bring up the sheet when the user selects the Adjust speed... menu item. You will end the sheet when the user clicks the OK button. It will look like Figure 20.1.

Your **AppController** will control the slider and the window, so you will need to add outlets for them. Also, your **AppController** will be sent a message when the user selects the Adjust speed... menu item or clicks the OK button, so you will need to add two action methods to the **AppController**.

Figure 20.2 presents the object diagram.

Add Outlets and Actions

Edit AppController.h.

```
#import <Cocoa/Cocoa.h>
@class BigLetterView;

@interface AppController : NSObject
{
    int count;        // How many times has the timer fired?
    int ticks;        // How high can "count" go?
    IBOutlet NSWindow *speedWindow;
    IBOutlet NSSlider *speedSlider;
```

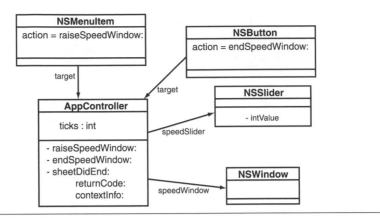

Figure 20.2 Object Diagram

```
    IBOutlet BigLetterView *inLetterView;
    IBOutlet BigLetterView *outLetterView;
    IBOutlet NSProgressIndicator *progressView;
    NSTimer *timer;
    NSArray *letters;  // The array of letters that the user will type
    int lastIndex;     // The index in the array of the
                       //    letter the user is trying to type
}
- (void)showAnotherLetter;
- (IBAction)stopGo:(id)sender;
- (IBAction)raiseSpeedWindow:(id)sender;
- (IBAction)endSpeedWindow:(id)sender;
- (void)sheetDidEnd:(NSWindow *)sheet
        returnCode:(int)returnCode
        contextInfo:(void *)contextInfo;
@end
```

Save the file.

Open `MainMenu.nib` and drag `AppController.h` into it.

Lay Out the Interface

Add a menu item to the main menu for your application (Figure 20.3).

Change the title of the menu item to Adjust Speed.... Control-drag from the menu item to the **AppController**. Set the action to be **raiseSpeedWindow:** (Figure 20.4).

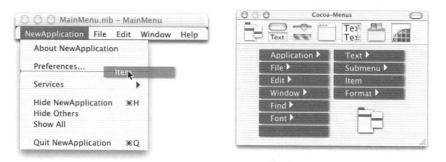

Figure 20.3   Add a Menu Item

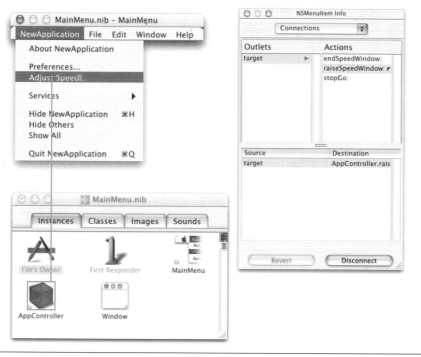

Figure 20.4   Connect the Menu Item

Create a new window by dragging one off the palette. Disable resizing for the window. Put a slider and a button on the new window. To label the left end of the slider "Fast" and the right "Slow", drop two uneditable textfields onto the window. Add a button and change its title to "OK". Inspect the slider and set its range of 5.0 to 40.0 (Figure 20.5).

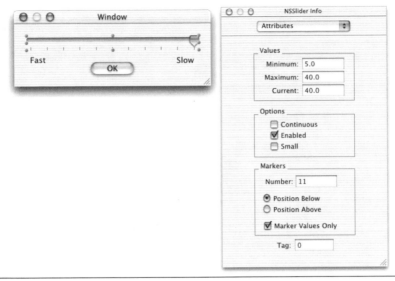

Figure 20.5 Inspect Slider

When the user clicks the "OK" button, you want the button to send a message to the **AppController** that will end the sheet. So control-drag from the button to the **AppController** to set the target. Choose **endSpeedWindow:** as the action (Figure 20-6).

In order to raise the window as a sheet, your **AppController** must have a pointer to it. So Control-drag from the **AppController** to the icon that represents the new window. Set this to be the speedWindow outlet (Figure 20.7).

For the **AppController** to read the slider, it must have a pointer to it. Control-drag from the **AppController** to the slider and set the speedSlider outlet (Figure 20.8).

Save and close the nib file.

Adding Code

In AppController.m, you defined a constant called TICKS. In the last section, the user got 10 ticks of the timer before the beep. In this section, you are going to make the ticks a variable. If the user is playing "Fast," they will get fewer ticks than if they are playing "Slow." You are going to read the ticks from the speedSlider. The first

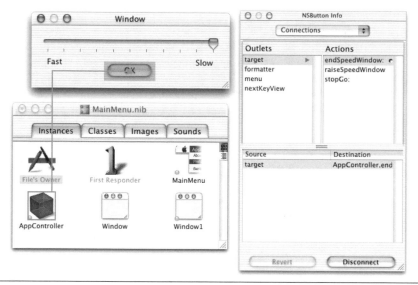

Figure 20.6   Set the Target of the Button

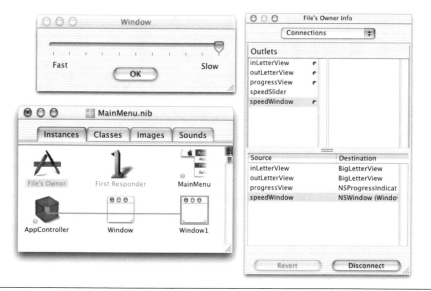

Figure 20.7   Connect speedWindow Outlet

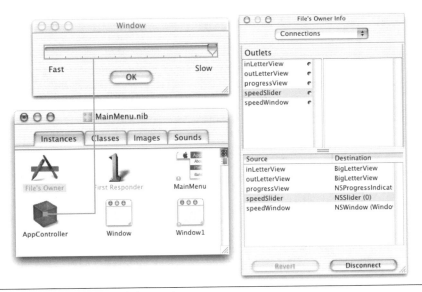

Figure 20.8   Connect speedSlider Outlet

step, then, is to go through `AppController.m` and replace the constant TICKS with the variable `ticks`. Delete the line that defines the constant TICKS.

In the init method, initialize `ticks` to be 10.

```
- init
{
    if (self = [super init]) {
        ticks = 10;
        letters = [[NSArray alloc] initWithObjects:@"a", @"s", @"d",@"f",
                                    @"j", @"k", @"l", @";",nil];
        lastIndex = 0;
    }
    return self;
}
```

When the user chooses the **Adjust Speed...** menu item, the `speedSlider` will be set so that it reflects the value of `ticks` and the sheet will run. Add this method to `AppController.m`:

```
- (IBAction)raiseSpeedWindow:(id)sender
{
    [speedSlider setIntValue:ticks];
    [NSApp beginSheet:speedWindow
        modalForWindow:[inLetterView window]
        modalDelegate:self
```

```
        didEndSelector:@selector(sheetDidEnd:returnCode:contextInfo:)
        contextInfo:nil];
}
```

Notice that you are attaching the sheet to the window that the inLetterView is on. The **AppController** is the modalDelegate, and it will be sent **sheetDidEnd: returnCode:contextInfo:** when the sheet is dismissed.

The sheet will end when the user clicks the OK button. Add this method to AppController.m.

```
- (IBAction)endSpeedWindow:(id)sender
{
  // Hide the sheet
  [speedWindow orderOut:sender];

  // Return to normal event handling
  [NSApp endSheet:speedWindow returnCode:1];
}
```

You could have also read the slider's new value in **endSpeedWindow:**, but you know that **sheetDidEnd:returnCode:contextInfo:** is going to be called. You are going to read the new value in that method. Add this method to AppController.m:

```
- (void)sheetDidEnd:(NSWindow *)sheet
        returnCode:(int)returnCode
        contextInfo:(void *)contextInfo
{
  // Read the slider's value
  ticks = [speedSlider intValue];

  // Reset the count
  count = 0;

  NSLog(@"sheetDidEnd: Return code = %d", returnCode);
}
```

For the More Curious: contextInfo

Notice the contextInfo parameter. This is a pointer to some data. You can supply it when you start the sheet, and the delegate will get the pointer when you end the sheet. For example, here the developer has started a sheet and put a phone number in for the context info:

```
[NSApp beginSheet:aWindow
    modalForWindow:someOtherWindow
```

```
        modalDelegate:self
    didEndSelector:@selector(didEnd:returnCode:phone:)
        contextInfo:@"703-555-6513"];
```

Later, in the **didEnd:returnCode:contextInfo:** method, the phone number will be supplied as the third argument.

```
- (void)sheetDidEnd:(NSWindow *)sheet
        returnCode:(int)returnCode
            phone:(NSString *)phoneNumber
{
  // Read the slider's value
  NSLog(@"sheetDidEnd: Phone number = %@", phoneNumber);
}
```

Notice that the context info and the **NSNotification**'s user info dictionary serve similar purposes.

For the More Curious: NSDrawer

A drawer is similar to a sheet in several ways: It is attached to a window, users can open and close it, and it has a content view that can be configured in Interface Builder (Figure 20.9).

A drawer is different from a sheet in that it is not a window: There is a class **NSDrawer**. Also, a sheet disables the window underneath, whereas a drawer simply

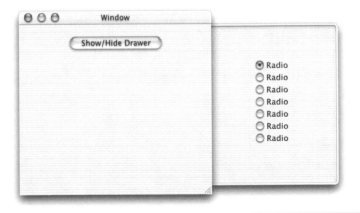

Figure 20.9   Example Drawer

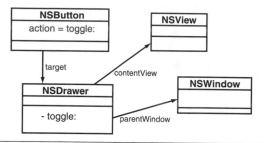

Figure 20.10   NSDrawer

augments the window it is attached to. Finally, creating a drawer is done differently than creating a sheet. In creating a drawer, there are three major players: the instance of **NSDrawer**, the content view of the drawer, and the window the drawer is attached to. You will typically also have a button or menu item for opening and closing the drawer. **NSDrawer** has an action method **toggle:** that will open the drawer if closed and close it if open (Figure 20.10)

In Interface Builder, there is a palette item that creates an **NSDrawer**, its parent window, and the drawer's content view, which will all be connected correctly. In Figure 20.11, I've added a button to the parent window and a matrix of buttons to the content view of the drawer.

Sometimes you will wonder whether a sheet or a drawer is more appropriate for your interface. Usually when a sheet is visible, the window beneath it is disabled. A drawer, on the other hand, is an extension to the window that the user may not always want to see.

Challenge

Put the speed adjustment on a drawer instead of a sheet.

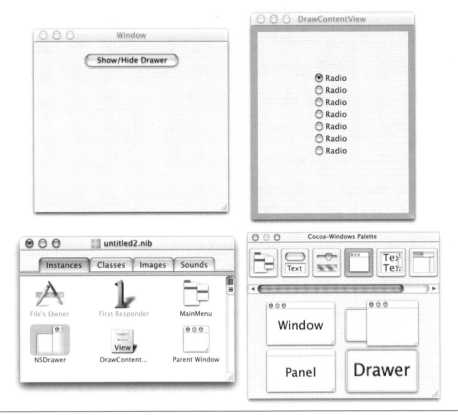

Figure 20.11   Example Drawer as Nib

Chapter 21
CREATING NSFORMATTERS

A formatter takes a string and makes another object. This is typically so that the user can type something that is more than just a string. For example, the **NSDateFormatter** when passed a string like "August 17, 1967" converts it into an **NSCalendarDate** object that represents the seventeenth day of August in the year 1967 (Figure 21.1).

Also, a formatter can take an object and create a string for the user to see. For example, imagine a text field that has an **NSDateFormatter**. When the text field is sent **setObjectValue:** with an **NSCalendarDate** object, the date formatter will create a string that represents that date. The user will see that string.

All formatters are subclasses of the **NSFormatter** class. Two of these subclasses come with Cocoa: **NSDateFormatter** and **NSNumberFormatter**. You used **NSNumberFormatter** in Chapter 4 to format the expected raise as a percentage.

The most basic formatter will implement two methods.

```
- (BOOL)getObjectValue:(id *)anObject
              forString:(NSString *)aString
      errorDescription:(NSString **)errorPtr
```

This message is sent by the control (like a text field) to the formatter when it has to convert aString into an object. aString is the string that the user typed in. The formatter can return YES and set anObject to point to the new object. If, on the other hand, the formatter returns NO, this indicates that the string could not be converted and that the errorPtr gets set to indicate what went wrong. Note that errorPtr is a pointer to a pointer. That is, it is a location where you can put a pointer to the string. anObject is also a pointer to a pointer.

```
- (NSString *)stringForObjectValue:(id)anObject
```

This message is sent by the control to the formatter when it has to convert anObject into a string. The string that is returned is the one the control will display for the user (Figure 21.2).

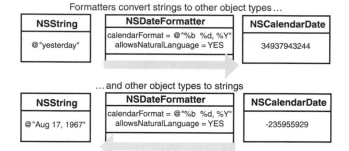

Figure 21.1   NSFormatter

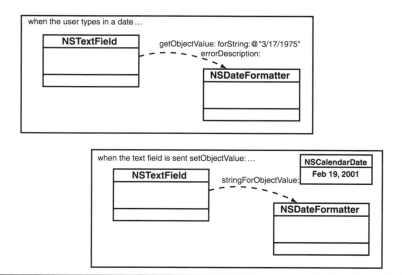

Figure 21.2   NSDateFormatter

A Basic Formatter

In this chapter, you will learn to write your own formatter class. You are going to create a formatter that will allow the user to type in the name of a color, and the formatter will create the appropriate **NSColor** object. Then you are going to set the background of the **BigLetterView** with that color object. Figure 21.3 shows what it will look like when you are done.

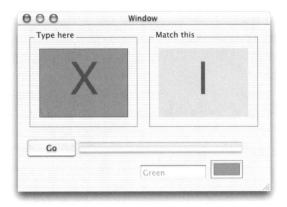

Figure 21.3   Completed Application

Edit the Interface File for the AppController Class

First you will add outlets and actions to your **AppController**. You are going to add a text field and a color well to the window. You will have outlets so that your **AppController** can send messages to the text field and the color well. You will have actions in **AppController** that will be triggered by the text field and the color well. Alter your AppController.h file to look like this:

```
#import <Cocoa/Cocoa.h>
@class BigLetterView;

@interface AppController : NSObject
{
    IBOutlet NSWindow *speedWindow;
    IBOutlet NSSlider *speedSlider;
    int count;
    int ticks;
    IBOutlet BigLetterView *inLetterView;
    IBOutlet BigLetterView *outLetterView;
    IBOutlet NSProgressIndicator *progressView;
    NSTimer *timer;
    NSArray *letters;
    int lastIndex;
    IBOutlet NSColorWell *colorWell;
    IBOutlet NSTextField *textField;
}
- (void)showAnotherLetter;
- (IBAction)stopGo:(id)sender;
- (IBAction)takeColorFromTextField:(id)sender; // Triggered by text field
- (IBAction)takeColorFromColorWell:(id)sender; // Triggered by color well
- (IBAction)raiseSpeedWindow:(id)sender;
```

```
- (IBAction)endSpeedWindow:(id)sender;
- (void)sheetDidEnd:(NSWindow *)sheet
        returnCode:(int)returnCode
        contextInfo:(void *)contextInfo;
@end
```

Editing the Nib File

Open MainMenu.nib. Drag the new AppController.h file into the nib file. Interface Builder will parse the file and add the actions and outlets to the **AppController** object (Figure 21.4).

Add a text field and a color well to the window. Set the target of each to the **AppController** object. The action for the color well will be **takeColorFromColor-Well:**. The action for the text field will be **takeColorFromTextField:**. Set the **AppController**'s textField outlet to the text field. Set the **AppController**'s colorWell outlet to the color well (Figure 21.5).

NSColorList

For this exercise, you will use an **NSColorList**. An **NSColorList** is a dictionary of color objects. It maps a name to an instance of **NSColor** objects. There are a couple of color lists that come standard with Mac OS X. In particular, the color list named "Apple" includes many of the standard colors, like "Purple" and "Yellow."

NSColorList is not a particularly useful class, but it makes this exercise very elegant. I am not going to spend much time talking about it.

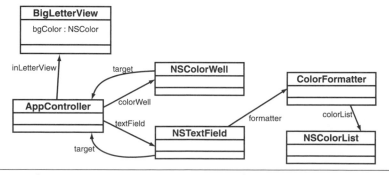

Figure 21.4 Object Diagram

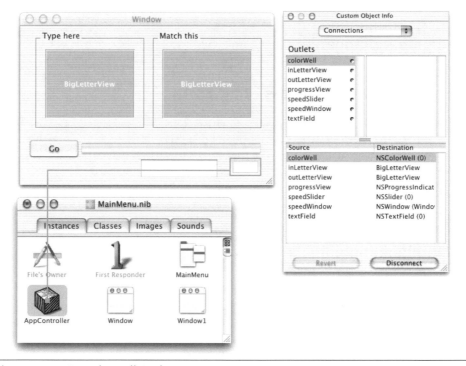

Figure 21.5   Set colorWell Outlet

Searching Strings for Substrings

When you have a string like "dakakookookakoo" and you are searching through it for a shorter string like "ka," the result will be an NSRange. The location is the first letter of the matching substring in the longer string. The length is the length of the substring.

Of course, there are a couple of options that you might want to set. For example, you might want to do a case-insensitive search. Or you might want to do a backwards search (from the end of the string instead of the beginning). To search backwards for the string "KA" in "dakakookookakoo" in a case-insensitive manner, you would use the following code:

```
NSRange aRange;
NSString *big = @"dakakookookakoo";
NSString *small = @"KA";

aRange = [big rangeOfString:small
                options: (NSCaseInsensitiveSearch | NSBackwardsSearch)];
```

At the end of this, aRange.location would be 10 and aRange.length would be 2.

If the substring is not found, the length will be 0.

Create a Subclass of NSFormatter

In Project Builder, create a new Objective-C class named **ColorFormatter**. Make **ColorFormatter** a subclass of **NSFormatter**. Give the class an instance variable of type **NSColorList**. Call the variable colorList.

```
#import <Foundation/Foundation.h>
@class NSColorList;

@interface ColorFormatter : NSFormatter {
    NSColorList *colorList;
}
- (NSString *)firstColorKeyForPartialString:(NSString *)string;
@end
```

Edit ColorFormatter.m to look like this:

```
#import <Cocoa/Cocoa.h>
#import "ColorFormatter.h"

@implementation ColorFormatter

- (id)init
{
    if (self = [super init]) {
      colorList = [[NSColorList colorListNamed:@"Apple"] retain];
    }
    return self;
}

// A private method
- (NSString *)firstColorKeyForPartialString:(NSString *)string
{
    NSArray *keys = [colorList allKeys];
    NSString *key;
    NSRange whereFound;
    int i, keyCount;
    keyCount = [keys count];

    // Loop through the color list
    for (i = 0; i< keyCount; i++) {
        key = [keys objectAtIndex: i];
        whereFound = [key rangeOfString:string
                    options:NSCaseInsensitiveSearch];
        // Does the string match the beginning of the color name?
```

```
                if ((whereFound.location == 0) && (whereFound.length > 0)) {
                    return key;
                }
        }
        // If no match is found, return nil
        return nil;
}

- (NSString *)stringForObjectValue:(id)obj
{
        // Find a string for the color "obj"
        float red, green, blue, alpha;
        float red2, green2, blue2, alpha2;
        NSColor *color2;
        NSString *key, *closestKey;
        float howClose, distance;
        int i, keyCount;
        NSArray *keys;
        closestKey = nil;
        // Is this a color object?
        if ([obj isKindOfClass: [NSColor class]]) {

            // Get the color components
            [obj getRed:&red green:&green blue:&blue alpha:&alpha];
            keys = [colorList allKeys];
            keyCount = [keys count];
            howClose = 3;

            // Loop through all the colors
            for (i = 0; i< keyCount; i++) {
                key = [keys objectAtIndex: i];
                color2 = [colorList colorWithKey:key];

                // Find the color components of the current color
                [color2 getRed:&red2 green:&green2 blue:&blue2 alpha:&alpha2];

                // How far is it from obj?
                distance = fabs(red2 - red) +
                           fabs(green2 - green) +
                           fabs(blue2 - blue);

                // Is this the closest yet?
                if (distance < howClose) {
                    howClose = distance;
                    closestKey = key;
                }
            }

            // Return the name of the closest color
            return closestKey;
        } else {
```

```
        // If not a color, return nil
        return nil;
    }
}
- (BOOL)getObjectValue:(id *)obj
            forString:(NSString *)string
    errorDescription:(NSString **)errorString
{
    // Look up the color for 'string'
    NSString *matchingKey = [self firstColorKeyForPartialString:string];
    if (matchingKey) {
        *obj = [colorList colorWithKey:matchingKey];
        return YES;
    } else {
        // Occasionally, 'errorString' is NULL
        if (errorString != NULL) {
            *errorString = @"No such color";
        }
        return NO;
    }
}
- (void)dealloc
{
    [colorList release];
    [super dealloc];
}
@end
```

You will need to get the formatter attached to your text field. Do it in the **awakeFromNib** method of **AppController**.

```
- (void)awakeFromNib
{
    ColorFormatter *colorFormatter = [[ColorFormatter alloc] init];
    [textField setFormatter: colorFormatter];
    // The formatter is retained by the text field
    [colorFormatter release];
    [textField setObjectValue: [inLetterView bgColor]];
    [colorWell setColor: [inLetterView bgColor]];
    [self showAnotherLetter];
}
```

Also in **AppController**, create the action methods.

```
- (IBAction)takeColorFromTextField:(id)sender
{
    NSColor *c = [sender objectValue];
    NSLog(@"taking color from text field");
```

```
    [inLetterView setBgColor:c];
    [colorWell setColor:c];
}

- (IBAction)takeColorFromColorWell:(id)sender
{
    NSColor *c = [sender color];
    NSLog(@"taking color from color well");
    [inLetterView setBgColor:c];
    [textField setObjectValue:c];
}
```

Be sure to import `ColorFormatter.h` at the beginning at `AppController.m`.

Build and run your application. You should be able to type in color names and see the background of the **BigLetterView** change. Also, if you use the color well, you should see the name of the color change in the text field.

The Delegate of the NSControl

You are probably wondering where the error string goes. The control can have a delegate. If the formatter decides the string is invalid, the delegate gets sent the message.

```
- (BOOL)control:(NSControl *)control
        didFailToFormatString:(NSString *)string
            errorDescription:(NSString *)error
```

The delegate can override the opinion of the formatter. If it returns YES, the control displays the string as is. If it returns NO, that means that the delegate agrees with the formatter: The string is invalid.

Implement this method in `AppController.m`.

```
- (BOOL)control:(NSControl *)control
    didFailToFormatString:(NSString *)string
        errorDescription:(NSString *)error
{
    NSLog(@"AppController told that formatting of %@ failed: %@",
            string, error);
    return NO;
}
```

Now open the nib file and make the **AppController** the delegate of the text field (Figure 21.6).

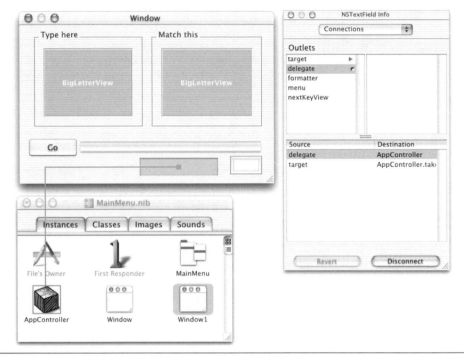

Figure 21.6   Connect the Text Field's delegate Outlet

Build and run your app. When validation fails, you will see a message on the console indicating what the string was and why it failed.

Checking Partial Strings

You might want to create a formatter that prevents the user from typing letters that are not part of a color name. To make the formatter check the string after every keystroke, implement the following method.

```
- (BOOL)isPartialStringValid:(NSString *)partial
    newEditingString:(NSString **)newString
        errorDescription:(NSString **)errorString
```

partial is the string, including the last keystroke. If your formatter returns NO, it indicates that the partial string is not acceptable. Also, if your formatter returns NO, it can also supply the newString and an errorString. The newString will appear in the control. The errorString should give the user an idea of what she or he did wrong. If your formatter returns YES, the `newString` and the `errorString` are ignored.

Add this method to your `ColorFormatter.m`.

```
- (BOOL)isPartialStringValid:(NSString *)partial
         newEditingString:(NSString **)newString
         errorDescription:(NSString **)error
{
    NSString *match;
    if ([partial length] == 0){
        return YES;
    }
    match = [self firstColorKeyForPartialString:partial];
    if (match) {
        return YES;
    } else {
        *error = @"No such color";
        return NO;
    }
}
```

Build and run your application. You will not be able to type in anything but the color names.

The Control's Delegate and Partial Strings

The delegate of the control also gets informed when a partial string is found to be invalid. Here is the message that the delegate will be sent:

```
- (void)control:(NSControl *)control
    didFailToValidatePartialString:(NSString *)string
            errorDescription:(NSString *)errorString
```

Implement the method in `AppController.m`.

```
- (void)control:(NSControl *)control
       didFailToValidatePartialString:(NSString *)string
       errorDescription:(NSString *)error
{
    NSLog(@"Formatting of partial string %@ failed: %@", string, error);
}
```

Build and run the application. You should see a message on the console when a partial string is found invalid by the formatter.

Formatters That Return Attributed Strings

Sometimes it is nice for the formatter to define not only the string that is to be displayed, but also the attributes of that string. For example, a number formatter might print the number in red if it is negative. To do this, you will use **NSAttributedString**.

Your formatter can implement:

```
- (NSAttributedString *)attributedStringForObjectValue:(id)anObj
                    withDefaultAttributes:(NSDictionary *)aDict
```

If the method exists, it will get called instead of **stringForObjectValue:**. Implement this method so that it displays the name of the color in that color.

```
- (NSAttributedString *)attributedStringForObjectValue:(id)anObject
                    withDefaultAttributes:(NSDictionary *)attributes
{
    NSColor *fgColor;
    NSAttributedString *atString;
    NSMutableDictionary *md = [attributes mutableCopy];
    NSString *match = [self stringForObjectValue:anObject];
    if (match) {
        fgColor = [colorList colorWithKey:match];
        [md setObject:fgColor forKey:NSForegroundColorAttributeName];
    }
    atString = [[NSAttributedString alloc] initWithString:match
        attributes:md];
    [md release];
    [atString autorelease];
    return atString;
}
```

Build and run the application. Note that the text field will not change colors until it gives up first-responder status.

Challenge

Color objects are from particular color spaces. Asking for the red, green, and blue components is only possible if the color is from an RGB-based color space, like NSCalibratedRBGColorSpace. So, if the user uses the color panel's CMYK view or Black/White view to choose a color, your formatter will fail to name the resulting color. Fix this problem.

NSColor has the following methods.

- (NSString *)**colorSpaceName**

Returns the name of the receiver's color space.

- (NSColor *)**colorUsingColorSpaceName:**(NSString *)spaceName

Returns a similar color from the color space named spaceName.

Chapter 22

PRINTING

C ode to handle printing is always relatively hard to write. There are many factors at play: pagination, margins, and page orientation (landscape versus portrait). This chapter is designed to get you started on your journey toward the perfect printout.

Compared to most operating systems, Mac OS X makes writing print routines considerably easier. After all, your views already know how to generate PDF, and Mac OS X knows how to print PDF. If you have a document-based application and a view that knows how to draw itself, you just implement **printShowingPrintPanel:**. In this method, you create an **NSPrintOperation** object and run it. The code would look like this:

```
- (void)printShowingPrintPanel:(BOOL)flag {
    NSPrintInfo *printInfo = [self printInfo];
    NSPrintOperation *printOp;
    printOp = [NSPrintOperation printOperationWithView:aView
                                         printInfo:printInfo];
    [printOp setShowPanels:flag];
    [printOp runOperation];
}
```

Adding Printing to TypingTutor

If your application is not document based, you will implement a **print:** method in the target of the menu item. For example, add the following method to your **AppController** class in your TypingTutor project.

```
- (IBAction)print:(id)sender
{
    NSPrintInfo *printInfo = [NSPrintInfo sharedPrintInfo];
    NSPrintOperation *printOp;
    printOp = [NSPrintOperation printOperationWithView:inLetterView
                                         printInfo:printInfo];
    [printOp setShowPanels:YES];
    [printOp runOperation];
}
```

Declare the method in AppController.h. Drag AppController.h into the nib file. Add a menu item called Print.... Make the **AppController** the target of the menu item, and set the action to **print:** (Figure 22.1).

Build the project and see that printing works. Unless you have a printer set up, you will only be able to preview what would have been printed (Figure 22.2).

To print all the views on the window, simply change the **print:** method to use the window's content view.

```
- (IBAction)print:(id)sender
{
    NSView *v = [[inLetterView window] contentView];
    NSPrintInfo *printInfo = [NSPrintInfo sharedPrintInfo];
    NSPrintOperation *printOp;
    printOp = [NSPrintOperation printOperationWithView:v
                                             printInfo:printInfo];
    [printOp setShowPanels:YES];
    [printOp runOperation];
}
```

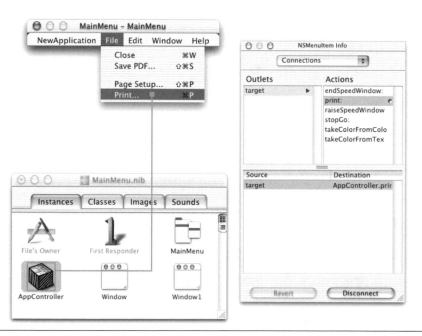

Figure 22.1   Connect Menu Item

Dealing with Pagination

What about multiple pages? A view, after all, only has a single page. How will you get a view to print multiple-page documents? Off-screen, you will make a huge view that can display all the pages of the document simultaneously (Figure 22.3). The print system will ask the view how many pages it is displaying. Then it will ask the view where each page can be found in the view.

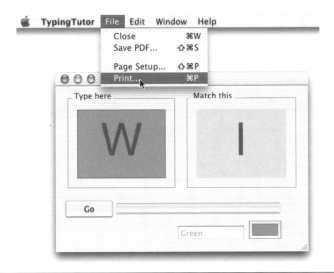

Figure 22.2   Completed Application

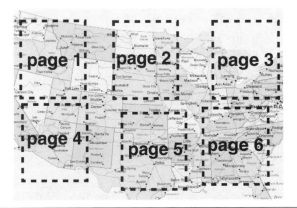

Figure 22.3   Each Page is a Rectangle on the View

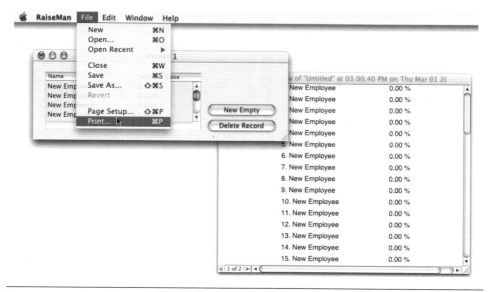

Figure 22.4   Completed Application

Your view, then, is going to have to override two methods:

```
// How many pages?
- (BOOL)knowsPageRange:(NSRange *)rptr;
// Where is each page?
- (NSRect)rectForPage:(int)pageNum;
```

As an example, you are going to add printing to the RaiseMan application. You will display the name and expected raise for 30 people on each page (Figure 22.4).

To do this, you will create a view that does the printing. The view will be big enough to display all the people simultaneously, but for each page there will be a rectangle that contains the information for 30 people. The view will be called **PeopleView** (Figure 22.5).

The code in MyDocument.m is actually pretty simple.

```
- (void)printShowingPrintPanel:(BOOL)flag {
    NSPrintInfo *printInfo = [self printInfo];
    NSPrintOperation *printOp;
    PeopleView *view;
    view = [[PeopleView alloc] initWithPeople:employees
                          printInfo:[self printInfo]];
    printOp = [NSPrintOperation printOperationWithView:view
                          printInfo:printInfo];
```

```
    [printOp setShowPanels:flag];
    [printOp runOperation];
    [view release];
}
```

You will have to import `PeopleView.h`. This is not so different from the TypingTutor example. There are slight differences, however.

- **NSDocument** implements **printDocument:** to call [self printShowingPrint Panel:YES], so your subclass of **NSDocument** is implementing **printShowing-PrintPanel:** instead of **print:**.
- The view that is doing the printing needs to be created. Usually you will create a view by calling **initWithFrame:**. In our **PeopleView**, you are going to create another constructor that takes the array of people and the print info object. The print info knows the paper size. Using the array of people and the print info object, you can figure out how big the frame should be.
- Notice that **NSDocument** has a method **printInfo** that returns the instance of **NSPrintInfo** for that document.

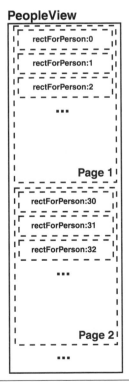

Figure 22.5   PeopleView

In the `MainMenu.nib` file, make the Print... menu item nil-targeted and set its action to **printDocument:** (Figure 22.6). (Remember that you set a menu item's target to be nil by dragging to the icon labeled First Responder.)

Create a class called **PeopleView** that is a subclass of **NSView**. `PeopleView.h` would look like this:

```
#import <Cocoa/Cocoa.h>

@interface PeopleView : NSView
{
    NSArray *people;      // Array of people to display
    int peoplePerPage;    // How many people on each page?
    int pages;            // How many pages?
    float rectHeight;     // How much vertical space does each person get?
}
- initWithPeople:(NSArray *)array printInfo:(NSPrintInfo *)pi;
- (NSRect)rectForPerson:(int)index;
@end
```

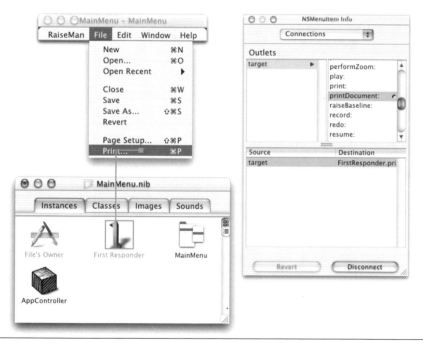

Figure 22.6   Connect Menu Item

In `PeopleView.m`, you will implement the **initWithPeople:printInfo:** method. This initializer will call **NSView**'s **initWithFrame:** method.

```
#import "PeopleView.h"
#import "Person.h"

@implementation PeopleView

- initWithPeople:(NSArray *)array printInfo:(NSPrintInfo *)pi
{
  NSRect theFrame;
  NSSize paperSize;
  peoplePerPage = 30;
  people = [array retain];

  // The operator will round down
  pages = [people count] / peoplePerPage;

  // So check to see if there was a remainder
  if ((([people count] % peoplePerPage) != 0) {
    pages = pages + 1;
  }
  paperSize = [pi paperSize];
  theFrame.origin = NSMakePoint(0,0);
  theFrame.size.width = paperSize.width;

  // The view is very tall: each page will appear
  // below the previous page
  theFrame.size.height = paperSize.height * pages;

  // Call NSView's initWithFrame: method
  self = [super initWithFrame:theFrame];

  // rectHeight is the vertical space that each person will get
  rectHeight = paperSize.height / peoplePerPage;
  return self;
}

// How many pages?
- (BOOL)knowsPageRange:(NSRange *)rptr
{
  rptr->location = 1;
  rptr->length = pages;
  return YES;
}

// In what rect will person 'index' get drawn?
- (NSRect)rectForPerson:(int)index
{
  NSRect theResult;
  NSRect theBounds = [self bounds];
```

```
      theResult.origin.x = theBounds.origin.x;
      theResult.size.width = theBounds.size.width;
      theResult.origin.y = NSMaxY(theBounds) - ((index + 1) * rectHeight);
      theResult.size.height = rectHeight;
      return theResult;
}

// Where will the drawing for page 'pageNum' happen?
- (NSRect)rectForPage:(int)pageNum
{
   NSRect theResult;
   theResult.size.width = [self bounds].size.width;
   theResult.size.height = rectHeight * peoplePerPage;
   theResult.origin.x = [self bounds].origin.x;
   theResult.origin.y = NSMaxY([self bounds]) -
                    (pageNum * theResult.size.height);
   return theResult;
}

// The method that does the drawing
- (void)drawRect:(NSRect)rect
{
    int i;
    NSRect aRect;
    NSMutableDictionary *attributes;
    NSString *raiseAsString, *printString;
    Person *aPerson;
    NSNumberFormatter *raiseFormatter;

    // Create a formatter that will format the expectedRaise
    raiseFormatter = [[NSNumberFormatter alloc] init];
    [raiseFormatter setFormat:@"0.00 %"];

    // Create the attributes dictionary for drawing the text
    attributes = [[NSMutableDictionary alloc] init];
    [attributes setObject:
                [NSFont fontWithName: @"Helvetica" size: 16]
                   forKey: NSFontAttributeName];
    [attributes setObject: [NSColor blackColor]
                   forKey: NSForegroundColorAttributeName];

    // Step through the list of people
    for (i = 0; i < [people count]; i++) {
      aRect = [self rectForPerson:i];
      // Only draw the people that are on the page being printed
      if (NSIntersectsRect(aRect, rect)) {
        aPerson = [people objectAtIndex:i];
        // Shift the rect to the right
        aRect.origin.x = aRect.origin.x + 150;
        // And make it narrower
        aRect.size.width = aRect.size.width - 400 ;
        // Format the float
```

```
        raiseAsString = [raiseFormatter stringForObjectValue:
                              [NSNumber numberWithFloat:
                                    [aPerson expectedRaise]]];

        // Create a string with the person's index and name.
        printString = [NSString stringWithFormat:@"%d. %@",
        i, [aPerson personName]];

        // Draw that string
        [printString drawInRect: aRect withAttributes:attributes];

        // Shift aRect to the right
        aRect.origin.x = aRect.origin.x + 250;

        // Draw the expected raise
        [raiseAsString drawInRect:aRect withAttributes:attributes];
    }
  }
  [attributes release];
  [raiseFormatter release];
}

- (void)dealloc
{
  [people release];
  [super dealloc];
}
@end
```

Build and run the app.

Challenge

Add a border around each page. Then add page numbers.

Chapter 23
UPDATING MENUS

In many applications, it is necessary to enable and disable menu items as the user interacts with the application. In particular, as the first responder changes, a menu item that is nil-targeted will need to be disabled if the responder chain does not respond to its action. By default, this is handled for you. When displaying itself, the menu item will automatically figure out if the current target has the appropriate action. If not, the menu item will be disabled.

When a menu item is deciding if it should be enabled, it will ask its target if it implements **validateMenuItem:**. If so, the target is sent **validateMenuItem:**. If the target returns YES, the menu item is enabled.

Thus, to enable and disable menu items, you are going to implement the following method:

```
- (BOOL)validateMenuItem:(NSMenuItem *)menuItem;
```

It will return YES if the menu item should be enabled.

Note that for nil-targeted actions, the member of the responder chain that would respond to the action is asked to validate it. So, for example, the window will be asked to validate **performClose:** (a window without a close button will invalidate this menu item). If a text field is selected, it will be asked to validate the **copy:** menu item. As the first responder changes, the new chain is asked to validate the respective menu items (Figure 23.1).

To review, a menu item will automatically enable or disable itself. First, it checks to see if its target implements the action. If not, the menu item is disabled. Otherwise, it asks the target if it responds to **validateMenuItem:**. If not, the menu item is enabled. Otherwise, it is enabled if and only if the target validates the menu item.

Making a BigLetterView Uncopyable

Notice that your TypingTutor program currently allows the user to simply drag or copy/paste the letter from the "Match this" **BigLetterView** to the "Type here" **BigLetterView**. This would be cheating, and you should prevent it (Figure 23.2).

You are going to add a BOOL instance variable called copyable to the **BigLetterView** class. If copyable is NO, you are going to prevent the user from dragging or copying

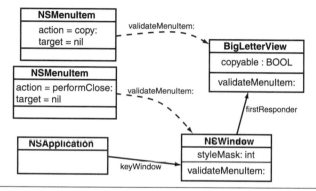

Figure 23.1   The Target Validates the Menu Item

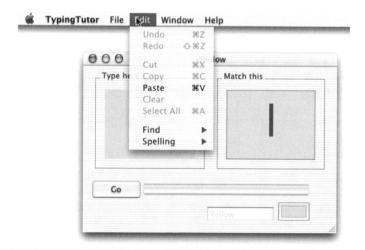

Figure 23.2   Completed Application

from the view. So start by editing the `BigLetterView.h` file to add the following instance variable.

```
@interface BigLetterView : NSView
{
    NSColor *bgColor;
    NSString *string;
    NSMutableDictionary *attributes;
    BOOL highlighted;
    BOOL copyable;
}
...
```

Next, add accessor methods for the variable in `BigLetterView.m`.

```
- (void)setCopyable:(BOOL)yn
{
    copyable = yn;
}
- (BOOL)copyable
{
    return copyable;
}
```

Also, declare these methods in `BigLetterView.h`.

In **initWithFrame:**, make the view copyable by default.

```
- initWithFrame:(NSRect)rect
{
    if (self = [super initWithFrame:rect]) {
      NSLog(@"initWithFrame:");
      [self prepareAttributes];
      [self setBgColor:[NSColor yellowColor]];
      [self setString:@" "];
      [self setCopyable:YES];
      [self registerForDraggedTypes:
              [NSArray arrayWithObject:NSStringPboardType]];
    }
    return self;
}
```

Make the "Match this" **BigLetterView** uncopyable in **AppController**'s **awakeFromNib** method.

```
- (void)awakeFromNib
{
    ColorFormatter *colorFormatter = [[ColorFormatter alloc] init];
    [textField setFormatter: colorFormatter];
    [colorFormatter release];
    [textField setObjectValue: [inLetterView bgColor]];
```

```
        [colorWell setColor: [inLetterView bgColor]];
        [outLetterView setCopyable:NO];
        [self showAnotherLetter];
}
```

In **BigLetterView**'s **mouseDragged:** method, start the drag operation only if the view is copyable.

```
- (void)mouseDragged:(NSEvent *)event
{
    NSRect imageBounds;
    NSPasteboard *pb;
    NSImage *anImage;
    NSSize s;
    NSPoint p;

    if (!copyable) {
        NSLog(@"Drag not permitted");
        return;
    }

    // Create the image that will be dragged
    anImage = [[NSImage alloc] init];

    // Get the size of the string
    s = [string sizeWithAttributes:attributes];

    // Create a rect in which you will draw the letter
    // in the image
    imageBounds.origin = NSMakePoint(0,0);
    imageBounds.size = s;
    [anImage setSize:s];

    // Draw the letter on the image
    [anImage lockFocus];
    [self drawStringCenteredIn:imageBounds];
    [anImage unlockFocus];

    // Get the location of the drag event
    p = [self convertPoint:[event locationInWindow] fromView:nil];

    // Drag from the center of the image
    p.x = p.x - s.width/2;
    p.y = p.y - s.height/2;

    // Get the pasteboard
    pb = [NSPasteboard pasteboardWithName: NSDragPboard];

    // Put the string on the pasteboard
    [self writeStringToPasteboard:pb];

    // Start the drag
```

```
    [self dragImage: anImage
        at:p
        offset: NSMakeSize(0, 0)
        event:event
        pasteboard:pb
        source: self
        slideBack: YES];
    [anImage release];
}
```

If you build and run the application now, the copy menu item will still be enabled. To disable the copy menu item, add a **validateMenuItem:** method:

```
- (BOOL)validateMenuItem:(NSMenuItem *)menuItem
{
    NSString *selectorString;
    selectorString = NSStringFromSelector([menuItem action]);
    NSLog(@"validateCalled for %@", selectorString);

    // By using the action instead of the title, we do not
    // have to worry about whether the menu item is localized
    if (([menuItem action] == @selector(copy:)) ||
        ([menuItem action] == @selector(cut:))){
        return copyable;
    } else {
        return YES;
    }
}
```

Build and run your application. Note that the Copy and Cut menu items are disabled when the uncopyable **BigLetterView** is selected.

Chapter 24
WORKING WITH NSTextView

NSTextView is a very smart class. It is basically a word processor. It deals with fonts, justification, rulers, graphics, spell-check, undo, drag-and-drop, and copy-and-paste. We could spend days discussing the text system. But for many uses of an **NSTextView**, all you need to do is read data from the view and insert data into the view.

When we talk about **NSTextView**, we are actually talking about a whole team of objects that make **NSTextView** work: An **NSTextStorage** (which inherits from **NSMutableAttributedString**) tracks changes to the text and informs the **NSLayout-Manager**. The **NSLayoutManager** lays out the text in a region that is defined by an **NSTextContainer**. The **NSTextView** is the view in which the text is rendered. You don't need to know anything about **NSTextContainer** or **NSLayoutManager** unless you are working on something where you need *a lot* of control over the text and its layout.

There is a class called **NSText** that is the superclass of **NSTextView**. It is terribly confusing to beginners because no one ever uses **NSText**. **NSText** existed before **NSTextView**, and it continues to exist to support people who might have used it at that time.

The data in a text view are typically read as one of three possible types.

- *A string*: In this case, you read and set the contents of the text view with an instance of **NSString**.
- *RTF*: Rich Text Format is a standard for text with multiple fonts and colors. In this case, you will read and set the contents of the text view with an instance of **NSData**.
- *RTFD*: This is RTF with attachments. Besides the multiple fonts and colors of RTF, you can also have images. In this case, you will read and set the contents of the text view with an instance of **NSData**.

NSTextView

Here are some of the commonly used methods on **NSTextView**.

- (NSString *)**string**

The text view's contents as a string.

- (void)**setString:**(NSString *)aString

Replaces the contents of the text view with aString.

- (NSRange)**selectedRange**

Returns the range of the current selection.

- (void)**setSelectedRange:**(NSRange)charRange

Sets the selection to the characters in charRange.

- (void)**replaceCharactersInRange:**(NSRange)aRange
                    withString:(NSString *)aString

Replaces the characters in aRange with aString.

- (void)**replaceCharactersInRange:**(NSRange)aRange
                    withRTF:(NSData *)rtfData

Replaces the characters in aRange with RTF text interpreted from rtfData.

- (void)**replaceCharactersInRange:**(NSRange)aRange
                    withRTFD:(NSData *)rtfdData

Replaces the characters in aRange with RTFD text interpreted from rtfdData.

- (NSData *)**RTFFromRange:**(NSRange)aRange

Returns an **NSData** object that contains an RTF stream aRange.

- (NSData *)**RTFDFromRange:**(NSRange)aRange

Returns an **NSData** object that contains an RTFD stream from aRange.

- (void)**scrollRangeToVisible:**(NSRange)aRange

Scrolls the text view in its enclosing scroll view so the first characters of aRange are visible.

- (void)**setFont:**(NSFont *)aFont **range:**(NSRange)aRange

Sets the font of characters within aRange to aFont.

- (void)**setTextColor:**(NSColor *)aColor **range:**(NSRange)aRange

Sets the text color of characters within aRange to aColor.

Messages the Delegate Will Be Sent

The delegate of the **NSTextView** gets informed of many things.

- (BOOL)**textShouldBeginEditing:**(NSText *)aTextObject

Sent the first time the user tries to edit the text in the text view after it has become first responder. If the delegate returns NO, the user will be unable to edit the text.

- (void)**textDidBeginEditing:**(NSNotification *)aNotification

Sent after the first change that the user makes after the view has become first responder.

- (void)**textDidChange:**(NSNotification *)aNotification

Sent each time the user changes the text in the text view.

- (BOOL)**textShouldEndEditing:**(NSText *)aTextObject

Sent when the text view is asked if it resigns as first responder. If the delegate returns NO, the text view refuses to give up first-responder status.

- (void)**textDidEndEditing:**(NSNotification *)aNotification

Sent when the text view has given up first-responder status.

```
- (NSRange)textView:(NSTextView *)aTextView
    willChangeSelectionFromCharacterRange:(NSRange)oldSelCharRange
                        toCharacterRange:(NSRange)newSelCharRange
```

Sent before the text view changes the selection. The delegate can return a new selection that will become the selection.

```
- (void)textViewDidChangeSelection:(NSNotification *)aNotification
```

Sent after the selection has changed.

```
- (BOOL)textView:(NSTextView *)aTextView
    shouldChangeTextInRange:(NSRange)affectedCharRange
        replacementString:(NSString *)replacementString
```

Sent before the user is allowed to replace the text in some range with another string.

Build the Editor with Which This Book Was Written

This book was written in SGML, the language on which HTML is based. SGML and XML are almost identical. Before marking up a document with SGML, you must decide on a *DTD*. A DTD (or document type definition) determines which tags may be used in the markup. A common DTD for technical documents is DocBook. This book is a DocBook document.

Before writing this book, I needed an editor. The exercise for this section is to write a simplified version of the DocBook editor with which this book was written (Figure 24.1).

Read, Write, and Edit Text Files

The first step is to write a simple text editor, like Apple's TextEdit. Create a new project of type Cocoa Document-based Application. This will create the skeleton of an application that can have multiple documents open at a time.

Open MyDocument.h and add an outlet for the text view and a variable for the string it is displaying.

Figure 24.1   Completed Application

```
#import <Cocoa/Cocoa.h>

@interface MyDocument : NSDocument
{
    NSString *string;
    IBOutlet NSTextView *textView;
}
@end
```

Open MyDocument.nib, and drop MyDocument.h into it. Delete the text field in the middle of the document window that says Your document contents here.

Drop a text view on the window, and resize it to fill the window. In the Attributes inspector, disable Multiple fonts allowed and enable Undo allowed (Figure 24.2).

In the size inspector, make the text view resize with the window (you are really setting the resize characteristics of the scroll view that the text view is inside) (Figure 24.3).

Your **MyDocument** object needs to know when the text has been edited, so make it the delegate of the text view. Double-click on the text view to select the text view. Control-drag to File's Owner and connect the delegate outlet.

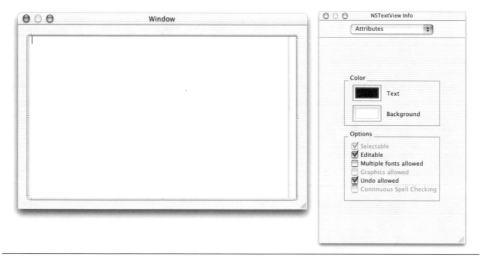

Figure 24.2   Inspect the TextView

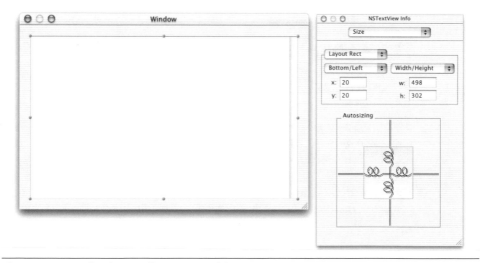

Figure 24.3   Make the ScrollView Resizable

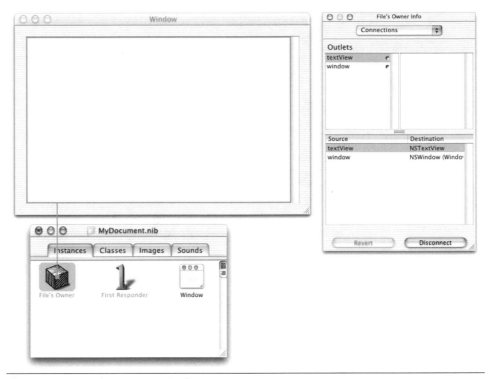

Figure 24.4   Set the textView Outlet

Your **MyDocument** object will also need to send message to the text view to implement loading and saving. Set the textView outlet of the File's Owner to be the text view (Figure 24.4).

Save and close the nib file.

Change the code in MyDocument.m.

```
#import "MyDocument.h"

@implementation MyDocument

- (NSString *)string {
    return string;
}
- (void)setString:(NSString *)value {
    [value retain];
    [string release];
    string = value;
}
```

```objc
- (void)updateString{
    [self setString: [textView string]];
}
- (void)updateView {
    [textView setString: [self string]];
}
- (NSString *)windowNibName {
    return @"MyDocument";
}
- (void)windowControllerDidLoadNib:(NSWindowController *) aController
{
    [super windowControllerDidLoadNib:aController];
    if (!string) {
        [self setString:
            @"<!DOCTYPE BOOK PUBLIC \"-//OASIS//DTD DocBook V3.1//EN\"[]>"];
    }
    // Large print for the myopic
    [textView setFont:[NSFont fontWithName: @"Courier" size:16]];
    [self updateView];
}
- (NSData *)dataRepresentationOfType:(NSString *)aType {
    [self updateString];
    return [string dataUsingEncoding:NSASCIIStringEncoding];
}
- (BOOL)loadDataRepresentation:(NSData *)data ofType:(NSString *)aType
{
    NSString *aString = [[NSString alloc] initWithData:data
                                    encoding:NSASCIIStringEncoding];
    [self setString: aString];
    [aString release];
    [self updateView];
    return YES;
}
- (void)textDidChange:(NSNotification *)aNotification
{
    [self updateChangeCount:NSChangeDone];
}
@end
```

Now you have a perfectly good text editor. Build it and run it. Create a new file, edit it, save it, close it, and open it again. Undo, redo, cut, copy, and paste should all work fine. Try control-clicking on the text view to bring up the standard text view menu. In the next section, you will replace that menu with another (Figure 24.5).

Note that because you haven't set the document types for your application, all the files will be saved with the ???? extension. This is fine for now.

Also note that spell-checking works.

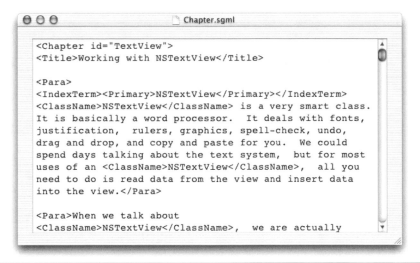

```
<Chapter id="TextView">
<Title>Working with NSTextView</Title>

<Para>
<IndexTerm><Primary>NSTextView</Primary></IndexTerm>
<ClassName>NSTextView</ClassName> is a very smart class.
It is basically a word processor.  It deals with fonts,
justification, rulers, graphics, spell-check, undo,
drag and drop, and copy and paste for you.  We could
spend days talking about the text system, but for most
uses of an <ClassName>NSTextView</ClassName>, all you
need to do is read data from the view and insert data
into the view.</Para>

<Para>When we talk about
<ClassName>NSTextView</ClassName>, we are actually
```

Figure 24.5   A Perfectly Good Text Editor

Adding a Context-Sensitive Menu

On Mac OS X, every view can have a menu associated with it. To get this menu, the user will control-click on the view. By default, the text view has a menu with standard text operations like cut, copy, and paste.

What will the menu do? When marking up an XML or SGML document, you will be wrapping text in tags like this: <Title>My Autobiography</Title>. So it would be convenient to be able to select a range of text and control-click to bring up a menu of what it could be wrapped in. When the user chooses a tag, the open tag will appear before the selection, and the close tag will appear after it.

You are going to create a subclass of **NSTextView**. When **MyDocument** receives notice that the nib file has been read, it will replace the instance of **NSTextView** with an instance of your subclass.

The object diagram is shown in Figure 24.6.

Open MyDocument.nib. Create a subclass of **NSTextView** called **SGMLView**. Add an action called **wrap:. wrap:** will be the action for all the menu items. Create the files SGMLView.m and SGMLView.h and add them to your project (Figure 24.7).

To swap the existing text view out and your **SGMLView** in, you will need an outlet to the **NSScrollView** that is in the window. So add an instance variable to MyDocument.h.

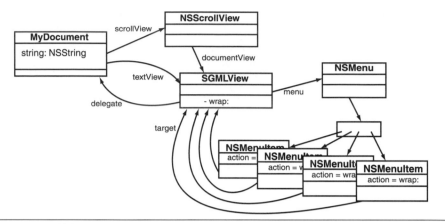

Figure 24.6   Object Diagram

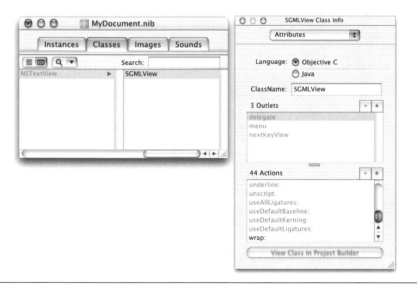

Figure 24.7   The Outlets and Actions of SGML View

```
#import <Cocoa/Cocoa.h>

@interface MyDocument : NSDocument
{
    NSString *string;
    IBOutlet NSTextView *textView;
    IBOutlet NSScrollView *scrollView;
}
@end
```

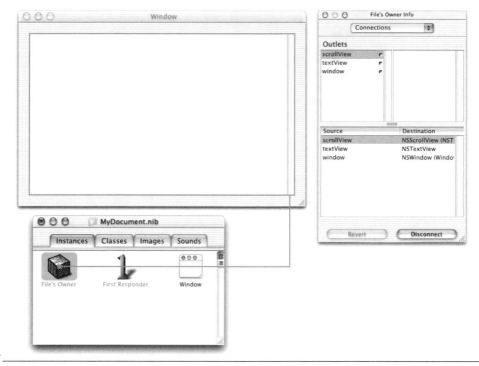

Figure 24.8   Set the scrollView Outlet

Drag MyDocument.h into the nib file. Connect the scrollView outlet to the scroll view (Figure 24.8). (Be sure that you have connected it to the scroll view, not the text view that it contains.)

Now you need to write the code that will swap out the **NSTextView** and swap in your **SGMLView**. This happens in the **windowControllerDidLoadNib:** method.

```
- (void)windowControllerDidLoadNib:(NSWindowController *) aController{
    NSSize contentSize;
    [super windowControllerDidLoadNib:aController];
    contentSize = [scrollView contentSize];
    textView = [[SGMLView alloc] initWithFrame:
            NSMakeRect(0, 0, contentSize.width, contentSize.height)];
    [textView setAutoresizingMask: NSViewWidthSizable];
    [[textView textContainer] setWidthTracksTextView:YES];
    [textView setDelegate:self];
    [textView setAllowsUndo:YES];
    [textView setRichText:NO];
    [textView setFont:[NSFont fontWithName: @"Courier" size:16]];
```

```
[scrollView setDocumentView:textView];
[textView release];
if (!string) {
    [self setString:
      @"<!DOCTYPE BOOK PUBLIC \"-//OASIS//DTD DocBook V3.1//EN\" []>"];
}
[self updateView];
}
```

Be sure to import SGMLView.h at the beginning of MyDocument.m.

You could build and run your application, but since you haven't overridden any methods in **SGMLView**, it will act just like an instance of **NSTextView**.

Adding the Menu

There is a dazzling array of DocBook tags, but you are going to use a few of my favorites. You could add them to the menu, one by one, but it will be much easier to create a property list containing them and read them at runtime.

It is common for a developer to want to create a text file that represents a list or dictionary. You can create a file called a *property list* (or plist), which represents any combination of **NSDictionary**, **NSArray**, and **NSString**. (In fact, there is a developer application called PropertyListEditor for creating and editing plists. You are not going to use it in this exercise, though.) Plists come in two styles: old-school and XML. In this exercise, you will create an old-school property list.

In an old-school plist, a dictionary appears in curly braces, an array appears in parentheses, and strings appear in quotes if they contain any white space. Here is a dictionary with two keys. One key is bound to a string, the other to an array of strings:

```
{
    pet = Rex;
    parents = ("Tom Hillegass", "Suzanna Hillegass");
}
```

In an XML plist, each token is wrapped in tags. Here is the same plist in XML format:

```
<?xml version="1.0" encoding="UTF-8"?>
<!DOCTYPE plist SYSTEM "file://localhost/System/Library/DTDs/PropertyList.dtd">
<plist version="0.9">
<dict>
```

```
<key>pet</key>
<string>Rex</string>
<key>parents</key>
<array>
<string>Tom Hillegass</string>
<string>Suzanna Hillegass</string>
</array>
</dict>
</plist>
```

If you were creating this plist in PropertyListEditor, it would look like Figure 24.9.

Property lists are nice, because they are easy to edit with a text editor and are easy to read in. To create a dictionary from a plist, you would use the following line of code:

```
NSDictionary *dict;
dict = [NSDictionary dictionaryWithContentsOfFile:@"/tmp/m.plist"];
```

Create a new empty file called `Tags.plist` (Figure 24.10).

This file represents a dictionary with one key: "tags". "tags" is associated with an array of strings. Add a plist containing my DocBook tags to `Tags.plist`.

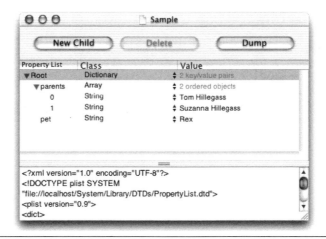

Figure 24.9   Property List Editor

Figure 24.10 Create a New File

```
{
    tags = (
        VariableList,
        ItemizedList,
        OrderedList,
        Section,
        ProgramListing,
        ScreenShot,
        Synopsis,
        Emphasis,
        GUIButton,
        GUILabel,
        GUIMenu,
        GUIMenuItem,
        ClassName,
        Function,
        Literal,
        Type,
        VarName,
        Application,
        Filename,
        VarListEntry,
        Title,
        ListItem,
        Para,
        KeyCap,
        Graphic,
        Quote,
        FirstTerm,
        IndexTerm
    );
}
```

Creating the NSMenu

Here is the code for reading in a dictionary from a property list, sorting the array, and creating a menu from it. Add this code to your SGMLView.m file.

```objc
- (id)initWithFrame:(NSRect)frame textContainer:(NSTextContainer *)tc {
    NSMenu *menu;
    NSMenuItem *item;
    int i;
    NSString *path;
    NSArray *tagArray;
    NSDictionary *defaultValues;
    if (self = [super initWithFrame:frame textContainer:tc]) {

        // Read the tagArray from the plist
        path = [[NSBundle mainBundle]
                        pathForResource:@"Tags" ofType:@"plist"];
        defaultValues = [NSDictionary
                        dictionaryWithContentsOfFile: path];
        tagArray = [defaultValues objectForKey:@"tags"];

        // Strings have a caseInsensitiveCompare: method
        // Use it to sort the array
        tagArray = [tagArray sortedArrayUsingSelector:
                            @selector(caseInsensitiveCompare:)];
        NSLog(@"tags = %@", tagArray);

        // Create the menu
        menu = [[NSMenu alloc] initWithTitle:@"Menu"];
        for (i = 0; i < [tagArray count]; i++) {
            // Create a menu item
            item = [[NSMenuItem alloc] init];

            // Set its attributes
            [item setTitle: [tagArray objectAtIndex: i]];
            [item setTarget: self];
            [item setAction:@selector(wrap:)];

            // Add it to the menu
            [menu addItem: item];

            // The item is retained by the menu
            [item release];
        }
        [self setMenu: menu];
        // The menu is retained by the view
        [menu release];
    }
    return self;
}
```

Add a **wrap:** method that prints out the name of the menu item that the user chose.

```
- (IBAction)wrap:(id)sender
{
    NSString *title = [sender title];
    NSLog(@"The user chose %@", title);
}
```

Build and run your application. You should get a menu to appear when you control-click in your **SGMLView** (Figure 24.11). When you choose an item from the menu, you should see a log statement.

Replace the Selection

Now implement the **wrap:** method. It needs to find the selection and replace it with a string that includes the opening and closing tags.

Figure 24.11   The Menu

```
- (IBAction)wrap:(id)sender
{
    NSString *title = [sender title];
    NSRange selection = [self selectedRange];
    NSString *wholeThing = [self string];

    NSString *oldString = [wholeThing substringWithRange:selection];
    NSString *newString = [NSString stringWithFormat:
            @"<%@>%@</%@>", title, oldString, title];
    [self insertText:newString];
}
```

Build and run your application. It should do everything right, but there is one tiny problem. If you control-click outside the selection, the selection changes before the menu appears.

Overriding menuForEvent:

Override **menuForEvent:** to prevent this problem from happening.

```
- (NSMenu *)menuForEvent:(NSEvent *)event {
    return [self menu];
}
```

(You could have done everything to this point without subclassing **NSTextView**. Overriding **menuForEvent:**, however, requires subclassing.)

Build it and run it. You should be able to select text and wrap it in DocBook tags.

Before you give it to your friends, be sure to set its document information. Choose Edit Active Target from the Project menu in Project Builder. Under the Application Settings tab, set the extensions to be "sgml" (Figure 24.12).

For the More Curious: The Field Editor

It takes a lot of smarts to lay out the characters in a text field. If every text field on a window had this kind of smarts, your application would take up a lot of unnecessary memory. After all, only one text field gets edited at a time. For efficiency, all the text fields on a window share one field editor. The field editor is an instance of **NSTextView**.

When a user selects and begins to edit a text field, the field editor takes over the processing of the events and drawing for that view. The field editor makes the text field its delegate (Figure 24.13).

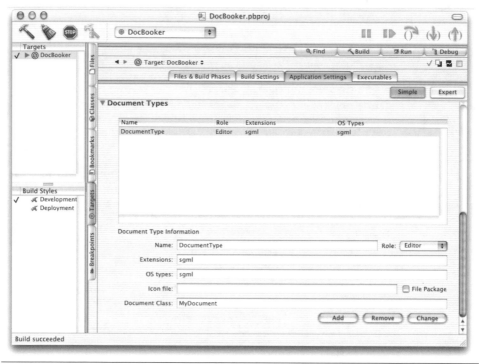

Figure 24.12 Set the Document Type Information

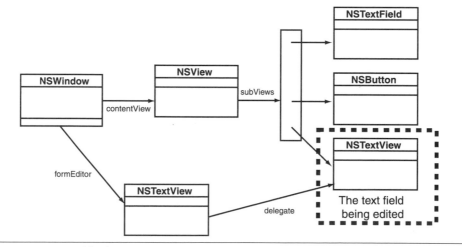

Figure 24.13 Field Editor

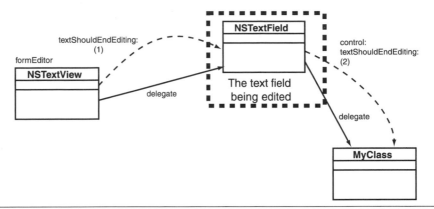

Figure 24.14   The Delegate of an NSControl

What happens if you want to create a delegate of the text field? For example, you want to receive the **textShouldEndEditing:** message from the field editor for a text field so that you can prevent the user from tabbing to another field (Figure 24.14).

When the user tries to change the first responder to another view, the field editor will send **textShouldEndEditing:** to its delegate (the text field). If the text field has a delegate, it will send that delegate the message.

```
- (BOOL)control:(NSControl *)textField
    textShouldEndEditing:(NSText *)fieldEditor
```

The delegate object can return NO, which will prevent the user from changing the first responder.

Here are a few other messages forwarded to you by the text field.

```
- (BOOL)control:(NSControl *)control
        textShouldBeginEditing:(NSText *)fieldEditor;
- (void)controlTextDidBeginEditing:(NSNotification *)aNotification;
- (void)controlTextDidChange:(NSNotification *)aNotification;
- (void)controlTextDidEndEditing:(NSNotification *)aNotification;
```

Chapter 25

USING JAVA WITH COCOA

O nce upon a time there was a fellow named Gosling who developed a language, a compiler, and a virtual machine. The marketing department at Sun Microsystems named the resulting product *Java*. After compiling the Java code into bytecodes, you could run it on any computer that had the virtual machine. Java became the hot thing to have on your résumé. Now everyone wants to use Java for everything.

Don't Use Java to Write Cocoa Applications

To please the many people who want to write applications in Java, Apple has done a clever hack that enables programmers to access the Cocoa frameworks from Java. The system that translates Java method calls into Objective-C calls is known as the *Java Bridge*.

The Cocoa frameworks were written in and for Objective-C. If you are going to write Cocoa applications, use Objective-C, C, and C++. Your application will launch faster and take up less memory than if it were written in Java. The quirks of the Java bridge will not get in the way of your development. Also, your project will compile much faster.

If you are going to write Java applications, use Swing. Swing, although not as wonderful as Cocoa, was written from the ground up for Java. Remember: The big selling point of Java is that applications written in Java are easily portable to any operating system. If you write a program with Cocoa, it will run only on Mac OS X.

Some people say: "But no one knows Objective-C." Programmers learn new languages all the time. Objective-C takes an afternoon to learn. If you are writing a Cocoa application, learning Objective-C is the least of your worries. Learning the frameworks that make up Cocoa will take much, much longer.

If You Must Use Java to Write Cocoa Applications

After that rant, I must admit that it is not actually that hard to write applications with Java and Cocoa. The engineers at Apple have done several clever things to make it easy. Remember the RandomApp example from Chapter 2? You are now going to write the same application in Java. Figure 25.1 shows what it will look like.

Create a New Project and Lay Out the Interface

Create a new project of type Cocoa-Java Application (Figure 25.2). Name it RandomJava.

Open MainMenu.nib. Drag a button out onto the blank window. Double-click on the button to change its title to Seed random number generator. Drag another button out, and relabel it Generate random number. Drop an uneditable text field and make it as wide as the window (Figure 25.3).

In the class browser, you can create a subclass of **java.lang.Object** and name it **Foo**. Add an outlet called textField and two actions called **seed()** and **generate()** (Figure 25.4).

Now create the file for the class **Foo**. Notice that a Foo.java file is created instead of a Foo.h file and a Foo.m file.

To create an instance of the class **Foo**, select **Foo** and choose Instantiate from the Classes menu.

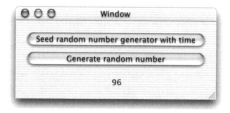

Figure 25.1   Completed Application

Figure 25.2   Choose the Project Type

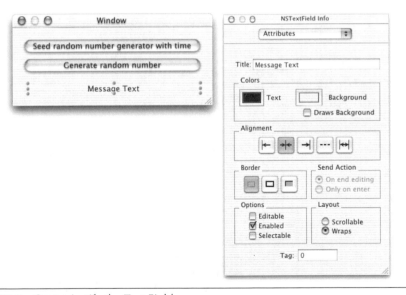

Figure 25.3   Center-justify the Text Field

Make Connections

Figure 25.5 is an object diagram of the objects that need to know about each other.

Control-drag from the **Foo** to the **NSTextField** (Figure 25.6).

Set the outlet textField. Control-drag from each of the buttons to the **Foo** class. Set the target and action of both buttons (Figures 25.7 and 25.8).

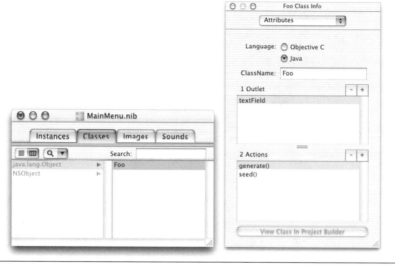

Figure 25.4   The Actions and Outlets of Foo

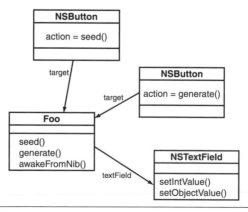

Figure 25.5   Object Diagram

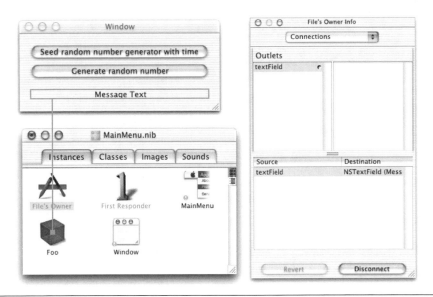

Figure 25.6   Set the textField Outlet

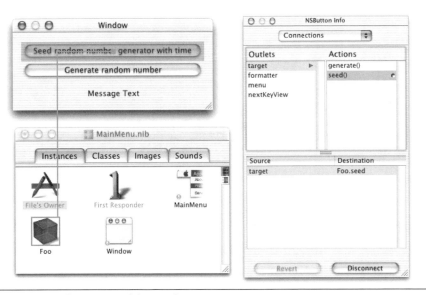

Figure 25.7   Set the Action of the Seed Button

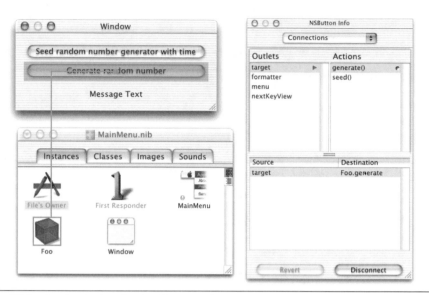

Figure 25.8   Set the Action for the Generate Button

Save your nib file.

Back in Project Builder

Make Foo.java look like this:

```java
import com.apple.cocoa.foundation.*;
import com.apple.cocoa.application.*;
import java.util.*;

public class Foo {

    private NSTextField textField;
    private Random aRandom;


    public Foo() {
        aRandom = new Random();
    }

    public void seed(Object sender) {
        Date aDate = new Date();
        aRandom.setSeed(aDate.getTime());
        textField.setStringValue("Generator is seeded");
    }
```

```
public void generate(Object sender) {
    int x;
    x = (Math.abs(aRandom.nextInt()) % 100) + 1;
    textField.setIntValue(x);
}

public void awakeFromNib() {
    textField.setObjectValue(new NSGregorianDate());
}
}
```

That should look familiar, but notice the oddity with the date. There are two different date classes: **java.util.Date** (which comes from Sun) and **com.apple.cocoa. foundation.NSGregorianDate** (which comes from Apple). All the Cocoa classes use **NSGregorianDate**. The **NSDateFormatter**, for instance, will not properly format a **java.util.Date** object. There is some of this sort of redudancy between the Java classes and the Java-fied classes from Cocoa's Foundation framework.

Build and run your application (Figure 25.9).

Once your application appears, seed the random number generator and generate a few random numbers. Congratulations, you have a working Java/Cocoa application.

Subclassing Cocoa Classes in Java

The next natural question is what to do if you wanted to create a subclass of another Cocoa class in Java; for example, if you wanted to create a subclass of **NSView** in Java. All the Cocoa classes are wrapped in Java classes. You may subclass the wrapper. In the class browser of Interface Builder, you can use the info panel to make the class a Java class (Figure 25.10).

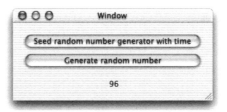

Figure 25.9 Completed Application

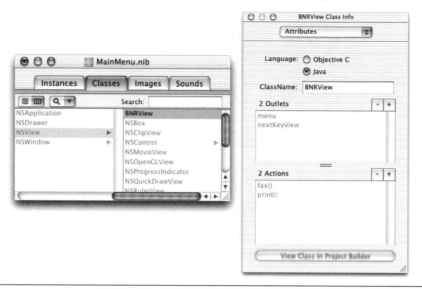

Figure 25.10   Setting the Language in the Class Inspector

Documentation

Another natural question is about documentation for the standard Java classes. If you already know the Java class libraries pretty well, you can use the application /Developer/Applications/JavaBrowser. If you are new to Java, you will want to buy a book or download documentation from the Internet.

Chapter 26

CREATING INTERFACE BUILDER PALETTES

In Interface Builder, there are several standard palettes. The palettes allow users to drag objects off the palette and drop them into their nib file. The palette also allows the user to inspect the attributes of that object and edit them. Finally, the palette allows the user to put the interface into test mode. The UI objects come alive and act as they would in an application.

When you save the nib file, you are archiving objects into a file. When you load the nib file into your application, you are unarchiving those objects. Some of the objects in the nib file are just placeholders. File's Owner, for example, is a placeholder for the object that will be supplied when the nib file is read in. Other objects, like the text fields, are actually archived into the file.

Until this chapter, all the instances of your custom classes have just been placeholders. When the nib file is read in, these instances are created with **alloc** and **init**. Then their outlets are set. On the other hand, when an instance of **NSTextField** is read in from the nib file, it is created with **alloc** and **initWithCoder:** because it was actually archived in the nib.

In creating a palette, you are creating a collection of classes that know how to archive themselves into a nib file and unarchive themselves when the nib file is read into the application. You will frequently also create inspectors for these objects. Inspectors allow the developer to set the instance variables of the objects inside Interface Builder.

The point of palettizing, then, is to make it easy for other people to use your classes in Interface Builder. For example, imagine you are the smartest programmer who works down at the nuclear power plant. You create a custom view class called **DangerMeter**. All the other programmers would like to use your **DangerMeter** in their nib files. They would like to be able to select the view and set the minRads and maxRads for the view in the inspector. If you are a kind programmer, you will palettize your view and create an inspector for it. While you are at it, you should also put

MeltdownTimer and **ExposureWarningView** in the palette. You can create inspectors for these classes, too.

Note that a palette is a type of bundle. There is some compiled code in the bundle that will be dynamically linked into Interface Builder. There will also be a couple of nib files: one for the palette and one for each of the inspectors. You can also have sounds and images in a palette.

Now that you have created a nifty view like **BigLetterView**, it is time to palettize it so that it will be easy for other people to use. This chapter will teach you how to do this. Notice from the description that you will have to do several things.

- Teach your object to archive and unarchive itself. This is how it will get in and out of the nib file.
- Create an inspector object for the view. For **BigLetterView**, you are going to let the user change the background color of the view and whether the view is copyable.
- Create two nib files: the one the user will drag the **BigLetterView** from, and the nib for the inspector (Figure 26.1).

Notice, also, that for your object to "come alive" in test mode, Interface Builder is going to have to dynamically link in the code for your objects. Loading code into a running application is somewhat dangerous, and until your project is bug free, you may crash Interface Builder a few times. This is expected. Also, once your code has been linked in, it cannot be unlinked. You will have to restart Interface Builder to test each new version of your palette. Debugging a palette can be a time-consuming process.

One palette can make several classes available to the user. Each of these classes will be represented by a view on the palette nib. Each of these classes may have a corresponding inspector. Each palette is controlled by a subclass of **IBPalette**. Each inspector is controlled by a subclass of **IBInspector**.

Add NSCoding Methods to BigLetterView

For your object to be saved to and read from a nib file, it must have coding methods. Luckily, **NSView** has taken care of most of the hard stuff. You will simply extend **NSView**'s **encodeWithCoder:** and **initWithCoder:** methods.

Add these methods to your BigLetterView.m file. You may notice that **initWithCoder:** and **initWithFrame:** have several similarities. When the view comes from a nib file, **initWithCoder:** will be called instead of **initWithFrame:**.

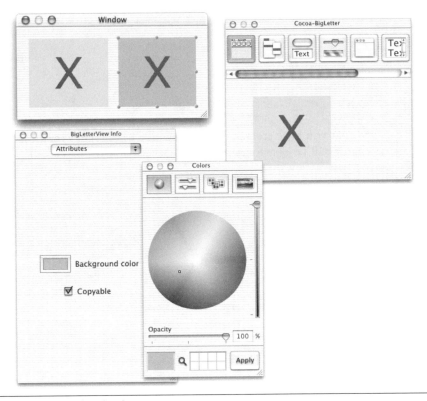

Figure 26.1   Completed Palette

```
- (void)encodeWithCoder:(NSCoder *)coder
{

    [super encodeWithCoder:coder];
    [coder encodeObject:bgColor];
    [coder encodeObject:string];
    [coder encodeValueOfObjCType:@encode(BOOL) at:&copyable];
}
- (id)initWithCoder:(NSCoder *)coder
{
    if (self = [super initWithCoder:coder]) {
      [self registerForDraggedTypes:
        [NSArray arrayWithObject: NSStringPboardType]];
      [self prepareAttributes];
      [self setBgColor:[coder decodeObject]];
      [self setString:[coder decodeObject]];
      [coder decodeValueOfObjCType:@encode(BOOL) at:&copyable];
    }
    return self;
}
```

Figure 26.2   Select Project Type

Make sure the project will compile. Close the project.

Create a Palette Project

In Project Builder, create a new project of type IBPalette (Figure 26.2). Name it BigLetter.

The new project is created assuming that the palette will have one view subclass called **BigLetter**. A palette can have many classes. Yours will have only the class **BigLetterView**. The new project assumes that you will also have one inspector class: **BigLetterInspector**. The new project assumes that you are creating one palette class: **BigLetterPalette**.

Select and delete files BigLetter.h and BigLetter.m. Notice that there are two nib files that were created automatically: one for the palette and one for the inspector.

Delete the line that imports BigLetter.h from BigLetterPalette.h and BigLetterInspector.m.

`BigLetterPalette.h` declares a category on the class **BigLetter**. Change it to be a category on **BigLetterView**.

```
#import <InterfaceBuilder/InterfaceBuilder.h>
#import "BigLetterView.h"

@interface BigLetterPalette : IBPalette
{
}
@end

@interface BigLetterView (BigLetterPaletteInspector)
- (NSString *)inspectorClassName;
@end
```

Also change it in `BigLetterPalette.m`.

```
@implementation BigLetterView (BigLetterPaletteInspector)
- (NSString *)inspectorClassName
{
    return @"BigLetterInspector";
}

@end
```

Drag `BigLetterView.h`, `BigLetterView.m`, `FirstLetter.h`, and `FirstLetter.m` into the new project from the Finder (Figure 26.3).

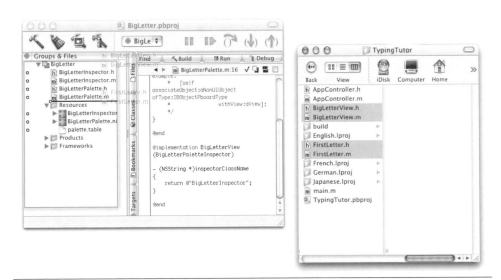

Figure 26.3   Add the BigLetterView Class and FirstLetter Category

Edit the Nib File for Your Palette

Double-click on BigLetterPalette.nib to open it in Interface Builder.

Drag BigLetterView.h into the doc window so that Interface Builder will know about your **BigLetterView** class. Drag a custom view onto the palette window and change its class to **BigLetterView** (Figure 26.4).

Set the File's Owner to be an instance of **BigLetterPalette** (Figure 26.5).

Control-drag from File's Owner to the palette window and set the original window outlet (Figure 26.6).

Save and close the nib file.

palette.table

When reading in a palette, Interface Builder will look for a file called palette. table. In this file, the palette declares which subclass of **IBPalette** to use, what nib file to read, and which classes in the palette should appear in the classes browser. You

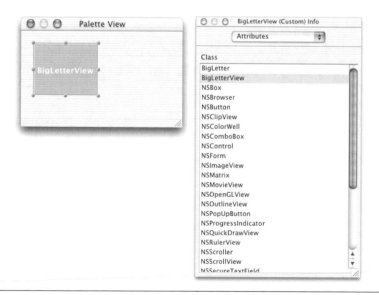

Figure 26.4   Add an Instance of BigLetterView to the Palette Window

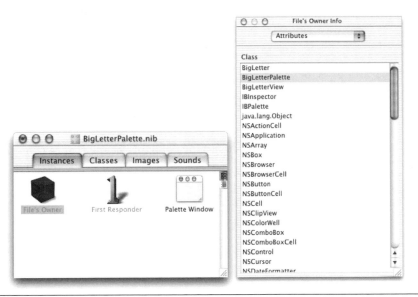

Figure 26.5   Set the File's Owner to be BigLetterPalette

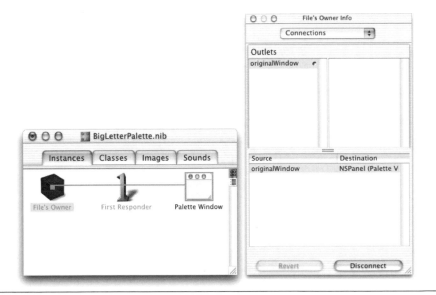

Figure 26.6   Set the originalWindow Outlet

can also specify images and sounds that you are including in the palette. It should appear under **Resources** in Project Builder's outline view. Edit the contents of the file to look like this:

```
<?xml version="1.0" encoding="UTF-8"?>
<!DOCTYPE plist SYSTEM
    "file://localhost/System/Library/DTDs/PropertyList.dtd">
<plist version="0.9">
<dict>
<key>Class</key> <string>BigLetterPalette</string>
<key>NibFile</key> <string>BigLetterPalette</string>
<key>ExportClasses</key>
<array>
<string>BigLetterView</string>
</array>
</dict>
</plist>
```

Build and Test

Build your palette. In your project directory is a directory called `build`. Your palette (`BigLetter.palette`) is there. You can load it from the Preferences panel of Interface Builder (Figure 26.7).

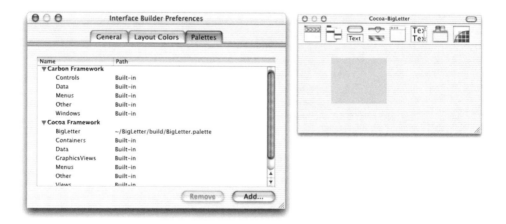

Figure 26.7   Load the Palette

If there are errors when it loads, you can see the messages using the Console application.

After your palette successfully loads, try creating a new nib file with two instances of your **BigLetterView**. Set the nextKeyView of each to the other. Run it in test mode and see if your view works. Make sure that you can tab between them.

Close the new nib file without saving it.

finishInstantiate

Notice that the **BigLetterView** appears without a letter in the palette. The user would guess its purpose more easily if the view drew itself with a letter. After the palette is loaded, the **IBPalette** object (in your case **BigLetterPalette**) gets sent **finishInstantiate**. This would be a good chance to set the string of the **BigLetterView** to be non-nil.

First, you will need to add an outlet from the palette controller object (**BigLetterPalette**) to the **BigLetterView**. Add the declaration of an instance variable to BigLetterPalette.h.

```
@interface BigLetterPalette : IBPalette
{
    IBOutlet BigLetterView *view;
}
@end
```

Drag BigLetterPalette.h from Project Builder into BigLetterPalette.nib in Interface Builder. Set the outlet to point to the **BigLetterView** in the window (Figure 26.8).

In **BigLetterPalette**'s **finishInstantiate** method, set the view's string.

```
- (void)finishInstantiate
{
    [view setString:@"X"];
    [superfinishInstantiate];
}
```

Build it. Quit Interface Builder. Start Interface Builder again. It will automatically reload the palette. You should see the "X" in the palette (Figure 26.9).

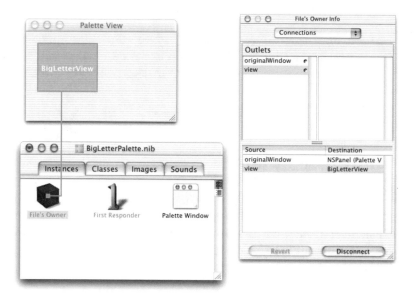

Figure 26.8   Set the View Outlet

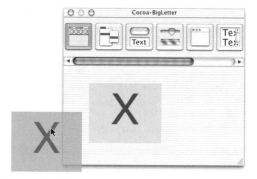

Figure 26.9   Working Palette

Adding an Inspector

It would be nice if anyone using your palette could select an instance of **BigLetterView** in their nib and see an inspector that would allow them to set the background color and copyability of the selected **BigLetterView** (Figure 26.10).

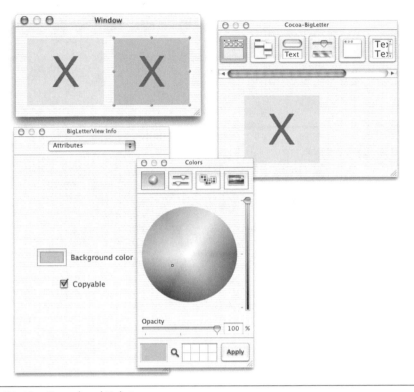

Figure 26.10   Completed Palette

Create a Nib File for Your Inspector

In Project Builder, double-click on BigLetterInspector.nib. Make the File's Owner an instance of **BigLetterInspector**. This inspector object will take information from the Info panel and set the instance variables of your object. It will also read the instance variables and set the UI objects in the Info panel. Drop a color well and a checkbox on the window (Figure 26.11).

Your inspector will need outlets for the color well and the checkbox. Add it to BigLetterInspector.h and name them colorWell and copyableCheckbox.

```
#import <InterfaceBuilder/InterfaceBuilder.h>

@interface BigLetterInspector : IBInspector
{
  IBOutlet NSColorWell *colorWell;
  IBOutlet NSButton *copyableCheckbox;
}
@end
```

Figure 26.11   Completed Interface for Inspector

Drag the `BigLetterInspector.h` into the nib file (Figure 26.12). Set the type of the File's Owner to `BigLetterInspector`. Connect the window outlet of the **BigLetterInspector** to the window (Figure 26.13).

Connect the `colorWell` outlet to the **NSColorWell** object (Figure 26.14).

Also connect the checkbox (Figure 26.15).

To an inspector, life consists mainly of responding to two messages: **ok:** and **revert:** (Figure 26.16). The message **ok:** tells the inspector to read the objects on the inspector panel and update the instance variables of the inspected object to match. **revert:** tells the inspector to read the instance variables of the inspected object and set the objects on the inspector panel to match.

When a user changes the color well in the inspector panel, you will want the inspected object (a **BigLetterView**) to have its instance variable (`bgColor`) updated. So set the `target` of the color well to be the File's Owner. The action is **ok:** (Figure 26.17).

Also, set the `target` of the checkbox to be the File's Owner. The action is again **ok:** (Figure 26.18).

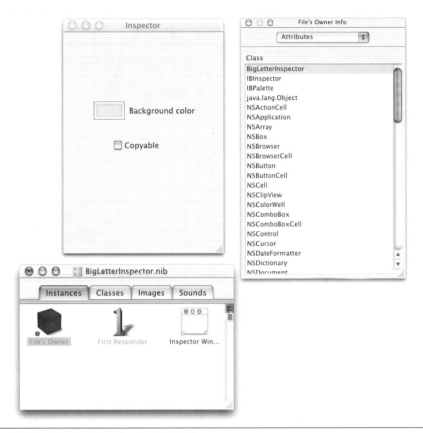

Figure 26.12   Set the Class for the File's Owner

Code for an Inspector

Your inspector will have three methods.

- **init** will read the nib file that you just created.
- **ok:** will read the color well and checkbox and set the bgColor and copyable instance variables of the **BigLetterView**.
- **revert:** will read the bgColor and copyable instance variables of the **BigLetterView** and set the color well and checkbox.

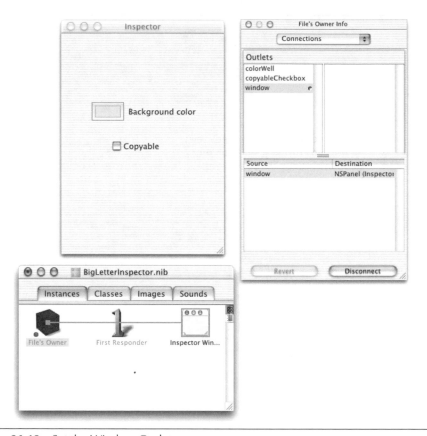

Figure 26.13   Set the Window Outlet

Here is what BigLetterInspector.m should look like:

```
#import "BigLetterInspector.h"
#import "BigLetterView.h"

@implementation BigLetterInspector

- (id)init
{
    if (self = [super init]) {
      [NSBundle loadNibNamed:@"BigLetterInspector" owner:self];
    }
    return self;
}
- (void)ok:(id)sender
{
    BigLetterView *selectedView;
```

```
        selectedView = [self object];
        [selectedView setBgColor:[colorWell color]];
        [selectedView setCopyable:[copyableCheckbox state]];
        [super ok:sender];
}

- (void)revert:(id)sender
{
        NSColor *color;
        BigLetterView *selectedView;
        selectedView = [self object];
        [copyableCheckbox setState: [selectedView copyable]];
        color = [selectedView bgColor];
        [colorWell setColor:color];
        [super revert:sender];
}
@end
```

Figure 26.14   Set the colorWell Outlet

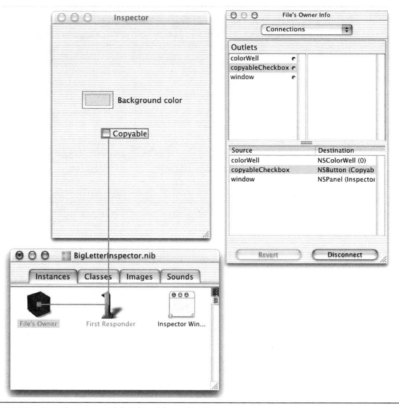

Figure 26.15   Set the copyableCheckbox Outlet

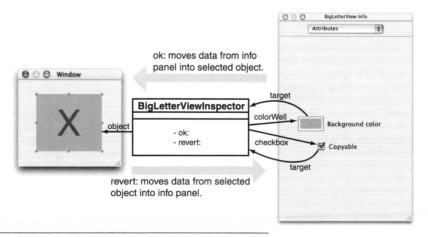

Figure 26.16   The Role of the Inspector

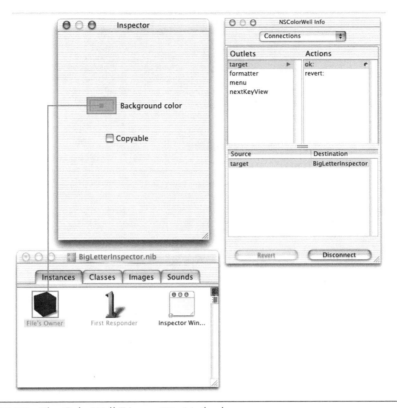

Figure 26.17   The ColorWell Triggers OK: Method

That's it. You have created a palette and an inspector. Compile the palette and restart Interface Builder. It should automatically reload the palette.

Note how the inspector allows you to choose the background color for the selected **BigLetterView**.

For the More Curious: How to Palettize Objects That Are Not Views

Views are easy to palettize. If you wanted to palettize something like your **Foo** class from Chapter 2, you would need to associate it with some view for the purpose of dragging. Most developers would use an **NSButton** as the view. It is easy to put an image or label on a button so that it will look like anything you want.

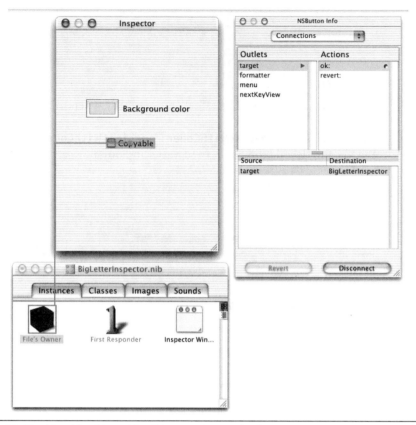

Figure 26.18   The Checkbox Also Triggers `ok:` Method

In your subclass of **IBPalette**, you will need an outlet to the button.

```
#import <InterfaceBuilder/InterfaceBuilder.h>

@interface BigLetterPalette : IBPalette
{
    IBOutlet BigLetterView *view;
    IBOutlet NSButton *button;
}

@end
```

In BigLetterPalette.m, in **finishInstantiate** you would associate the button with a **Foo** object.

```
- (void)finishInstantiate
{
```

```
    [super finishInstantiate];
    [self associateObject:[[Foo alloc] init]
                ofType:IBObjectPboardType
             withView: button];
}
```

finishInstantiate will be called automatically when the palette is loaded.

You will also need **encodeWithCoder:** and **initWithCoder:** methods that properly encode and decode the textField outlet in Foo.m.

```
- (id)initWithCoder:(NSCoder *)coder
{
    if (self = [super init]) {
      textField = [[coder decodeObject] retain];
    }
    return self;
}
- (void)encodeWithCoder:(NSCoder *)coder
{
    [coder encodeObject: textField];
}
```

Finally, you would declare that **Foo** implements the **NSCoding** protocol.

```
@interface Foo : NSObject <NSCoding>
```

After building and loading the palette, you could drag from the button to the nib's doc window. The image of the button would become the symbol representing the **Foo** object. Just as in Chapter 2, you would make it the target of two buttons and set the text field outlet. Niftiest of all, your entire RandomApp application would work in Test Interface mode.

Challenge

Add your formatter to your custom palette. You will need to use the IBFormatter-PboardType when you associate the formatter with a button. Also, make sure that **ColorFormatter**'s **initWithCoder:** method properly initializes the colorList. (It doesn't have to decode it from the coder; just make sure its colorList is initialized after calling [super initWithCoder:coder].)

When you have completed this challenge, you will be able to drop your formatter on text fields and table view columns as you did with the number formatter while creating the RaiseMan application.

Chapter 27

THE END

When I teach a class, it always ends with the "Feel-Good Talk," which has the following parts.

- The knowledge you have received from this experience never comes easy. You have learned a lot of stuff. Be proud.
- The only way to solidify what you have learned is to write applications. The sooner you start, the easier it will be.
- There is still much more to learn, but you have crossed the hump in the learning curve. It will be easier from here. Once again, the only way to progress is to write applications.
- As a speaker, I'm available for weddings, parties, bar mitzvahs, etc. I also offer five-day classes at the Big Nerd Ranch. For a schedule, please see the Big Nerd Ranch Web site (http://www.bignerdranch.com).

The final part of the "Feel-Good Talk" is a listing of resources that will help answer your questions as they arise. As with any programming topic, your answers will be found in a hodgepodge of online documentation, Web sites, and mailing lists.

- If you have a question about Cocoa, the first place to check is in the reference. All the classes, protocols, functions, and constants are listed there. Look in `/Developer/Documentation/Cocoa/Reference/`.
- If you have a question about Objective-C, the first place to check is in the Objective-C reference. Look in `/Developer/Documentation/Cocoa/ObjectiveC/`.
- If you have a question about Project Builder or Interface Builder, the first place to check is in the developer tools reference. Look in `/Developer/Documentation/DeveloperTools/`.
- Don't be afraid to experiment: Most questions can actually be answered by creating a tiny application. Creating this application will probably take you less than 15 minutes.
- The Web site for this book (http://www.bignerdranch.com/Book) has the answers to many questions and several fun examples.

- There are two Web sites that are gradually accumulating good articles for Mac OS X developers: StepWise (http://www.stepwise.com/), which is geared toward more experienced Cocoa programmers, and CocoaDevCentral (http://www.cocoadevcentral.com/), which is targeted at beginners. You might also check the *MacTech Magazine* site (http://www.mactech.com/).
- You can search the archives of the MacOSX-dev mailing list at the OmniGroup Web site (http://www.omnigroup.com/). It is a very active mailing list, and searching it can be rather tedious. Apple also has a mailing list for Cocoa developers. You can join the cocoa-dev mailing list at Apple's list server (http://lists.apple.com/). Both lists are archived at http://cocoa.mamasam.com/.
- If you have exhausted all other possibilities, Apple's Developer Technical Support will answer your questions for a fee. They've answered lots of questions for me, and I find them to be consistently knowledgeable and helpful.

Finally, try to be nice. Help beginners. Give away useful applications and their source code. Answer questions in a kind manner. It is a relatively small community, and few good deeds go forever unrewarded.

Thanks for reading my book!

INDEX

Learn Mac OS X Programming at the Big Nerd Ranch for 10% Off

Mention this coupon to get a 10% discount on tuition for any scheduled class on Mac OS X programming. Classes are five days long, and are taught by this book's author, Aaron Hillegass. Room, board, and mountain vistas are included.

Please find a schedule of our programs on our web site: http://www.bignerdranch.com/.

Space is limited. Please call now to reserve a seat: (404) 210-5663.

BiG
nerD
ranch